LOCAL GOVERNANCE IN NORTH-EAST INDIA

LOCAL GOVERNANCE IN NORTH-EAST INDIA:
A Case of Dismal State in Mizoram

C. Nunthara

GYAN

ISBN: 978-81-212-1274-8
Price: ₹ 1080
First Published, 2015

Published by
Gyan Publishing House
23, Main Ansari Road
Daryaganj, New Delhi-110002
Phones: 23282060, 23261060
Fax: 91-11-23285914
E-mail: books@gyanbooks.com

Laser Typesetting: Rajender Vashist, Delhi
Printed at: Chawla Offset Printers, Delhi

Cataloging in Publication Data--DK

Courtesy: D.K. Agencies (P) Ltd. <docinfo@dkagencie

Nunthara, C., 1944- **author.**

Local governance in North-East India : a case of disn
Prof C. Nunthara.

pages cm

Includes bibliographical references (pages) an
ISBN 9788121212748

1. Local government--India--Mizoram. 2. Decentrali
India--Mizoram. 3. Local finance--India--Mizoram. 4. L
Mizoram--Statistics. I. Title.

DDC 320.80954166 23

Contents

Preface

India is a large country and federal in its governmental structure. Our Constitution bestows a clear mandate for democratic decentralisation through the Directive Principles of state Policy which insists the state to promote Panchayati Raj Institutions, and now more specifically through the 73rd and 74th constitutional amendments which seek to create genuine grass roots democracy through a medium of active local self-governments in both urban and rural areas. Consequent upon the constitutional amendments the panchayats have acquired constitutional legitimacy. However, most panchayats continue to be treated as agencies of the state government for implementation of certain prescribed schemes. It was in this backdrop that the Institute of Social Sciences, New Delhi, took interest in bringing out a volume *Status of Panchayati Raj in the states of India, 1994,* and *Status of Panchayati Raj in the states and Union Territories of India. 2000.* I was involved in both the volumes in writing the situation in Mizoram. The Institute subsequently organised an all-India project on initially termed, *'Inclusion of Excluded Communities'* in trying to unmask the concrete reality of the functioning of the 73rd constitutional amendment in different states. I was involved again to make a study of grass-roots reality in the case of Mizoram and Arunachal Pradesh, even though 73rd amendment has not been operative in Mizoram. This has given me enough awareness and curiosity to delve deeper into the problem.

It was then that the University Grants Commission awarded me the esteemed Emeritus Fellowship in 2011 which provided me to take a comprehensive study in a broader perspective of the problem encountered in Mizoram. The field work was carried out during 2012-2013. The present volume is, therefore, a result of this study. If the constitutional mandate to create genuine grass roots democratic local self-governments has not been fully implemented in some states, it is a non-starter and a sad case in Mizoram. This may be because of ignorance on the part of the state legislature and bureaucrats coupled with the usual lack of political will and lack of public awareness. The volume is intended to instill fresh awareness and inspire and motivate meaningful responses.

I am indebted to many people who helped me tremendously during the course of field investigation in Mizoram. I have visited all the eight district headquarters and met and studied with officials in different departments having a direct concern and association with the village councils; visited 31 village councils throughout Mizoram, discussed with them their problems, their aspirations and the actual functioning of the village councils in the Autonomous District Council areas, non-District Council areas, and in the Hmar Peoples' Movement affected areas. It will not be possible to mention individual names, but I am sincerely grateful to all the village council members and other informants in the villages and I do have a heart-felt sympathy for them all, and also the officials in the district headquarters. Apart from officials in the district headquarters, I am also grateful to officials in Aizawl in the departments of Local Administration Department, Rural Development Department, NLUP implementation wing, Urban Development, Transport Department, Excise Department, Taxation Department, different departments in the Secretariat and Aizawl Municipal Council, for their untiring and persistent help.

C. Nunthara

List of Tables

1

Introduction

1.1. Theoretical Orientation

In the understanding of classical tradition, development is equated with growth, and that a quantum increase in the production of goods and services would bring development. It was also assumed that the trickledown effect of growth would lead to equitable sharing of benefits, resources and opportunities in the society. But the process did not yield the desired result to humanity in the developing countries. Development in these countries immediately after the second world war have shown that socio-economic deprivation of substantial section of their population continued or rather increase in proportion. There has thus been a perspective shift in conceptualising development. *The Human Development Report* 1990, states that *"people must be at the centre of all development. The purpose of development is to offer people more options. One of their options is access to income-not as an end in itself but as a means of acquiring human well-being. But there are other options as well, including long life, knowledge, political freedom, personal security, community participation and guaranteed human rights. People cannot be reduced to a single dimension as an economic creature. What makes them and the study of development process fascinating is the entire spectrum through which human capacities areexpanded and utilised."* (UNDP 1990). Thus, according to United Nations Development Programme (UNDP), at all levels of development, basic human needs to lead a long and healthy life, to acquire knowledge, and to have access to resources needed for a decent standard of living- must be met. Indication of the vulnerability to corruption and bureaucratic inefficiency resulting in service diversion, limited access and high prices which accompanies centralised mechanisms has been amply demonstrated by thus 2004 *World Development Report* which stated, *"Too often service fail poor people – in access, in quantity and in quality (World Bank, 2004).*

The world had witnessed increasing centralisation and concentration of power and authority after the first world war, and particularly during the decades- the 1940s and 1950s- in both developed and underdeveloped countries. However, in developing countries, debates over the overall functioning of government focused on the role and effectiveness of central power and authority in promoting economic and social progress and the advantages of decentralising authority to sub-national units of administration, local governments, and other agents of the state. In other words, governments around the world started to realise that centralised government have failed to deliver public services, and in order to boost delivery system and efficiency and to extend service coverage by giving more responsibility to local government units, decentralisation of power, authority, and resources has been recommended during decades 1960s and 1970s. Decentralisation was defined as the transfer of authority, responsibility, and resources through de-concentration, devolution or delegation from the centre to the lower levels of administrative units. During 1970s and 1980s, the process of globalisation also forced governments of developing countries to recognise the limitations and restrictions of central economic planning and trickle-down theories of economic growth toward meeting basic human needs and growth-with-equity objectives. Participatory development also led to increasing calls for decentralisation. There has thus been a paradigm shift in development strategies for the disadvantaged section of the society. In the background of declining access of a large section of the population to the means of livelihood security, education, healthcare facilities, housing and other basic needs, the philosophy of social justice was integrated in the development discourse since 1970s.

It was in this backdrop that the World Development Report, 1997 re-emphasised the need for an effective new role of the state for social and economic development. The state is central in the process, not as a direct provider of development but as a partner, medium and facilitator. The world is changing, and with it the ideas about the state's role in economic and social development. In view of the growing lack of confidence in governance by private investors, increase in corruption and poverty, technological changes, growing discontent of the people, growing grassroots mobilisation, and increasing pressure of the civil society, a redefinition of state's role and responsibilities has been suggested as a means to solve some of these problems. Along with this, the concept of governance also expanded to include not only the government but other societal institutions, including private sector and civil associations. Debate shifted from mere allocation of responsibilities within government to how strongly the state should intervene in economic activities, is the government inhibiting or promoting growth and social development, and the appropriate roles of government, private sector and civil society.

As the concept of decentralisation evolved over the past half century, Shabbir Cheema and Deniis A. Rondinelli (2007) observe, *"The first wave of post-world war II thinking on decentralisation, in the 1970s and 1980s, focused on de-concentrating hierarchical government structures and bureaucracies. The second wave of decentralisation, beginning in the 1980s, broadened the concept to include political power sharing, democratisation, and market liberalisation, expending the scope of private sector decision-making. During 1990s, decentralisation was seen as a way of opening governance to wider public participation through organisation of civil society."* By the 1980s, government pursued three forms of decentralisation namely, de-concentration, devolution and delegation. De-concentration sought to shift administrative responsibilities from central ministries and departments to regional and local levels through field offices of national departments and transferring some authority for decision making to regional field staff. Devolution aimed to strengthen local governments by granting them the authority, responsibility, and resources to provide services and infrastructure, protect public health and safety and formulate and implement local policies. National government, through delegation, shifted management authority for specific functions to semiautonomous or parastatal organisations and state enterprises, regional planning and area development agencies. While the three forms of decentralisation processes are important, greater application of devolution has been lately emphasis. Decentralisation is to ensure grass roots participation in decision-making process. It has to ensure participation, responsiveness and efficiency and makes public governance closer to the people.

For Pranab Bardhan and Dilip Mookherjee (2006), the dimensions of design of decentralisation will include the following:

(1) ***Constitutional Authority:*** Do the local governments have an independent authority enshrined in the constitution, or do they exist at the mercy of upper-level governments (which may be the state government). In India, although we have 73rd and 74th constitutional amendments, the state government, in many cases, are still reluctant to bring about grassroots transformation in real term. In Mizoram, the 73rd amendment is inapplicable, and the state legislature has been doing nothing to ensure legislative provisions.

(2) ***Electoral Process*:** Are key officials elected directly or indirectly? Is there any restriction on electoral contestants or electoral mobilisation efforts? Are there adequate safeguards to ensure the conduct of free and fair elections, including the use of secret ballots and the absence of intimidation of voters, manipulation of voters' list, or election machinery?

(3) ***Range of Expenditure and Management Responsibilities Devolved*:** What are the precise decisions to be devolved to local governments? Do they include local infrastructure such as sanitation, water, irrigation, roads and public buildings; primary education and healthcare, and local welfare programmes such as pensions, housing, and special benefits for the disabled or the poor? Can the local government decide on allocation of fiscal resources across these areas and across citizens or localities within the community? Is there significant ambiguity in the allocation of responsibilities across different tiers of the governments? What autonomy the local governments have over hiring, firing and paying of personnel? Situation seems to differ from state to state, and in Mizoram there is simple lack of autonomy of the local governments in all spheres.

(4) ***Financial Devolution*****:** To what extent can local government raise resources either through local taxes, user fees or borrowing? What is the extent of autonomy accorded to them over such decisions, for example, what portion of local government budget are self-financed, and who sets local tax rates or user-fee schedules? How are fiscal transfers from upper-level governments determined, and how much scope is given to local governments to affect these transfers via processes of decentralised budgeting or planning? Are the transfer formula-bound or subject to political discretion of upper-level government officials or negotiation between upper and lower levels. In most states in India, decentralised budgeting and planning is still weak, and absence in Mizoram.

(5) ***Authority and Competence of Local Officials*****:** Is the decentralisation both *de jure* and *de facto*? Or do decisions continue to be taken by upper levels of government? How has the balance of actual control rights shifted from central bureaucracies to elected local government officials?

The decentralisation process is at the *de jure* level and there does not seem to be significant shift of powers to elected local government officials in India.

(6) ***Information and Oversight Mechanism*****:** Are local citizens and leaders likely to be sufficiently informed? Do citizens have access to information concerning local government budgets or the actions of government officials? Are local government officials subject to oversight of Citizen Oversight Committee or upper-level governments? Are there channels or forums allowing citizens to communicate their priorities and concerns to elected officials? Many of these will be affected by the design of decentralisation while some of them are context variables reflecting underlying community characteristics.

They continued to explore on the types of decentralisation on the basis of whether they have been comprehensive or piecemeal, uniform or uneven across the country, or whether they gradually evolved or represented a "big bang" reform. In terms of design of decentralisation, three different kinds can be observed: (a) Comprehensive big bang political-cum-economic devolution such as Bolivia, Indonesia, and post-1994 South Africa; (b) Comprehensive political devolution–partial and uneven economic devolution such as Brazil and India; (c) Limited political devolution, more significant administrative and economic devolution such as China, Pakistan, Uganda, and pre-1994 South Africa.

Type-A decentralisation represents countries with comprehensive big bang decentralisation implemented simultaneously throughout the entire country. In Bolivia, it was introduced in the face of rising political competition from ethnically based populist groups in an effort to legitimise and consolidate its power among its rural constituents. In Indonesia, it was an aftermath of the transition to democracy following the collapse of the Suharto regime, and weakening of the power of the central government *vis-à-vis* regional interest. In both cases, the previous centralised regime had been associated with high inequality in interregional allocation of funds, poor service delivery and high level of corruption. Substantial amount of funds have been transferred to local governments, 20 per cent of the total government expenditure in Bolivia and 30 per cent in Indonesia.

Type-B represents Brazil and India. These are large democracies with a high degree of heterogeneity and sharp inequality across regions and across levels of economic and social well-being. Regional governments are an important intermediate tier between national and local governments. Regions or states in these countries are larger than many independent countries of the world. The extent and nature of decentralisation is chosen by each region independently, resulting in a gradual and uneven pattern across the country, subject to significant learning and discussion. The result is considerable heterogeneity in the extent and nature of responsibilities transferred, fiscal and administrative capacity government, planning and budgeting systems. Local governments in Brazil have greater fiscal authority and autonomy. In India, local governments are devolved significantly less spending or allocation responsibilities. It is surprisingly, the only country in their study where local governments have no jurisdiction over the administration of primary education and health. In most Indian states, the devolution of administrative responsibility over most infrastructure and welfare programmes has been *de jure* rather than *de facto*, with state bureaucracies continuing to retain their power over these programmes. Both countries share similar failures in social service delivery from centralised economic administration over the previous two or three decades, with frustrating lack of progress in reducing poverty and limiting social exclusion.

Type-C represents countries such as China, Uganda, and Pakistan where decentralisation has been employed as an instrument of consolidation and legitimisation of non-democratic political power at the national level. Pakistan and Uganda are examples of military dictatorships utilising local governments as a way of neutralising the potential for political opposition from ethnic and regional groups according to divide and rule strategy of the colonial regime. China is larger country characterised by long tradition of centralised political power. The common feature of these decentralisations is that local governments are subordinate to the dominant power at the national level, have no independent or very limited constitutional authority/ protection and can be dismissed or neutralised by higher level government. Local governments depend on grants devolved from upper levels, and are assigned the role of delivering wide range of local services. Pakistan represents cases where state bureaucrats have become subordinate to elected district officials. China represents another case where local government officials are not elected and subordinated to upper level government officials.

In contrast to type-B which are uniform with respect to the extent of political decentralisation but non-uniform with respect to economic decentralisation, type-C are non-uniform with respect to political decentralisation and more uniform with respect to economic decentralisation. Type-A decentralisation are uniform in both dimensions. Common to all three forms of decentralisation is the feature that local governments typically have limited authority over personnel they hire, especially with respect to pay and service conditions. Salaries of the personnel represent a significant part of their costs they have limited control over. The bulk of their expenditure (over 70 per cent) are in the form of transfer fiscal received from upper level government. This gives rise to problems that each local government vying with others to receive more fiscal transfer by demonstrating exceptional need or manipulating processes of political bargaining.

The fall of authoritarian regimes in Latin America in the 1980s and in Central and Eastern Europe in 1990s and the spread of democratic principles in East Asia brought renewed interest in decentralisation. The International Monetary Fund, the World Bank and other International development agencies also prescribed decentralisation as the structure needed to strengthen democracy and promote good governance. Governments in developing countries were also pressurised to decentralise by ethnic and religious/cultural groups seeking greater autonomy. In Africa, pressure for decentralisation came from tribal minorities and economically peripheral ethnic groups. Growing discontent with the inability of the central government bureaucracies to deliver effectively almost any kind of service to local areas fueled the decentralisation movement. Calls for devolution and autonomous rule also came from minority groups in Belgium, Quebec, Wales, Scotland, Malaysia, Mexico, Philippines, India, Yugoslavia, Baltic countries and countries of former Soviet Union (Cheema and Rondinelli, 2007). Decentralisation occurs in Latin America, Africa, Asia and Eastern Europe. The initial changes were initiated in the 1970s, picked up momentum in the 1980s and accelerated in the 1990s (Cheema and Mookherjee, 2006).

In reassessing decentralisation, Cheema and Rondinelli (2007) states that in one form or another, both democratic governance and decentralised government have been adopted by many countries over the past quarter of a century. They expressed *'By early 1990s, all but twelve of the seventy-five countries with a population of more than five million had undertaken some form of decentralisation. At the end of 1990s, about 95 per cent of the countries with democratic political systems had sub-national units of administration or governments. By the early 2000s, there were more democratic states in the world than non-democratic ones. Freedom Houseranked 89 of the 192 countries that it surveyed as "free" and 54 as "partly free"(four billion people, or 63 per cent of the world's population, live in these countries). At least 119 of those countries were deemed to be formal electoral democracies'*. The impact of decentralisation on citizen participation varies from country to country depending mainly on the type of decentralisation used and the political situation in the country. In Africa questions were raised about whether decentralisation can increase efficiency in service delivery, empower local groups and facilitate popular participation. Available evidence point to the fact that many of the failures of decentralisation are due less to the inherent weaknesses in the concept itself rather than to government's ineffectiveness in implementing it. Like any participation for fundamental change, decentralisation meets resistance from those whose interest is served by the concentration of power and resources in the centre government.

In the 21st century the global de-concentration of economic activity has given new resources and new pressures on local governments to perform their administrative roles more effectively. The United Nations Development Programme(UNDP) re-conceptualised in the 1990s the concept of governance, defining it as "the exercise of political, economic and administrative authority in the management of a country's affairs." The UNDP thus perceives governance as those institutions and processes through which government, civil society organisations and the private sector interact with each other in public affairs through which citizens articulate theirinterests, mediate their differences, and exercise their political, economic and social rights. Decision-making in public affairs is no longer considered the monopoly of government but the right and obligation of citizens through social organisations and the private sector. Good governance implies effective and efficient management of public resources and an adequate response to critical societal needs. It also denotes democratic forms of relationships between the governed and the governors, relationships that have built-in mechanism for public participation, accountability and transparency. Democratic governance, therefore, implies the creation of channels for –public participation in decision-making, to abide by the rule of law, to increase transparency in public procedures, and to hold officials accountable-so that it will strengthen institutional framework for citizen participation in economic and political processes, and promotes universal human rights and values as ends in themselves.

Currently, the popular terminology of reforms in the third world countries is expressed as 'good governance' reforms. It may also be called 'democratic governance'. The new governance archetype is said to mark 'perhaps the greatest political revolution of our times' (Dahl and Linblom cited by Salamon, 2002). The new approach shifts the focus from control of large bureaucratic organisations to enablement skills. The skills are meant to engage partners arranged horizontally in networks and to bring multiple stakeholders together for a common objective in a situation of interdependence (Salamon, 2002:16). This is currently promoted by the trinity of World Bank/ International Monetary Fund/ World Trade Organisation. In connection with the third world, good governance is to ensure accountability, transparency and efficiency in public service along with protection of civil and human rights and maintaining rule of law through an independent judiciary (Oommen, 2004:146). Governance is conceived as encapsulating government but going beyond an covering non-governmental agencies as well to meet the needs and aspirations of the citizens. The relation between the state and civil society is recast from the previous confrontational orientation into a mutual, shared, collaborative mode.

The current use of the concept has been raised by the World Bank in 1989 in connection with the issue of improving development performance due to a crisis of governance in sub-Saharan Africa in which the Bank's programmes of adjustment and investment were not proving effective. This gives rise to a push for "good governance" as sound development management which was defined as the manner in which power is exercised in the management of a country's economic and social resources for development (World Bank, 1992). Later, the Bank convoluted its view in the 1992 report of Governance and Development, when it stated, "*Governance, in general, has three distinct aspects: (a) the form of political regime(parliamentary or presidential, military or civilian, and authoritarian or democracy); (b) the processes by which authority is exercised in the management of a country's economic and social resources; and (c) the capacity of governments to design, formulate, and implement policies, and in general, to discharge governmental functions* (World Bank, 1992).

The term 'good governance' was also used at the second United Nations conference on least-developed countries held in 1990. The concluding remark of the conference was thus, "Good governance is basic to the economic and social progress of all countries". The General Secretary, Kofi Annan, also discourses that 'Good governance is perhaps the single most important factor in eradicating poverty and promoting development' (UNDP, 2020:51). The debates on good governance is all about what makes institutions and rules more effective including transparency, participation, responsiveness, accountability and the rule of law. It is partly about having efficient institutions and rules that promote development and ensuring that public services live up to their names. This will entail protecting human rights, promoting wider people's participation and achieving more equitable economic and social outcomes. On the other hand, the Economic and Social Commission for Asia and the Pacific (ESCAP), a UN organisation, observes governance as 'good' only if measures are taken to minimise corruption and there is inclusion of the voices of the most vulnerable sections of society including minorities in decision-making.

1.2. The Indian Scene

In terms of overall growth rate, after reforms have been introduced, it has been a remarkable success. Despite urbanisation, around 70 per cent of India's population continues to live in villages and about 60 per cent of workforce sustains itself from agriculture and related activities. The world is looking India as potentially the biggest growth, next to China, in the coming decades.The interaction between urban and rural growth and sustainability is going to be critical here. Preventing environmental degradation and lessening vulnerability of the poor will be key intervention that will determine the quality of life. If India is to meet the growing expectation of investors over the world, the key question will be how it manages its rapid urbanisation. It is now accepted that the constitutional divides of subjects between union and states has been insolvent, and what matters is not the subjects but the functions under each subject. Thus, union government should perform those tasks which cannot be performed effectively at the state level, and the states should do the same in relation to local governments. That is the principle of decentralisation envisioned in 73rd and 74th amendments. After a shaky start and stagnation in the years following Independence, growth rates has developed into high gear during the 1980s and following years. Table 1.1

shows growth rates among selected countries in Asia during 1981-2008.

Table 1.1: Growth Rates (per cent) for Selected Countries in Asia, 1981-2008

Country	*1981-90*	*1991-97*	*199*
India	5.6(5.4)	5.3 (5.7)	5.7(
China (Mainland)	8.9(8.8)	10.3(10.2)	8.0(
China (Hongkong)	6.3(6.2)	5.5(5.3)	2.2(
Singapore	6.9(7.5)	8.4(8.2)	2.7(
Bangladesh	3.9(4.0)	4.5(4.5)	5.0(
Indonesia	5.3(5.4)	6.7(6.8)	4.0(
Korea	8.3(8.3)	6.7(6.8)	3.9(
Malaysia	5.8(6.2)	8.8(9.0)	2.7(
Thailand	7.6(7.3)	6.5(7.6)	4.7(
Pakistan	6.0(6.0)	4.1(4.2)	3.5(
Sri Lanka	4.2(4.3)	5.1(5.1)	3.8(

Source: International Financial Statistics, IMF.

[***Note***: The figures in brackets represent the winsorised growth rates (i.e., calculated by omitting the highest and lowest observations over each sub-period)].

Table 1.2. Represents the growth rates in India's successive Five Year Plan periods.

Table 1.2: Growth Rates in India Over Successive Plan Periods

Plan Period	*Annual Growth rate of GDP (Factor Cost) %*
I 1951-1956	3.6
II 1956-1961	4.2
III 1961-1966	2.8
IV 1969-1974	3.3
V 1974-1979	4.8
VI 1980-1985	5.6
VII 1985-1990	6.0
VIII 1992-1997	6.7
IX 1997-2002	5.5
X 2002-2007	7.6
2005-2006	9.5
2006-2007	9.7
2007-2008	9.2
2008-2009	6.7

Source: Basu and Maertens (2007); RBI (2010a): appears in India Development Report 2011 edited by D.M. Nachane.

In spite of growth, according to an estimate made by Polaski *et al* (2008). 792 million Indians constituting 73 per cent of the total population, survive on less than $1 per day, while 94 per cent of the population live on less than $2 a day. The initial steps in the liberalisation were taken in the 1980s mainly as a result of balance of payment crisis of 1991,which forced India to approach IMF for assistance. As a response to IMF urging and also because of the general disheartening attitude towards existing policies, the government of India made a distinctive break to launch an ambitious reforms programme across several areas necessitating democratic decentralisation and good governance.

In recent decades, multilateral and bilateral development agencies come forward with 'good governance' package and helping or forcing introduce it in the third world countries. The Government of India also has paid special attention to governance reforms. The Tenth Five Year Plan of India (2002-2007) has a full chapter on Governance and Implementation. It says that governance issue is at the forefront of the development agenda. It states, "*Governance relates to the management of all such processes that, in any society, define the environment which permits and enables individuals to raise their capability levels, provide opportunities to realise their potential and enlarge the set of available choices. These processes, covering the political, social and economic aspects of life impact every level of human enterprise, be it the individual, the household, the village, the region or national level... It covers the state, civil society and the market, each of which is critical for sustaining human development (GOI, 2002a).* The state is then considered responsible for creating a conducive political, legal and economic environment for building individual capabilities and encouraging private initiative. The role of civil society is to facilitate the mobilisation of public opinion and people's participation in economic, social and political activities. Governance, according to chapter 6 of Tenth Five Year Plan, thus, includes– people's participation, decentralisation, right to information, civil society involvement, civil service reforms (rightsising, transparency, accountability, professionalism) procedural reforms, judicial reforms (speedy delivery of justice), using information technology, empowerment of the marginalised. The policy thrust area for each ministry/ department of the Centre Government is identified. In case of almost all ministries/departments one item is common that is, institutional reform in terms of decentralisation, simplification, transparency, accountability and e-governance. Different societies and different social theorists may have different interpretations of what constitutes the acceptable core of 'good governance'. The contemporary usage of the term captures elements of institutional change that have become part of the reality of the world economy and society today. It warns us that governance is more than what government simply do. It asks how power in society is exercised in both form and practice (Doornbos, 2001:96).

According to 2006 Transparency International Corruption Perceptions Index, Finland Iceland and New Zealand are considered to be the world's least corrupt countries and Haiti to be the most corrupt. It defines corruption as the abuse of public office for private gain and measures the degree to which corruption is perceived to exist among a country's public officials and politicians. It is a composite index, drawing on 12 polls and surveys from nine independent institutions. Only 163 of 193 countries are included due to the absence of reliable data from the remaining countries. The score range from 10 (corruption free) to zero (highly corrupt). A score of 5.0 is considered the borderline figure distinguishing countries in terms of serious corruption problem. India figure at No. 70 with a rating of 3.3. It shows that corruption is a serious problem in India. What about 'good governance' which our Eleventh Five Year Plan categorically emphasis the relevant portion of which are reproduced below:

- The government at all levels must be accountable and transparent. Closely related to accountability is the need to eliminate corruption, which is widely seen as a major deficiency in governance. Transparency is also critical, both to ensure accountability and also to enable genuine participation.
- The government must be effective and efficient in delivering social and economic public services, which are its primary responsibilities. This requires constant monitoring and attention to the design of our programmes. In our situations, where the responsibility for delivery of key services such as primary education and health is at

the local level, this calls for special attention to ensuring the effectiveness and efficiency of local governments.

- Governments at lower levels can only function efficiently if they are empowered to do so. This is particularly relevant for the PRIs, which currently suffer from inadequate devolution of funds as well as functionaries to carry out the functions constitutionally assigned to them
- An overarching requirement is that the rule of law must be firmly established.
- Finally, the entire system must function in a manner which is seen to be fair and inclusive. This is a perceptional issue but it is real nonetheless. Disadvantaged groups especially the SCs, STs, minorities and others, must feel they have an equal stake and should perceive an adequate flow of benefits to ensure the legitimacy of the state.

So what are the barriers to good governance? Here the Second ARC observation may be, once again, helpful which are:

(1) ***Attitudinal Problems of the Civil Servants:*** There is growing concern that civil servant and administration have become inflexible, self-perpetuating and inward looking. A study of centre for media studies reveals that majority of citizens are not satisfied with the delivery of public services. In seven of the 11 departments surveyed, less than one-third of the citizens are satisfied with services delivered. Even in essential services like Public Distribution System (PDS), hospitals, electricity and water supply, only 30-40 per cent are happy with the services, and in need-based services like police, judiciary and municipalities, less than 20 per cent are satisfied. The civil servants' attitude is of indifference and insensitivity to the people's needs. There is a mind-set in which officers distinguish themselves as dispensing favours to the people rather than serving them.

(2) ***Lack of Accountability:*** Reason for inefficiency is hold to be inability within the system to hold the civil services accountable for their actions. This is very often because of the fact that authority is divorced from accountability. The complacency that the system breeds has resulted in employees adopting a pathetic attitude towards citizens and their grievances.

(3) *Red Tapism:* Bureaucracies are expected to adhere to rules and procedures which are important for good governance. But a common complaint pertained to excessive red-tapism and the long time taken to get even routine work done. The sixth Central Pay Commission observes, *'For the common man, bureaucracy denotes routine and repetitive procedures, paper work and delays. This, despite the fact that Government and bureaucracies existto facilitate the citizens in the rightful pursuit o their legal activities. Rigidities of the system over centralisation of powers, highly hierarchical and top down method of functioning with a large number of intermediary levels delaying finalisation of any decision, divorce of authority from accountability and the tendency towards micromanagement, have led to a structure in which form is more important than substance and procedures are valued over end results and outcomes. Non-performance of the administrative structures, poor service quality and lack responsiveness, and the subjective and negative abuse of authority have eroded trust in governance systems which needs to be restored urgently".*

(4) ***Low Level of Awareness to the Rights and Duties of Citizens:*** Low level of awareness about their rights prevents citizens from holding erring government servants to account. At the same time low levels of compliance of Rules by the citizens also act as an impediment to good governance.

(5) ***Ineffective Implementation of Laws and Rules:*** There is a large body of laws legislated in the country for purposes of maintaining public order, safety, sanitation and hygiene, protecting rights of citizens, and so on. Effective implementation will improve the welfare of all citizens and encourage each citizen to contribute towards development of society. But effective implementation is simply lacking

(6) ***Need for Reforms:*** The poor image of government in the minds of the people points to inefficient and ineffective administration, and the need for substantial reforming of our governance system.

Thus, a sound legal framework is the basic requirement. This will give rise to strong and effective institutional mechanisms to ensure that the rule of law is maintained and the rights of our citizens are well protected and human dignity upheld.

In India, it is observed that certain economic reform measures were initiated by Centre Government in the 1980s. However, systematic and far-reaching agenda of reforms unfolded with the Balance of Payment (BoP) crisis of 1991. The reforms package first formed conditionality's attached by the IMF and World Bank as contributor of the financial loans provided to the country to overcome the crisis. Subsequently, other major multilateral and bilateral agencies such as Asian Development Bank (ADB), United States Agencies for International Development (USAID), Department for International Development, UK (DFID), and Netherlands Organisation for International Cooperation (NOVIB) that operate in India, made governance reforms an important part of their agenda. These external agencies are directly involved in pushing and facilitating reforms both at the centre and the state levels in the country. The ruling regime in the country have carried forward the reforms agenda in a determined manner even after overcoming the external BoP of 1991 and despite opposition from certain sections of the society. Reforms started systematically at the Central level, and have later moved on to the state level since the second half of 1998 (Howes, *et al.*, 2003). However, the tempo and depth of reforms vary at the state level. Some states have moved faster like Andhra Pradesh (Mooij, 2003; Rao, 1998) and Gujarat (Dholakia, 2000, 2003), while some are very slow like Bihar and some may be in the middle (Nayar, 2004).

As the horizon of the concept of governance expanded, it has ramification on the rationale and forms of decentralisation. Decentralisation now includes not only the transfer of power, authority and responsibility within government, but the sharing of resources for determining public policy within the society. Decentralisation of government and devolution of functions and power are important measures. Encouraging people's participation in development projects is given attention both in the government and externally funded projects. The state is getting decentralised both vertically and horizontally. All the measures of governance reforms need critical appreciation. The reforms are being implemented at different levels- centre, state and local levels But the pace and speed of reforms differ across different spheres—economic, social, cultural, political, and also across different sectors. The implications of reforms have some commonalities and also certain variations reflected in terms of human development, human rights, equity and empowerment.

In conformity with the Directive Principles of State Policy concerning establishment of panchayats as units of local self-government, a determinate rural sector initiative, the Community Development Programme was launched in 1952. In 1953, the National Extension Service was again introduced aiming primarily at transfer of scientific and technical knowledge to agriculture, animal husbandry and rural craft sectors. In 1956, the second Five Year Plan recommended the village panchayats should be organically linked with popular organisations at higher levels, and in stages should take over the entire general administration and development of the district or the division excluding the functions of law and order, administration of justice, and selected functions pertaining to revenue administration. This had consequently induced appointment of Balwantrai Mehta Committee in 1957. The recommendations of the Committee had an impact and in 1959 the panchayat system was at work in some form in almost all states, although the higher tier had not been set up in Kerala and Jammu and Kashmir. By the end of 1980s, except Meghalaya, Nagaland, Mizoram and Union Territory of Lakshadweep, all other states and UTs had enacted legislation for the creation of panchayati raj institutions. In 14 states/UTs there was a three tier system, in four states/UTs it was a two tier structure and in nine states/UTs only one tier functioned.

In 1959, the first Administrative Reform Commission suggested that the main executive organ of the panchayati raj system should be located at the district level and not at the Block level. In 1977, Ashoka Mehta Committee was appointed, and it also recommended the district as the first point of decentralisation below the state level. With minor variations introduced by subsequent committees in the 1980s, the recommendations of Asoka Mehta Committee were well received and led many states to introduce appropriate Amendments in their Panchayati Raj Acts. Karnataka, Maharashtra, Andhra Pradesh, West Bengal and Gujarat embraced the new arrangement but U.P., Bihar, Punjab and Haryana held back. The committee was of the view that panchayat empowerment was not of much use unless it received constitutional standing.

Hence, there was a need for introducing a constitutional amendment on the subject. Although a number of committees were formed between 1978 and 1986 to look into various aspects of strengthening local self-government institutions, only minor suggestions were made, and with some modifications, Asoka Mehta Committee recommendations form the basis of the PRI format in existence in the country today.

The 73rd and 74th constitutional amendments constitute a landmark in the process of democratic decentralisation in India. In terms of these amendments the responsibility for taking decision regarding activities at the grassroots level which affect people's lives would rest directly upon the elected members of the people themselves. The intentions of the Amendments is to assign a position of command to them in the democratic framework of the country. But local government is a state subject under Schedule VII, the actual implementability of the provisions is dependent on the intentions and strength of the state panchayati raj enactment. However, the challenge is to ensure a design of the state law which is in total harmony with the spirit of the amendments.

Thus, Indian Constitution, both through Directive Principle of State Policy and the 73rd and 74th amendments provides a clear mandate for democratic decentralisation. It thus seeks to create institutional framework for grassroots democracy through the medium of genuine self-governing local bodies in both rural and urban areas. It is stated that while in USA local government revenue accounted for 15 per cent of the total government revenues in 2001, the corresponding figure in India was merely three per cent. Even after the 73rd and 74th amendments the transfer of funds, functions and functionaries has been nominal in most states except Kerala. Throughout 1970 and 1980s, a process of centralisation of functions such as water supply and sanitation in the hands of parastatals (water boards and authorities) has led to massive decline in the role and status of local bodies, which is now sought to be reversed. Such reversal is facing inevitable hurdles and snags from established institutional structures at the state government and district levels, and this has to be overcome.

After the Ministry of Panchayati Raj was set up in 2004, the panchayat agenda has received a much wider public attention.

The Ministry has been pursuing three broad aspects of panchayat agenda: empowerment, enablement and accountability. The Ministry is particularly giving

importance to building and strengthening institutions, systems, and processes to ensure efficiency, transparency and accountability. Creation of ombudsman, social audit, model accounting system would also set a need paradigm of accountability. MGNREGA, which mandates panchayats as the principal planning and implementing authorities, has given high visibility to the panchayats. There are, however, many unfinished agenda such as:

- Panchayats are very often unable to function efficiently due to insufficient funds, staffing, office space and infrastructure;
- True integrated decentralised planning is yet to happen largely due to non-cooperation from the line Departments.
- Devolution of the three–'Fs' to the panchayats is highly uneven across states since Article 243G gives discretion to the states;
- Implementation of PESA needs urgent attention which will address people's disaffection in tribal/forest Areas. PESA was enacted in 1996 which extended Part IX of the Constitution to Schedule V Tribal Areas and promotes people centric governance. This may be extended to non-council areas of Mizoram.
- Elected village councils in the Sixth Schedule Areas and non-Sixth Schedule Areas of North East States, particularly Mizoram, need to be established for meeting the aspirations of the people.

Local government is sometimes treated as synonymous with decentralisation, but the two are quite apart particularly when the local situation itself is plagued with sharp hierarchical divisions. Functions should be ideally performed according to the principle that the central authority should have a subsidiary function performing only tasks which cannot be performed effectively at the local levels. That is the decentralisation envisaged in the amendments which now need to be implemented in full. The second Administrative Reforms Commission identified core principles which are: (i) application of the principle of subsidiarity in the context of decentralisation; (ii) clear delineation of functions of local governments *vis-à-vis* state governments and among different tiers of the local governments; (iii) effective devolution of these functions and resources accompanied by capacity-building and accountability; (iv) integrated view of local services and development through convergence of programmes and agencies; and (v) citizen centricity.. Since all the fifteen reports and the recommendations of the Second Administrative Reforms Commission have been examined by the Core Group on Administrative Reforms, and Group of Ministers (GoM) have also considered the recommendations, and are now in various stages of implementations, the core principles may be crucial guidance for State Finance Commission:

(a) ***Subsidiarity*** : The central idea of subsidiarity is that citizens as sovereign and stake-holders arethe final decision-makers in democracy. Citizens are also customers of all servicesprovided by the State. Subsidiary principle stipulates that functions shall be carried out closest to citizens at the smallest unit of governance and delegated upward only when local units cannot perform the tasks.

(b) ***Democratic Decentralisation***: Subsidiarity can be applied only through effective decentralisation. It is because of this that 73rd and 74th amendments were enacted in 1992. Effective decentralisation from states to local governments should be the cardinal principle of administrative reforms. Such decentralisation should be influenced by four guiding norms. (i) There should be a clear link in the minds of the citizens between their votes and the consequences in terms of public good it promotes; (ii) Decentralisation promotes fiscal responsibility provided there is a clear link between resource generation and outcomes in the form of better services; (iii) In centralised structures, the closer government process is to the citizen, the greater the participation, stakes and understanding of the issues. Therefore, if democracy is to be real, the locus of power should shift as close to the citizen as possible in order to facilitate direct participation, constant vigil and timely intervention; (iv) All governance processes are about fulfilling the citizen aspirations and needs. Only in effective

and empowered local governments can the positive power to promote public good be reinforced and the negative impulses to abuse authority curbed.

(c) ***Delineation of Functions***: In Federal governmental arrangement, the roles and responsibilities of various tiers of government have to be clearly defined. India's constitution enumerates the subjects under state control under List II of the Seventh Schedule. Where a subject requires a federal and state jurisdiction, it is included in List III, and clear principle define the extent of authority of the Union and the states. However, in respect of local governments, there are complications: (i) Since all local governments' subjects are also state subjects, there must be clear delineation of the state and local government in respect of each of the subjects/functions. Otherwise needless confusion and undue interference by the state will be inevitable. In many of these functions state may have to play vital and legitimate role. For example, while school education may be a subject of devolution, the framing of courses, setting standards and conduct of common examinations should fall under state purview. (ii) Within local governments there is a need for clear functional delineation among the various tiers. For example, while school management can be entrusted to local government, most staffing and academic matters would fall within the purview of the higher tiers of local government.

(d) ***Devolution in Real Terms***: The principles of subsidiarity and democratic decentralisation cannot be operationalised by mere creation of elaborate structures and periodic elections. Devolution, to be real, demands that local government should be effectively empowered to frame regulations, take decisions, and enforce their will within their legitimate sphere of action. Such empowerment should be clearly and unambiguously defined by the constitution and state legislatures. Empowerment remains deceptive and misleading unless public servants entrusted with the discharge of responsibilities are fully and permanently under local government control, subject to protection of their service conditions.

Fiscal devolution to the local governments must also meet two norms: (i) In order that local government must be able to fulfill its obligations, there must be room for flexibility through untied resources in order to establish priorities, and devise new schemes and allocate funds. (ii) There must be both opportunity and motivation to mobilise local resources through local taxes, cess and user fees, subject to norms of financial decorum and accountability.

Equally important is building of capacity of local government to discharge their responsibilities effectively. Real empowerment will entail not only devolution and capacity building, but strategies be evolved to overcome the resistance of the state executives and governments as the compulsion of real politics often prevents the possibility of any serious measures to enable local governments to function as institutions of self-governance.

(e) ***Convergence***: *First,* with rapid urbanisation and increase of peri-urban areas to be taken into account in city planning and development, there need to be greater institutional convergence between rural and urban local governments. *Second,* parastatal bodies function independent from local governments and are directly accountable to the state government. In this way local governments are deprived of their important functions. Proliferation of parastatals is in breach of the principle of subsidiarity and thus slabs effective citizen's participation in the management of these services. The local functions of all these authorities need to be devolved on local governments. *Third,* citizens must be able to interact with all service providers through a single window as far as possible. Increasingly, all over the world, several disparate services provided by different agencies of government, are available to citizens under one roof. In Germany, for instance, local government is the point of contact in obtaining passport through the actual service is provided by the federal government. *Fourth,* empowerment of stake-holders and local governments should be seen as continuum. But the local government and empowered group of stake-holders cannot function in isolation. Just

as the tiers of the local government function in close coordination, local government and empowered stake-holders group should work in concert. The larger functions of support, coordination and policy will be with the local governments and the actual day-to-day management and service delivery will be the responsibility of the stake-holders. This convergence between the empowered stake-holders' groups and the local governments should be a key feature in decentralisation.

(f) ***Citizen Centricity*:** The citizen is at the heart of democracy. Thus, all governance institutions particularly local governments, should be judged by the satisfaction of citizens and direct empowerment of people. Therefore, measurement of citizen's satisfaction as the consumer of public services is an important one. Report cards, citizens' feedback at delivery and service counters for the citizens' voice to be heard needs to be institutionalised in decentralised governance. *Second*, social audit through reliable and trustworthy based community organisations, civil society groups and prominent citizens would ensure citizen centricity. Through gram sabha comprising of all residents, the citizens, as stake-holders, can participate in decision making. This can be done even at the level of urban local councils. The most important form of citizens' participation is a community of clearly identifiable stake-holders in the delivery of a specific service. The second Administrative commission is of the opinion that empowerment of stake-holders and local government must be seen as continuum and that there should be no cause for conflict between stake-holders and local government. Effective empowerment of stake-holders accompanied by mechanisms of coordination with local government is key principle to be followed.

The panchayats at present, except in some states, are performing and functioning sub-optimally. The root cause of this is that panchayats are not seen as local governments with clear roles, and lead to:

- Inadequate devolution–as many states are not taking effective steps to devolve the three Fs to local governments to enable them to discharge their responsibilities.

- Parallel system and set up under various centre/state developmental programmes further drained strength of the local government and depleted their functional space or even encroach upon their political space.
- In some states the village panchayats have been placed in a position of subordination. Panchayats officials have to spend extraordinary amount of time visiting Block offices for funds and technical approval. This is the normal case in Mizoram. This control of bureaucracy distort the role of elected representatives
- Activities permitted under the tied funds/schemes are not always appropriate for the specific rural areas. This results in unsuitable activities.
- Empowering the gram sabha could have been a powerful weapon for transparency, accountability, and involvement of marginalised sections. But many states Acts do not spelt out the powers of gram sabhas nor have any procedures been laid down for the functioning of these bodies or penalties for the officials.

1.3. The Problem, Issues and Objectives

It may be recalled that the Constitution of India had given almost unlimited power to the state government in respect of local self-governing institutions.It may establish or abolish these institutions. The states had absolute authority over devolution of powers and functions.This discretionary power has been used to centralise power at almost all levels. The 73rd amendment to the constitution was to put an end to this.

Mahatma Gandhi, who strongly believed in *Gram Swaraj*, pleaded for the transfer of power to the rural areas. Villages should govern themselves through elected bodies to become self-sufficient. This will be the very foundation of democracy in independent India. But the draft constitution in 1948 had no place for panchayati raj Institutions. Gandhi severely criticised this and called for immediate attention. The President of the Constituent Assembly, Dr Rajendra Prasad, drew the attention of the Law Minister, Dr B.R. Ambedkar, to this lacuna, initiating discussion and debate both within and outside the constituent Assembly. As a result, panchayat finds a place in the Part IV of the constitution containing the non-mandatory Directive

Principles of the State Policy. The amendment which was eventually numbered as Article 40 of the Directive Principles of the State Policy states, " *the state shall take steps to organise village panchayats and endow them with such powers and authority as may be necessary to enable them function as units of self-government*". Rural problem was accordingly tackled through community development programme in 1952 and National Extension Service in 1953 but more or less failed miserably due to the absence of effective instrument for people's participation.

In order to boost participation, strong local level government was realised early. Thus, Balwantrai Mehta Committee was appointed in 1957 to look into the problems of democratic decentralisation in independent India. This was followed by the appointment of Ashok Mehta Committee in 1977, GVK Rao Committee in 1985, Singhvi Committee in 1986 which recommended that panchayati raj institutions should be constitutionally recognised and protected. Prime Minister Rajiv Gandhi was driven by a vision to provide the people with representative administration in his address to the Nation in January, 1985. His vision was that people must determine their own destinies and said, "*to the people of India, let us ensure maximum democracy and maximum devolution. Let us give power tothe people*". Following these circumstances, Rajiv Gandhi influenced the introduction of the 64th amendment bill on local government on the 15th May, 1989 in Parliament, but failed. But in September 1991, a fresh bill was introduced, and it was passed in 1992 as the 73rd amendment Act, 1992, and came into force with minor modifications on 24 April, 1993.

As far as local governance is concerned, Article 244 of the Constitution envisions three categories of Tribal Areas, such as:

(1) Areas notified as 'Scheduled Areas in the specified States in Fifth Schedule,

(2) Areas listed as 'Tribal Areas' in the Sixth Schedule in North Eastern Region,

(3) Areas not covered in the above two categories.

Sixth Schedule provisions concern 'administration of tribal areas' and Fifth Schedule relates to 'administration and control of Scheduled areas and Scheduled Tribes', but there is no special schedule for the rest. Thus, the legal framework of local self-government in North-east India may follow the following typologies:

(1) Sixth Schedule Frame in Meghalaya, parts of Assam, parts of Mizoram and parts of Tripura;

(2) State Legislature Frame in Nagaland and non-council Areas in Mizoram;

(3) National Frame in Arunachal Pradesh, Sikkim, Manipur excluding hill areas, non-council areas in Assam and Tripura.

This entails that different constitutional measures is necessary for implementing reform in the specified areas. Mizoram falls under the first and second categories, i.e., Sixth Schedule Frame and State Legislature Frame.

The 73rd Amendment Act is an attempt to restructure the PRIs to reach the grass root level. The bill for the first time gave constitutional status to panchayati raj institutions and it becomes mandatory on all state governments to implement it. It brought about uniformity in structure, composition, powers and functions of panchayats. It gave impetus to local government to promote social and economic development and improvement in living condition of rural India. But the general impression in many states is still that these institutions are viewed as implementing agencies for developmental activities and that they are not given the status of decentralised political institutions. But there are many states on the path to fulfilling Article 243G which provides that state legislature should 'endow panchayats with such powers and authority as may be necessary to enable them to function as institutions of self-government', and the same Article also indicates that 'powers, authority and responsibility of panchayats prescribes that panchayats will plan for, and implement schemes relating to economic development and social justice'. The Eleventh Schedule lists 29 functional items which are to be entrusted to the panchayats, and states are on their path to devolve these functions. I have given introduction to the panchayati raj institutions because the Mizoram Finance Commission Act, 2010 states, *to enable all the local bodies to have financial autonomy to perform functions analogous to the functions of other local bodies constituted under Constitution Part IX and Part IX-A while retaining the distinctive tribal identity.* The understanding seems to be that the recommendations may be at *par* in regard to the devolution of the three Fs (Functions, Functionaries and Finance).

Notwithstanding anything contained in the provisions, the Constitution 73rd Amendment Act, 1992 under its Article 243M states that the Act in its present form will not apply to (a) the Scheduled Areas and the Tribal Areas referred to in Clause (2) of Article 244 (b) of the Constitution (b) the States of Nagaland, Meghalaya, and Mizoram (c) the hill areas in the State of Manipur for which District Council exist (d) Panchayats at the district level in the hill areas of Darjeeling district of West Bengal. Clause (4) of Article 243 M, however, *provides that the Amendment may apply to Nagaland, Meghalaya and Mizoram provided that the Legislative Assembly of the concerned State passes a resolution to that effect by a majority of total membership of that House and by a majority of not less than two-thirds of the members of that House present and voting*. This means that the Centre Government is not going to impose externally the provisions contained in the Part IX of the Constitution, but that the state and the State Finance Commission may take initiative in order to accrue the benefits of these provisionseither by formal recommendations or by legislation or both. It may be pertinent to recall here what the Prime Minister, Manmohan Singh, proclaimed in his speech on the occasion of National Panchayati Raj Diwas in New Delhi on 24th April, 2013. He stated that 'the bureaucracy is still unwilling to share its power with elected local bodies' and he called for 'immediate change in this mindset'. He also said, "The Centre will implement Rajiv Gandhi Panchayat Empowerment campaign under the 12th Plan to strengthen panchayats. We have allotted more money this time to help the states in their initiatives to strengthen Panchayats and budgetary support for this purpose has been increased by around ten times at Rs 6,437 crores from Rs 660 crores in the 11th Plan. I hope the state government will use this fund thoroughly in strengthening institutions of local self-government. It is our promise that the central government will provide all possible help to states so that our development process becomes more inclusive and sustainable". The new government at the Centre under Narendra Modi is also currently committed to bring about better governance.

Historically, right from the initiation of the province of Assam in 1874, some parts of its were administered under the

Scheduled District Act, 1874. There were the Backward Tracts which included (a) the Lushai Hills, (b) the Naga Hills, (c) the Garo Hills, (d) the North Cachar Hills, (e) the British portion of the Khasi and Jaintia Hills and the eastern Frontier Tracts of Lakhimpur, Balipara and Sadhiya. There were complete statutory bar to the legislative authority of the legislature within the backward areas. The Centre Government said that the area of Assam was so large that a scheme of centralisation was best arrangement. In course of time the Backward Tracts were replaced by what was known as Excluded Areas. The Constituent Assembly formed Advisory Committee on Fundamental Rights and Minorities. The task was to suggest plan for the administration of these areas. In 1947, the Advisory Committee set up three sub-committees. One of the sub-committee submitted its report on July 28, 1947. The other sub-committees also finalised their repots within two months. On the suggestion of the chairman a joint meeting was held. The result was that the failure of these areas lay in development and not in isolation. However, they distinctly made it clear that excluded and partially excluded areas needed separate treatment even in states other than Assam, and made their suggestions. But the reports were never considered by the Constituent Assembly (Hidayatullah, 1979: 44). There was thus, Tribes Advisory Council where the Fifth Schedule will be in operation, and in Assam the tribal areas were divided into two parts. With the first part there were to be Autonomous District and Autonomous Regions. Mizoram was in the first category and Arunachal, for example, was in the second category. Mizo Hills fell under the Sixth Schedule provisions. The Sixth Schedule provision is a very elaborate one, and has undergone many changes since it was first enacted. The changes were made through constitutional amendments, Parliamentary legislation, Presidential Order and Centre Government Notifications.

In pursuance of paragraph 11 of the Sixth Schedule to the Constitution, the Lushai District (Village Councils) Act, 1953 was passed by Mizo District Council, which received the assent of the Governor of Assam on November 19, 1953 and published in Assam Gazette on the 9th of December, 1953. Section 1(2) of the Act states that, 'it extends to the Lushai Hills District except the areas under the jurisdiction of the Pawi-Lakher Regional

Council' and Section 3(2) provides the size of the village councils in consonance with the size of the village. Section 23 of the Lushai Hills District (Village Council) Act, 1953, has given power to the village council to make rules. Section 23(2) stipulates, "in particularly and without prejudice to the foregoing powers such rules may prescribe:

(a) Control, preservation and use of timbers and other forest products except the reserved forests, ordinarily utilised for building purposes such as canes, sungrass, siallu, laisawral etc.;

(b) Maintenance, preservation and improvement of good water supply;

(c) Control of stray animals within its jurisdiction and at night within the village Ram (land);

(d) Ngawidawh (fish trap),

(e) Extraction of Khamkhuai (species of bees)".

In addition to this power, the Administration of Justice Rules, 1953 had given certain judicial functions to the village councils. Section 6 of the Rules conferred the establishment of village courts. Section 14 of the Rules stated that the village council court shall try suits and cases of the following nature in which both the parties belong to the Scheduled Tribes or tribes residents within its jurisdiction–(a) cases of civil and miscellaneous nature falling within the purview of village or tribal laws and customs (b)criminal cases falling within the purview of tribal laws and customs and offences of petty nature, simple assault and hurt, affront and affray of whatever kind, drunken or disorderly brawling, public nuisance and simple cases of wrongful restraint.

However, after the Assam Reorganisation (Meghalaya) Act, 1969 (55 of 1969) this has been drastically changed. The village councils try only such suits and cases which are not excluded from their jurisdiction by the rules made by the Governor and the District Councils. Also, if any law made by the District Council or a Regional Council is repugnant to any provision of law made by the state legislature, the law or regulation or rules made by the councils to the extent of repugnancy will be void and the law mad by the legislature will prevail in Meghalaya and Mizoram. The Governor, therefore, has the overriding power to annul any Act or resolution of a District Council if it is likely to endanger, according to him, the safety of India or is likely to prejudice public order and may take such steps as he thinks necessary, and he may even assume all or any of the powers of the Councils.

The Sixth Schedule divided Tribal Areas into Part A and Part B as follows:

Part A: (1) The United Khasi-Jaintia Hills District; (2) The Garo Hills District; (3) the Lushai Hills District; (4) The Naga Hills District; (5) The North Cachar Hills; (6) The Mikir Hills.

Part B: (1) North Eastern Frontier Tract including Balipara Frontier Tract. Tirap Frontier Tract, Abor Hills District and Mismi Hills District; (2) the Naga Tribal Areas.

Today, the Tribal Areas are as described in the Table as Part I, Part II, and Part III. Part I are the territories in the state of Assam; Part II concerns the state of Meghalaya and Part III relates to Mizoram which run as follows:

Part I: (1) North Cachar Hills District; (2) The Mikir Hills.

Part II: (1) The Khasi Hills District (2) The Jaintia Hills District (3) The Garo Hills District.

Part III: (1) The Pawi District (2) The Lakher District (3) The Chakma District.

The names of the Pawi District, the Lakher District and the Chakma District in the state of Mizoram came by the Mizoram District Council (Miscellaneous Provisions) Order, 1972. The name Mizo District was omitted by the Government of Union Territories (Amendment) Act, 1971 (83 of 1971). It dissolved the Mizo District Council, and the Autonomous Regions in Mizoram became Autonomous Districts. Thus, in so far as the Sixth Schedule is concerned, it now governs only the areas shown in Parts I, II and III.

Under this condition, Roy Burman (1995) observes, "Those who are aware of the socio-political cross-currents in North-east India know that the Sixth Schedule in its present form has reached a road block in the harmonious functioning of the state government and the Autonomous District Councils". Under the Sixth Schedule, the Autonomous District Council was the authority to design the nature of decentralisation of power at the village level as was done in Mizoram. The village councils in Mizoram enjoyed a high degree of autonomy in village administration including judicial matters. However, the situation changed drastically with the emergence of Union Territory status of Mizoram in 1971 and subsequent statehood in 1987, and the revocation of Mizo District Council. The village councils have been functioning directly under the state government through the Local Administration Department as its nodal agent. Bureaucrats, as state agents, seem to have free play in the actual functioning of the village councils. Immediately after statehood, other functional and line departments are also infiltrating in the affairs of the village councils. The autonomy of the village council has been slowly eroded, and the functional role of the village council become ambiguous and ambivalent. During a course of field survey of some village councils during 2001-2002, village council members are complaining that the state government, through its bureaucratic representatives, has given them more responsibilities than they can handle, and without attendant powers and authority-administratively, politically and financially. This project is, therefore, an attempt to see the level of truth in this, and to delineate the true nature of village council in Mizoram from empirical and actual case situations- is it merely an agent of the state government for implementation of certain programmes or does it truly function as government in the local situation in the true sense of the term 'government'?

The study is, thus, a departure from the general broad framework of studying panchayati raj institutions. It focused on the actual functioning of village councils in Mizoram. Mizoram, along with other hill areas specified in Article 243M, is outside the purview of the 73rd constitutional amendment. The 73rd amendment, 1992 under its article 243M states that the Act in its present form will not apply to (a) the scheduled areas and the tribal areas referred to in Clause (2) of the Article 244(b) of the constitution, (b) the states of Nagaland, Meghalaya and Mizoram, (c) the hill areas in the state of Manipur for which district councils exist, (d) Panchayats at the district level in the hill areas of Darjeeling district of West Bengal. Clause (4) of the Article 243M, however, provides that the amendment may apply to Nagaland, Meghalaya and Mizoram, provided that the legislative assembly of the concerned state passes a resolution to that effect by a majority of total membership of that House and by a majority of not less than two-thirds of the members of that

House present and voting. Reorganisation of North-east India and the subsequent termination of Mizo District Council when Mizoram became UT in 1971 and the centralisation of power by the state government machineries in relation to village councils needs special attention.

It is to remember here that the Indian masses had been subjected to ruthless exploitation by the imperial rulers and their India allies. This has been continuing even after Independence because of a policy of centralisation by the framers of the constitution and subsequently by the ruling elites in Independence India. Many studies have confirmed this. And the only way to end this, according to Ghosh (2000:2) is *"when every villagers recognises his own strength and becomes conscious that he is the maker of his own destiny."*

The village councils in Mizoram is a very peculiar one. It is different from panchayati raj institutions elsewhere in India, and it is a variant of village councils under Sixth Schedule provisions *per se.* Without the intermediary channel of the district council, it has been losing its autonomy and viability. If panchayati raj institutions are considered agencies of the state government especially in regard to regulatory functions, village councils in Mizoram are agents of the state government in developmental functions and to a lesser degree at the level of regulatory functions. The powers and authority of panchayats in relation to social service activities are almost absent in village councils. However, the judicial powers of the village councils following traditional social customs is, nonetheless, absent in the case of panchayat system. A combination of village council's judicial power and the Sixth Schedule provisions and the 73rd constitutional amendment as far as development and social service functions are concerned can go a long way in fulfilling the aspirations of the people of Mizoram and elsewhere.

The objectives of the present study is :

(1) *Todelineate the functioning of village councils in Mizoram before and after the abolition of Mizo District Council in 1971.* Relevant questions may be: What is the nature of autonomy enjoyed by the village councils in Mizoram before and after 1971? What type of changes can be observable in the matter of state intrusion into the affairs of the village councils after 1971?

(2) *To assess the performance of village councils in regard to 'regulatory' functions and 'developmental' functions after reorganisation of North-east India.* Relevant questions may be: What is the nature of developmental functions enjoyed by village councils? Is it satisfactory? What power do village councils enjoy in order to discharge its regulatory functions? It will also take into consideration, as far as possible, the role of women in local governance, and relationship between the existing land tenure system and the prospects of rural development.

(3) *To appraise and assess the nature of urban local government.* There are 24 notified town/urban areas in Mizoram including Aizawl. Of these, only Aizawl has Municipal Council and the rest continued to have village councils. Relevant questions may be: What is the nature of urban local bodies in Mizoram?

1.4. Methodology

Village councils in Mizoram used to enjoy a high level of autonomy in village administration including judicial matters before the abolition of Mizo District Council. However, the situation changed tremendously after the emergence of Union Territory of Mizram in 1971 and statehood in 1987, leading to revocation and dissolution of Autonomous Mizo District Council. The matter of village governance has been left to the LAD of the government of Mizoram since then. In actual reality, it seems that other functional departments are also involved in the affairs of the village councils as the volume of developmental activities increased. With the dissolution of Mizo District Council, the gap between the state government machineries and the village councils become widen and the space, thus, created has been more or less occupied by bureaucrats and politicians. As such, development packages seem to have been thrown into them, and the people largely do not involve and freely participate in the programmes. They are not, thus, highly motivated. This must have impinged on the progress of developmental processes. There does not seem to be any devolution of functions, functionaries, and finance.

The proposed study is empirical in nature, and as such collection of primary data have been undertaken from the field situation. It is thus based on extensive field investigation of selected village councils. Altogether 31 village councils from different parts of Mizoram(at least two from each district). During 2012 two village councils each in seven districts such as Champhai (Zote, Ngur), Lunglei (Luangmual, Thuampui), Lawngtlai (Thingkah, Chawntlangpui), Saiha Zero Point, Saihatlangkawn), Serchhip (Chhiahtlang, New Serchhip), Mamit (New Mamit, Rawpuichhip) and Kolasib (Thingdawl, Lungdai) have been visited. In 2013, during the third and final phase of fieldwork, four more village councils in Mamit district, (West Phaileng, New West Phaileng, Lallen, Damparengpui) two more village councils in Kolasib district (Nisapui, Bukpui), two more village councils in Serchhip district (Keditum, Khawlailung) and nine village councils in Aizawl district (Samlukhai, Chamring, Sumsuih, Muallungthu, Muthi, Sakawrdai, Zohmun, Vaitin, Sailutar) have been visited. Besides, five urban local councils have also been visited. I have carefully discussed the problems with the council members, conducting questionnaire to the council members, and to the public in 31 villages from different parts of Mizoram. The primary data collected is supplemented by a wide range of secondary data.

The book is an attempt to see the problems in Mizoram from the perspectives of: (i) Global transformation towards decentralisation and good governance; (ii) India's commitment to decentralisation as enshrined and envisioned in the 73rd and 74th constitutional amendments; (iii) Weaknesses of state legislative provisions in Mizoram and some other states in India; (iv) Reluctance of politicians and bureaucrats in devolving functions, funds and functionaries to local governments mainly due to lack of political will, and lack of public awareness. It is expected that this book will call to mind the educated elites, politicians, bureaucrats, and the public in general in India, and in particular Mizoram and North-east India, to have a fresh and meaningful look into the reality of the problems in our local government system.

The book is divided into nine chapters. Chapter one is introductory highlighting the theoretical perspective in decentralisation and good governance and the problems encountered in India. Chapter two is about Mizoram, history of governance in the traditional set-up leading to the present situation. Chapter three spells out local government in India with 73rd constitutional amendment and decentralisation processes. Chapter four is empirical in nature *vis-a-vis* devolution of functions, functional activities and the role of parastatals. Chapter five is all about the pathetic condition of service delivery, and chapter six specifies the financial position and source of funds of local governments in Mizoram. Chapter seven is all about the way expenditures are maintained and protracted on different functional areas. Chapter eight is on general observation and chapter nine contains recommendations.

2

Local Government in Mizoram

2.1 Land and the People

Mizoram lies in the southernmost corner of North-east India. It is bounded on the north by the Cachar district of Assam, on the east and south-east by Myanmar and on the west by Tripura and Bangladesh. More than 75 per cent of its boundaries are bounded by foreign countries. It covers an area of 21,081 square kilometers. It used to be the largest district of Assam in geographical area, but population-wise the smallest district. On the whole, Mizoram enjoys a fairly pleasant weather, and there is slight change of temperature during summer and winter. The whole area consists of small ranges of hills running in the north-south direction in parallel series, separated from one another by narrow valleys. The general level of these ranges is about 3,000 feet high in the west, and slowly rises as one goes eastward where there are ranges over 6,000 feet high, and the climate also according becoming cooler, In fact there are peaks over 8,000 feet high in the Chin Hills of Myanmar bordering Mizoram.

Due to the steepness of the ranges of hills and the continuous clearings of the forest for *jhumming* and excessive monsoon rains, the alluvial soil in the hills have been washed away. The soil is generally loose, porous, sandy loam but clayey in the lower elevation. As such, the water holding capacity is low. The soil in the lower valley sides are however alluvial. The nature of the soil is a direct result of excessive erosion brought about by continuous practice of shifting cultivation.

Mizoram continues to be sparsely populated This may be because of the bad communication system, rugged hills and different terrain and remoteness from the rest of the world. But the demographic data has shown a steady increase in population. District-wise population can be seen in Table 2.2.

Table 2.1: Population Trend in Mizoram

Sl.No.	*Year*	*Males*	*Females*	*T*
1.	1901	39,004	43,430	
2.	1911	43,028	48,176	
3.	1921	46,653	51,754	
4.	1931	59,186	65,218	
5.	1941	73,855	78,931	
6.	1951	96,136	100,066	
7.	1961	132,465	133,598	
8.	1971	170,824	161,566	
9.	1981	257,239	236,518	
10.	1991	358,078	330,778	
11.	2001	459,109	429,464	
12.	2011	552,339	538,675	

Source: *Statistical Handbook, Mizoram, 2012.*

With the exception of few immigrants after independence, the entire population can be said to consist of Mizo tribe. But the term, 'Mizo' is a relative one and may or may not include all the hill men residents of Mizoram. The Chakmas and Reangs are now considered formal residents of Mizoram as far as political structure is concerned, but remain largely to be socially distinct tribe having no common culture and normative social customs with the Mizos. The Chakmas are immigrants from Bangladesh largely after independence, and have not generally adaptive to the Mizo social norms. They have their own distinct culture and religious life totally different from those of the Mizos. They are followers of Buddhism and their societal form takes a Buddhist cultural form. The Reangs are a semi-nomadic people and are scattered along the small strips of valleys on either banks of the western rivers, and generally have no social contact with the Mizos.

Table 2.2: District-Wise Population, 2011 Census

Sl. No.	*District*	*Area (sq.km)*	*Population*			*% d g ra*
			Persons	*Males*	*Females*	
1	Mamit	3,025	85,757	44,567	41,190	3
2	Kolasib	1,382	83,054	42,456	40,598	2
3	Aizawl	3,576	404,054	201,072	202,982	2
4	Champhai	3,185	125,370	63,299	62,071	1
5	Serchhip	1,421	64,875	32,824	32,051	1
6	Lunglei	4,536	154,094	79,252	74,842	1
7	Lawngtlai	2,557	117,444	60,379	57,065	3
8	Saiha	1,399	56,366	28,490	27,876	1
TOTAL		**21.081**	**1,091,014**	**552,339**	**538,675**	**2**

Source: *Statistical Handbook, Mizoram, 2011.*

Barring the Chakmas and the Reangs, we may take the term 'Mizo' to include those who are living in Mizoram and adjacent areas and who identify themselves as Mizo. The Census report often classify the Lais (Pawis) and the Maras (Lakhers) of the south Mizoram as belonging to separate tribal groups different from the Mizos. However, the Lais and Maras, collectively known as the 'Shendus' by the British in the early period of colonisation and which also includes a number of other sub-tribes (Reid, 1942:1) inhabiting the southern area of Mizoram in those days, usually identify themselves as belonging to the Mizo community depending on the social context and rewards. In both social and political spheres, the Lais readily adapt themselves to the Mizo normative rules where the Maras are less adaptive to the Mizo way of life. This was instrumental in the creation of United People's Party formed by the Mara Students Union in order to create political image in the 1987 Assembly elections. The social adaptive nature of the Lais may be attributed to the presence of a number of Lai residents among the dominant Lusei group under the Lusei chiefs in the traditional setting. The dialect of the Lai has also close affinity with the language commonly spoken by the Mizos, that is, Duhlian or Lusei language.

Table 2.3: Distribution of Population by Tribal Groups, 1961

Name of Group	*Population*
Mizo/Lusei	213,261
Chakma	19,337
Any Kuki tribes (including Reangs)	11,677
Lakher (Mara)	8,790
Pawi (Lai)	4,587
Hmar	3,119
Others	243

Source: *Census of India, 1961, District Census handbook, Lushai Hills, p. 172.*

The seemingly small number of the Lais, Maras and the Hmars may be noted. This was mainly due to the fact that an alarmingly large number of these sub-groups returned themselves in the census category of Mizo/Lusei, while in fact the actual population of Mara was larger than that of the Chakmas. The Mizos are broadly divided into two major sub-group categories-the Lusei and non-Lusei or Awzia. 'Awzia' simply means those who speak dialect other than the Lusei. Member of the Awzia group are, thus, people who have dialect of their own different from the Lusei, and different from each other. While the different non-Lusei clans may be said to form a separate social group of their own, different clans of the Lusei formed one single group by virtue of the common language they have in Lusei. Coupled with this was the administrative skills which ultimately become instrumental in assimilating the non-Lusei clans to the Lusei way of life (Skakespeare, 1901:145).

Luseis are divided into twelve or more major clans while the non-Luseis are divided into sixteen or more major clans. Different versions of clan division and counting of number of sub-clans have been invented by different writers and informants giving rise to different conceptions of clan division. Each of the major clans has been sub-divided into a number of minor clans totaling about 349 (Zatluanga, 1968). The Lusei, as a group, was considered the dominant group in political sphere and wielded prestige in the social realm. The Lusei, under Sailo chiefship, wielded political power for several years, and as a consequent the British named Mizoram the Lushai Hills.

Just as the population of Mizoram could almost be considered as consisting one tribal form, the religion of the hills could be considered as one, that of Christianity. The Mizos in general have forsaken their traditional religion in favour of Christianity. Only minor tribal groups like the Chakmas and the Reangs and members of out-group living as permanent residents during the British period returned themselves as non-Christians. In 1961, the per centage of Christianity in Mizoram was 88.06. However, the figure only for the Lushai/Mizo was 206,484 or 97.01 per cent. Table 2.5 may be seen for this. This remains more or less constant. The impact of Christianity on the spread of education may also be noted. The percentage of total literates in 1901, in Mizoram was 2.95 per cent while it was 6.75 per cent in neighbouring Khasi and Jaintia hills. This can be seen from Table 2.3. By 1961, the percentage of literacy in Mizoram increased to 51.24 whereas it was only 37.15 per cent in Khasi and Jaintia hills. And in 2011 provisional census figure the per centage of literates in Mizoram jumps to second place in India at 91.58 per cent, which is next to Kerala (93.91 per cent).

Table 2.4: Number of Total Literates per 10,000 of Total Population in the Mizo Hills and United Khasi and Jaintia Hills

Year	*Total literates*		
	Mizo Hills	*K & J Hills*	*Mizo*
1901	295	672	2.95
1911	472	651	4.72
1921	743	905	7.43
1931	1,267	1,094	12.6
1941	2,312	1,615	23.1
1951	3,651	2,296	36.5
1961	5,124	3,715	51.2

Source: Census of India, 1961,Vol III, Part A- General Report, pp. 166-67.

Table 2.4 shows population by decadal growth in Mizoram with contrasting figure from Meghalaya whereas Table 2.5 indicates distribution of Tribal Groups by religion.

Table 2.5: Distribution of Tribal Groups by Religion

Tribal Groups	*Name of Religion*			
	Animist	*Buddhist*	*Christian*	*Hindu*
Lushai/Mizo	140(0.05)	3,304(1.55)	206.484 (97.01)	2,795 (1.31)
Chakma	-	15,367 (79.47)	3,421 (17.69)	466 (2.41)
Any Kuki Tribe(including Reang)	5,409 (46.32)	-	-	6,263 (53.68
Lakher	-	-	6,633 (75.46)	2,056 (24.54
Pawi(lai)	-	-	4,578 (99.800)	9(0.20
Hmar	-		2,768 (88.74)	384(1
Others	-	-	190(95.95)	8(4.05
Total	**5,549 (2.09)**	**18,671 (7.02)**	**229,847 (86.39)**	**11,945 (4.49)**

Source: Census of India, 1961, District Census Handbook, Mizo Hills, Table C-V.

2.2 Traditional Governance

Traditional political institutions centred round chiefship to which all the legal authority was attached. The chief was the guardian of the people, head of the village, leader in war, owner of the village land, protector and father of the subjects (Sinha, 2012).The chief was the secular head of the village or cluster of villages, but he was not the ritual head of the village. The Mizos and all the related tribes claim to have originated from what they have called 'Sinlung' or 'Chhinlung'. Different interpretations have been given to Chhinlung tradition. It might have been the present Tailing or Sinlung in the south-west China (Songate, 1956:6) or it might have been Sining in central China (Pudaite, 1963:21), or still it might have been taken from a Chinese King Chien Lung (Vanlawma, 1972:1). The Mizos firmly believed that the term 'Chhinlung', whether a place or a person's name, originated from China and that the Mizos and all the related tribes claim to have originated from China.

From Chhinlung (Vanlawma, 1972), they were said to have forced to lead a nomadic life by their inability to repulse their enemies. This has been confirmed by many folklores and traditional songs common among the Mizos, Hmars and other related Kuki tribes. This can be taken as illustrious of the common origin of all the Kuki tribes. Their nomadic movement took them to the present Shan State of Myanmar. The movement from Shan state must have dispersed them into sub-groups. This was considered to be an outcome of Shan aggression.Thus while the main group settled down in Khampat, sub-groups such as the Hmars, Thados, Pangs, Darlawngs, Mirawngs and others continued their westward movement and reached the hitherto unoccupied hill ranges of Indo-Burma borders. The solidarity developed during Chindwin and Kabaw valley settlement was broken and was not completely revived even after the British rule. Although neighboring people called them by different names at different times, the Mizos had common ancestor and falls under the following sub-tribes- Chin, Old Kuki, Thado Kuki, Lusei Kuki, Kuki in Tripura, Kuki in Assam, Kuki in Manipur, Mizo in Myanmar, Arakan, Bangladesh and Tripura (Nunthara, 2013). Both inter-tribal and intra-tribal conflicts forced some groups to migrate into the present Mizoram. The last batch to cross river Tiau to enter Mizoram was the group who claim themselves to be 'Lusei' in the beginning of Seventeenth century. The Lusei group were stronger and superior with their powerful Sail chiefs. The rudimentary and elementary form of polity that emerged at this time is very much akin to what Claessen and Skalnik call 'early state' in terms of what they call the inchoate, typical and transitional type.

The Sailos must have established their rule in Mizoram between 1580 and 1600 or 1550 (Vanlawma, 1975, Thangliana, 1992). Even after British consolidation, the Sailos were permitted to function as chiefs for 60 years when chiefship was abolished in 1954. Each of the indigenous non-Lusei clans had its own customary ritual head called 'Puithiam'(priest), apart from the Lusei priest who was the village priest. The Lusei also had their own religious priest called 'Sadawt'. The Lusei clans were not supposed to use the services of the non-Lusei priests and the members of the non-Luseis were denied the use of Lusei priest. The chief had some control and influence over the village priest. The village priest, at the direction of the chief, could be called upon to conduct ceremonies that concerned the entire village.

The chief was the proprietor of the village land. He had the right to collect taxes on bees and salt springs not only from his subjects but also from members of other villages who had made use of these. He had to see that outsiders did not encroach the land, and preserve the land form wasteful use. The chief was also the traditional legal head and authority. He had the power over life and death, ostracism and the right to demand free labour for the construction of his house. He was traditional village head in all spheres and had final authority except in ritual matters. However, although the legislative power and executive function were vested in the chief, he was guided by the traditional normative rules. Traditional convention required the chief to appoint elders to assist him in administration.The presence of elders or advisers each representing a cluster of locality or clan in the village meant that the chief had to consult them, and respect their ideas and advice. The elders were influential men in their respective clan or localities and rich in local standard. The chief also had to respect the wishes of the village youths who were the backbone of his power and glory. Moreover, the people could always shift their allegiance to other chief by migrating in another village if the chief become dictatorial. Because of these customary constraining elements, the chief could not be dictatorial and iron-handed.

The chief had to see that his chiefdom is economically self-sufficient. He would go round the village to see if they were village youth loitering in the street, and if found one, he would say, 'young man it is good to rest once in awhile, but we must see that we reap harvest big enough to feed our neighbouring villages'. He would always try to instill the value of hard work and endurance. He was monarch in his own respective areas and together dominates and controls the whole of Mizoram. Although Sailo chiefs had their respective chiefdoms and internally divided among themselves, all of them together held Mizoram as one powerful Sailo kingdom. This process could have culminated in one powerful Sailo kingdom had it not been prevented by the British intervention. Thus, the Mizo social and political formation at the dawn of British entry suggested that there was a rudimentary form of social categorisation and specialisation and division into rulers and the ruled. The political organisation was centering on the chief and his council of elders and political activities had been sometimes centralised as it was in the case of Selesih Confederacy and later on the fight with the Chin, Suktes, Paihtes and the British in order to safeguard Mizoram as a whole. At other times, at the level of domestic arrangement it may be localised, and citizenship is largely on residence and birth in the territory. All the Sailo chiefs recognised Mizoram as their recognised legal territory. However, the type of political organisation in around 1850 is reflected in the report of Col. Lister quoted in Alexander Mackenzie which reads, "*The Lushais are a very powerful tribe under the Government of six sirdars, of whom one is the acknowledged chief. They all have their separate cantonments with number of dependent villages attached. In these cantonments the fighting men reside; in the dependent villages are located the ryots, who are merely used as coolies, and for tilling the soil. They consist, in many instances, of the captives they have brought away in their different expeditions, a great par of them probably taken as mere children and gradually reconciled to their captivity.*

The rich societal structure evolving during the Sailo period can be gained from an account made by Rev. Liangkhaia (1988) reflecting the characteristics of the society. *First,* they recognised the importance of children, and one among the major festivals,

Chapchar Kut, was meant mainly for children. Second, tremendous efforts that were put on the training of the youth to be brave, chivalrous and dedicated to the society was remarkable. *Zawlbuk*, bachelor's dormitory was crucial here. One important contribution of Zawlbuk is in the shaping of social mores and perpetuation of traditional customary laws. It came into being to serve the needs of the society and perform important educative functions to the youth. Zawlbuk is the organisation through which Mizo's social life rotated. It was a training ground for warfare, discipline, defense of the village, hunting, dance, other cultural activities, and a spirit of sacrificial deeds for others. 'Val Upas' (elderly members) would instruct the youth and became an important place for socialisation process. A cherished term 'tlawmngaihna' a combination of chivalry, gallantry, bravery, meekness, dedication, civility, respect for elders may be said to have originated from Zawlbuk. Third, the way the society looked after widows and destitute is also remarkable. The Chief and Zawlbuk system patronised and supported widows and the poor and the helpless ones. Fourth, respect shown to elders was inherent in the process of socialisation of children. Fifth, the emphasis on hard work and endurance. The chief himself took responsibility to see the survival of the social form through these social characteristics. So, under chiefship, everybody care for the 'welfare of the society'. Thus, even though in a rudimentary form, service delivery to the citizen was very efficient and effective.

The chief court functioned as the highest legal authority. It tried all kinds of cases from petty thefts to rape case and cases involving capital punishment. Besides, elders the chief usually had some other assistants such as the Tlangau (village cryer), the Thirdeng (village blacksmith). The Tlangau had a right to collect a small basket full of rice per household annually and the blacksmith had the right to demand a portion of the wild animals killed as well as sacrificial killing of a pig by any family. With the abolition of chiefship, the political functions of the chief were taken over by the District Council and the village councils. But, with the absence of traditional propriety and sanction, the village councils have no arbitrary power beyond those sanctioned by the rules. In the situation, the village councils, in the beginning, found it difficult to exercise even those powers sanctioned by the rules, and in the absence of clear roles, the position of village council is ambiguous, indistinct and confusing.

At the time of abolition of chiefship in Mizoram, there were 309 dethroned chiefs in Mizoram as follow:

Table 2.6: Number of Chiefs Dethroned in Mizo Hills

Name of Clan	*Number of Chiefs dethroned*	*Name of Clan*
Sailo	169	Chenkual
Pawi	27	Khiangte
Fanai	19	Palian
Lakher	15	Tlanglau
Hmar	12	Tuikuk
Hualngo	10	Pachuau
Zadeng	8	Hauhnar
Ralte	7	Tlau
Chawngthu	6	Hnamte
Thangluah	6	Gurkha
Zahau	6	Chakma
Paihte	4	**GRAND TOT.**

Source: *Zahluna in Patnaik(ed) MIZORAM: Dimensions and Perspectives, 2008 (pp.264-65).*

The administration of villages in Mizoram by 309 hereditary chiefs had been replaced and taken over by the village councils.

2.3 Sixth Schedule and Village Councils

At the dawn of British colonisation of Mizoram, it was ruled by the Sailo chiefs. Analysis of tribal political organisation very often characterised the tribals' social division and social change in terms of contact with the caste-Hindu plains. But Mizos are characterised by their traditional political independence largely stemming from their geographical isolation, and this have shaped their social organisation and nature of their identity very much like the Bhils in the pre-Rajput conquest.

Under the Sixth Schedule provision, the first general election to the Lushai Hills District Council was held on 4 January, 1952. The Lushai Hills District Council was then inaugurated on 26th April, 1952 at Aizawl by the Chief Minister of Assam. In response to the political demand of the inhabitants of the remote southern Mizoram, Pawi-Lakher Regional Council was inaugurated with headquarters at Saiha on 23rd April, 1953 by Ch. Saprawnga, Parliamentary Secretary to the Government of Assam.

In pursuance of Paragraph 11 of the Sixth Schedule to the Constitution of India, the Lushai Hills District (Village Council) Act, 1953 was passed by the Luhsai Hills district Council, and received the assent of the Governor of Assam on the 19 November, 1953, which was subsequently published in Assam Gazette on 9 December, 1953. The Act provided for the establishment of village council in Mizoram as per Clauses (e) and (f) sub-paragraph (1) of paragraph 3 of the Sixth Schedule which empowers the District Council to make laws with respect to the establishment of village or town committees or councils and their powers and any other matters relating to village or town administration, including village or town police and public health and sanitation.

The Act also specifies the functions of the village council as follows:

(1) The village council or any officer of the state government authorised (by the state government) shall allot a particular region within the boundaries of each village for jhum each particular year, and the distribution of the jhum-plots shall be done in accordance with the laws framed by state government under paragraph 3(1) (d) of the Sixth Schedule to the Constitution of India;

(2) The village council shall have powers to enforce 'Hnatlang' in the interest of the public whenever occasion demands provided that no discrimination shall be made on grounds of religion or caste or class or any of them;

(3) Any person who does not comply with the order of 'Hnatlang' shall be liable to 'run' either in kind or in cash which may be fixed by the government, by order, from time to time, not exceeding (Rs 50 per hnatlang day) unless he has been exempted from hnatlang under section 9(1) or has obtained commutation under Section 9(3).

Regulation of Hnatlang: (1) Each Council shall have power to exempt any person or persons from Hnatlang at its own discretion. The reason for exemption shall be recorded in writing. No person who is 60 years or above shall be compelled to do any Hnatlang; (2)Any person below 15 years shall not be allowed to represent in the Hnatlang; (3)Every person shall have the option of commuting his obligation to render service under hnatlang on payment of cash compensation in lieu of it at a rate to be fixed by the village council not exceeding (Rs 25) per hnatlang day.

***Collection of Taxes*:** (1) The state government or any officer authorised by it in this behalf, shall either appoint tax collectors or allot the work of collection of taxes to suitable persons, specifying their duties and any other matters connected with the collection of taxes; (2) Collection of taxes shall be done strictly in accordance with rules or under instructions and directions given by the state government or authorised by it in that behalf. Responsible for the sanitation of the village. A sanitation committee shall be appointed by the village council if necessary.

In exercise of the powers conferred under sub-paragraph (4) of paragraph 4 of the Sixth Schedule to the Constitution of India, the Lushai Hills District Council, with the previous approval of the Governor of Assam, made the Lushai Hills Autonomous District (Administration of Justice) Rules, 1953. The Rules provided for three classes of courts to be constituted by the District Council for the trial of suits and cases between the parties all of whom belong to the Scheduled Tribe or Tribes within the Lushai Hills Autonomous District: (1) Village Courts, (2) Sub-ordinate District Council Courts, (3) District Council Court. The village council for each Village or a smaller body consisting of not less than three members of the council as elected by the council in this behalf shall sit as the village court; provided that where the village council sits itself as a court, the quorum to constitute a court shall be three members or half of the total number of members of such council, whichever is greater.

Provided further that until such time a village court or courts is or are constituted under this Rule, the Headman of a village either recognised or appointed as such by the District Council, shall exercise the powers of a village court under these Rules. The jurisdiction of a village court shall extend to the hearing and trial of suits and cases arising within the territorial limits of the village.

A village court shall try suits and cases of the following nature in which both the parties belong to a Scheduled Tribes resident within its jurisdiction:

(a) Cases of civil and miscellaneous nature falling within the purview of village or tribal laws and customs.(b) Criminal cases falling within the purview of tribal laws and customs and offences of petty nature, such as petty theft and pilfering, mischief and trespass of petty nature, simple assault and hurt, affront and affray of whatever kind, drunken or disorderly brawling, public nuisance and simple cases of wrongful restraint: provided that the village court shall not be competent to try offences in respect of which the punishment of imprisonment is obligatory under the Indian Penal Code.

A village court shall not be competent to pass a sentence of imprisonment in any criminal cases. It shall have power to impose a fine for any offence it is competent to try, which may expend to Rupees five hundred according to the nature of offence. It may award payment in restitution or compensation to the aggrieved or injured party in accordance with the customary law.

In a civil case, a village court shall have power to award all costs, as also compensation to those against whom unfound or vexatious suits and cases have been instituted before the court. The fines and payments imposed and ordered under sub-rule (1) and (2) may be enforced by distrait of the property of the offender.

A village court shall have power to order attendance of the accused and the witnesses to be examined in the case and to impose a fine not exceeding Rupees one hundred on any person willfully failing to attend when so ordered.

If any person on whom a fine or any payment has been imposed by a village court fails to deposit the amount at once or within such time as the village court may allow, the Court shall report the matter to the Chief Executive Member for necessary action to realise the fine or duties in such manner as it may deem fit unless the accused person gives notice to appeal such decision.

Where a village court is of the opinion that the sentence it is competent to pass is insufficient in the circumstances of the case it shall without delay refer the case to the competent court, and the court shall dispose of the case in accordance with these rules.

Subject to Rule 31, an appeal shall lie to the Sub-ordinate District Council Court or Additional Sub-ordinate District Council Court, as the case may be, from a village court within the jurisdiction of the Sub-ordinate District Council Court or Additional Sub-ordinate District Council Court concerned, against any order or sentence in a criminal case, or against any decision in any other case, provided the appeal is preferred within sixty days of the conviction or sentence or decision of the village court excluding the time for getting copies of the order or decision appealed against. The Sub-ordinate District Council or Additional Sub-ordinate District Council Court while hearing the appeal may either decide the appeal after perusal of the records of the case or may try the case *de-novo*.

2.4 MNF Uprising and Dislocation of Local Governance

In order to preserve and maintain Mizo identity among the newly awakened educated middle class, the Mizo Cultural Society was established in 1959. Mr R.B.Chawnga, the first president of Mizo District Council sub-Court, Aizawl, became its first President and R. Zuala, a senior government employee in the Deputy Commissioner's office, became its Secretary. In 1959-1960, Mizoram was severely hit by a popular famine known as 'mautam'. Mautam means flowering of bamboos producing seed like grain which caused multiplication of rats and pests. Earlier a flowering of bamboos and significant scale of famines had taken place, for example, in 1911-12 (Patnaik and Lathakima, 2008). Rats would appear in the jhum field overnight and would eat away the paddy bringing great havoc to the farmers. The Mizo Cultural Society, thus, held a conference in early 1960 which was followed by a grand procession and demonstration while the Chief Minister of Assam, B.P. Chaliha, and Williamson Sangma, a Garo minister, were visiting Mizo Hills. The Mizo District Council took a negative note and its disapproval of the procession. This resulted in prohibition of membership in the society for government employees. It also resulted in the demolition of R.B. Chawnga from the rank of first class officer to the rank of second class officer. Mr Laldenga, a district council cashier clerk, was on leave at that time and had to resign on charge of misappropriation of district council funds which had never been proved. Laldenga became the secretary of the society. With the government's hostile attitude, the society was soon defunct.

But the famine situation was getting more acute that the leaders of the Mizo Cultural Society decided to create the Mizo National Famine Front in the middle of 1960 to render voluntary services to the famine incapacitated people and protest against the ill-treatment of the government of Assam. R. Dengthuama became its first President and Laldenga its secretary. Mizo youth were voluntarily involved in relief works in towns and remote villages. The people fondly remembered the volunteers delivering food stuff in their villages and gave all the credits to Laldenga and his band of volunteers (Jagdish and Lalthakima, 2008:15).

When the famine was over in 1961, the members of the MNFF met at J. Manliana's residence at Aizawl and decided to transform the MNFF into a political party. Laldenga, however, did not agree to the proposal of demanding full independence, but a separate Mizo state within India. But other members believed that they had to take an extreme step in order to win the people's confidence and support. The Mizo Union was involving itself with the hill state movement with the All Party Hill Leaders Conference (APHLC), and any political aspiration must supersede the aspiration of the Mizo Union. Laldenga ultimately had given consent to independent movement on October 28, 1961. On the same night, eight people gathered at Ladenga's residence and formed a new political party called 'Mizo national Front (MNF)' which was to have lasting impact on Mizo politics. Laldenga was appointed its chairman, R. Vanlalawma its secretary and A. Rohnuna, the joint secretary.

The MNF had series of public meetings in 1961 and 1962 and called for Greater Mizoram and secession from India. They argued that the Mizo had been given separate administration by the British, and the Mizos have the right to be separated from what they call 'Indian colonialism', especially as they had been completely marginalised and neglected particularly during the famine situation. The independent Mizoram would comprise of all the Mizos in Mizoram, Manipur, Cachar, Tripura, Bangladesh and Burma across international boundary they would emphasised. The wider application of the term 'Mizo' to include all the sub-ethnic groups of Kuki-Chin group in the continuous settlements became convenient tool for imparting the idea of Greater Mizoram. This has given rise to stress on differential variation between in-group and out-group members. This was also facilitated by the failure of Assam state government to take immediate relief measures to the famine-stricken Mizo people reinforcing the condition of already existing distrust towards out-group members. The MNF leadership was able to exploit this by emphasising the relative strong qualities of the Mizos as against the caste-ridden Hindu society. It is, thus, not only material domination but also the cultural domination that the Mizo and other social entities in the North-east fear. The MNF leaders accordingly preached the social and cultural danger of remaining a part of India, particularly taking care to emphasise the destructive elements of Hindu culture to the Mizo Christian community. They, thus, emphasise the cultural and social factor which is also evident in the Memorandum submitted to the Prime Minister of India in 1965 and the Declaration of Independence signed by 61 signatories. The MNF, thus, emphasised that the Mizo stood as a nation even before the British came having a nationality distinct and separate from that of India. The only aspiration of the Mizo people, they would say, is the creation of Mizoram, a free and sovereign state to govern herself, to work out her own destiny as political self-determination is the birth-right of any nation group. The Mizos should not be deprived of such God-given national birth-right.

The MNF drew support from all sections of the population and in particular from the dethroned chiefs and their followers and younger generation. They were secretly making negotiation with the then East Pakistan for supply of arms and other material help. When the Government of India intended to move in the 18th Battalion Assam Rifles to help the 1st Assam Rifles to keep law and order situation in Mizoram, it was a good excuse for the MNF and was, thus, compelled to strike before the 18th Battalion reached Aizawl. And on the night of February 28, 1966, the Aizawl Treasury was looted and telephone exchange was put out of action. The scheduled MNF meeting on March 1, 1966 was cancelled, and MNF MLA J. Manliana was recalled from Shillong, and the MNF declared Independence. The MNF attacked at several places throughout Mizoram. The culvert between Vairengte and Lailapur gate in Cachar district was blown up and the Aizawl-Silchar road was blocked at several places. Aizawl was attacked on March 3, 1966 and the Assam Rifles post fell thereby leaving only Assam Rifles barrack. The MNF volunteers virtually captured many places throughout Mizoram including Aizawl town until there was air shelling on March 5, 1966. Three Jets strafed the MNF positions on March 5, 1966 and a number of light bombs dropped. As many as five air raids were carried out on March 5, 1966 and the Aizawl main *bazaar* was completely burnt down.

The advancing army column reached Aizawl on March 6, 1966 and Aizawl was recaptured. Lunglei was recaptured on March 13, 1966. But the interior villages were still under the MNF control and only after two months had some of the important centres freed of the MNF occupations, and normal administration reestablished. The suffering cries of the people had also forced the MNF to reduce ambush and arms combat with the security forces.

The MNF was declared unlawful by an Extraordinary Gazette Notification of the Government of India published on March 6, 1966, which reads that the MNF activities were "prejudicial to the security of the Mizo District in the state of Assam and the adjoining parts of the territory of India. The Centre Government, by affecting necessary amendment, has ordered that Rule 32 of the Defence of India Rule, 1962 shall be applicable to the MNF. Rule 32 of the DIR as amended provides that no person shall:

(a) manage or assist in managing any organisation to which this rule applied;

(b) promote or assist in promoting a meeting of any members of such an organisation or attend any such meeting in capacity;

(c) publish any notice or advertisement relating to such meeting;

(d) invite persons to support such an organisation or otherwise assist the operation of such organisation.

The Mizo Union hold outstanding position in Mizoram politics due to its anti-chief policy.It had made,accordingly a sweeping victory in the 1962 District Council elections in which it had won 16 of the 22 elected seats. The 1967 elections to the District Council were postponed in Mizoram due to the disturbed situation. The term of the then existing Council, elected in 1962, was extended till 1970 when fresh elections were held. During 1966-69, normal political activities were suspended and for the first time the Mizo Union lost majority position in the District Council in 1970 when the Congress emerged as the ruling party. However, the Mizo Union was able to retained its dominant position in the village council elections in 1971. Results of the three village council elections(1960, 1963 and 1971) may be seen below.

Table 2.7. Results of Three Village Council Elections Immediately before Attainment of UT Showing Comparative Strength of Different Political Parties

Parties	
	196(
Mizo Union	280
UMFO	83
Congress	-
Public	-
Independents	18
Drawn	-
UMMP(created by the Mizo Union & one factional group of Mizoram Congress in 1971	-
Total	**381**

Source: *Personal Record of Bonthanga Poonte(L) State Social Welfare Officer, Mizoram*) (appeared in C. Nunthara's *Mizoram: Society and Polity,* 1996).

Variation in the number of village councils was due to the creation of new village councils in 1963 in some of the big villages on the one hand, and grouping of villages after 1967 which reduced the total number of village councils in 1971. However, after returning of normal activities in 1972, people started going back to their original villages and subsequently recognised to have their own village councils. As such, the total number of village councils in 1994 had been massively increased from 158 in 1971 to 681 village councils in 1994.

In spite of army column operations against the MNF underground, many of the interior village remained to be under MNF control throughout 1966. The army was asked to by the central government to deal with the situation on March 2, 1966, and the 61 Mountain Brigade was moved from Tripura. During the first month, all the posts which had fallen to the MNA were taken back. But the casualties were heavy. During the next eight months, the army was joined by two more army battalions (18 Punjab and 9 Bihar). By the end of April, the MNF dispersed themselves in smaller units and merged with the population. They then launched guerrilla attacks on the Security Forces often inflicting substantial damages and casualties. It was in this situation that the army proposed that insurgency could not be controlled without more troops for operations and without resorting to resettlement of villages in order to isolate the insurgents from the populace. The proposal to resettle the villages was opposed by the Assam government particularly the Governor, B.K. Nehru, and the centre ministries of Home and Finance. But the army's persistence resulted in the clearance of the scheme by the Centre Government on December 5, 1966. The army called it "Operation Accomplishment" and on January 3, 1967 AIR announced the decision of the government to group villages in Mizo Hills for security reasons. The same day formal orders were issued by B.C. Carriapa, Commissioner of Division of Cachar and Mizo Hills and ex-officio Centre Government Liaison Officer for Mizo Hills, under Rule 57 of the Defence of India Rules, 1962, directing inhabitants of 100 villages along Vairengte-Aizawl-Lunglei road to move to 18 selected grouping centres, and authorised the army to remove them by use of 'minimum force'.

During the following months after the outbreak of violence in February, 1966, the law and order situation was most critical and to cope with this various orders were passed like the declaration of Mizo Hills as disturb area, promulgation of Armed Forces (Special Power) Act, declaration of offences section 188 and 505 of IPC as cognizable, prohibition orders on Arms, ban on wearing uniforms resembling army/police uniforms, ban on articles such as torchlights, jungle boots, etc. The grouping scheme which had four distinct categories involved a total of 2,36,162 population and 463 villages relocated to 101 grouping centres during 1967-1970. Incidents of stray cases of relocation by the army without any order continued even after this. The grouping scheme, because of stray cases of relocation, ultimately involved 516 villages evacuated and regrouped into 110 grouping centres, while 138 villages were excluded from the scheme. Jafa (2010) quotes incidence of grouping of villages recorded by an army officer in charge of actual shifting operation in summary form below: "*Darzo is one of the riches villages. There were ample stores of paddy, fowls and pigs. We arrived in the village around ten in the morning. My orders were to get the villages to collect whatever moveable property they could, and to set their own village to fire at seven in the evening. I also has orders to burnt paddy and other grain that could not be carried.. to keep food out of the reach of insurgents.. it was obvious they could not vary away even one fourth of paddy on store. Night fell and I had to persuade the villagers to come out and set fore on their homes. Nobody came out. I had to order my soldiers to enter and force the people out. Every man, woman and child came out with as much belongings as they could. But they wouldn't set fire to their own homes. Ultimately I lit a torch myself and set fire to one house. I knew I was carrying out orders, and would hate to do so if I had my way. My soldiers also started torching other houses. There was absolutely confusion Women were wailing and shouting and cursing. Children were frightened and cried. Pigs were running about, mithuns were bellowing, dogs were barking. One little girl run into her burning house and soon darted out holding a kitten in her hands.*

When it was time for the world to sleep, we marched out of Darzo-soldiers in front, with the Mizos following, and the rear brought up by more soldiers. I hated myself that night. I had done the job of an executioner. That night when I saw children as young as three years carrying huge loads on their heads for fifteen miles with very few stops for rest, their nose running, their little feet faltering, with pregnant women hardly able to carry their burden up the hill from Mat river valley- for the first time in my life as a soldier I did not feel the burden of the haversack on my own back. It was a miracle that we reached Hnahthial without a casualty, or perhaps the Mizos are a very tough people, physically and emotionally.

But there was something more to be carried out. I called the Darzo VCP(Village Council President) and elders and ordered them to sign a document saying that they had voluntarily asked to be resettled in Hnahthial PPV under the protection of the security forces as they were being harassed by the insurgents. Another document stated that they had burnt down their own village, and that no force or coercion was used by the Security Forces. They refused to sign. After one hour called them again one by one. On my table was a loaded revolver, and in the corner stood tow NCOs with loaded sten-guns. This frightened them and one by one they signed both the documents."

Such was the magnitude and extent of grouping of villages.The initial dislocation in jhum cycle and disruption of rural economy has been tremendous. It also has lasting impact of occupational structure of the population leading to large-scale unemployment situation. It destroyed the consistency of jhum cultivation, and without any infrastructure development in the villages, acquiring new occupation was not easy. Life was, therefore, precarious, unsteady and uncertain. One of the immediate impact has been large-scale migration to urban areas in search of commercial openings. The percentage of urban population in Mizo Hills in 1961 was 5.36 which suddenly jumped to 46.09 per cent in 1991 and 49.5 per cent in 2001 and 52.9 per cent in 2008 and 51.5 per cent in 2012. The scheduled village council's elections could not be held in 1966 as all normal political activities have been suspended. The terms of village councils and District Council have been extended. All normal life in grouping centres has been disturbed. By 1971, most of the uprooted villages have gone back to their original villages, but these hamlets have not been given civic amenities or village council in 1971.

In the grouping centres, dusk to dawn curfew imposed in and around grouping centres drastically reduced the time available for agriculture works and greatly distressed people-habitat integration. The protracted and prolonged counter insurgency measures also have stretched physical and societal distress and agony suffered by the people. Traditional Mizo social organisation centred on basic values such as bravery, chivalry and agricultural work. These basic values giving rise to societal norms were endorsed by the village solidarity. Members of the village councils in the grouping centres virtually complain the existence of village sub-group rivalry within the grouping centres in matters connected with the administration of the church, schools and politics. This had been enhanced by the method of concentration of members of regrouped village in one block or locality. People retained the sentimental bond of their old village which may sometime cut across familial ties. This helped in deteriorating village solidarity and harmony at the grouping centres.

Regrouping of villages thus destroyed the very fabric of society. Chivalry in Mizo conceptual understanding was a combination of gallantry, bravery, politeness, gentility, kindness, consideration for others, and most of all respect for elders. A Mizo understanding of tlawmngaihna subsumes all these attributes. These basic societal values were upheld by the common occupation in jhum cultivation which was harshly disrupted by grouping of villages without providing alternative occupations. Thus, grouping of villages, military frustration and harassment and dusk to dawn curfew have resulted in the dislocation of the normal functioning of village councils in the rural areas.

2.5 UT/State and Village Councils

When normalcy returned in 1967, the Congress started revamping the party. The president, A. Thanglura, on becoming MLA in Assam State Assembly, was stationed in Shillong. Dengthuama was appointed Convener of the party and later elected president in December, 1968. Strife within the party resulted in factional rivalry, one group led by Dengthuama and the other group led by Hrangchhuana, original treasurer of the party. Assam Pradesh Congress Committee (APCC) president, Bhagawattti, visited Mizo Hills and made Hrangchhuana Convener of the Mizo District Congress Committee (MDCC), and later *ad-hoc* president of the MDCC.The faction led by Dengthuama predominated the Mizo District Council membership, and all the top offices including the CEM (Chief Executive Member) were occupied by them. The factional group led by Dengthuama called themselves Mizoram Congress while the group led by Hrangchhuana was characterised by them as *vai Congress* or stooge of Assam Congress. This group claimed themselves to be representatives of Mizo identity in line with the MNF.

The factional rivalry culminated in the Hrangchhuana faction seeking alliance with the Mizo Union resulting in the no-confidence motion against the faction led by Dengthuama in the District Council. The Congress led by Dengthuama was defeated and the Congress led by Hrangchhuana with the help of the Mizo Union became the ruling group. However, friction soon developed because of the failure to accommodate Mizo Union leaders as promised in the new Council. The Mizo Union then sought alliance with the Dengthuama's group. Thus, on March 8, 1971, the Congress led by Hrangchhuana was defeated. The

Mizo Union and the faction led by Dengthuama then formed a coalition government called 'United Mizo Parliamentary Party' (UMPP). Ch. Chhunga, a Mizo Union president, became the CEM. During the tenure of the Ch. Chhunga, the first elections to the village councils after the MNF uprising were held in 1971 in which Mizo Union retained its strong position by capturing 66 of the 158 village councils. The Mizo Union gradually dominated the UMPP. The UMPP, in its session, held in April 14, 1971, passed the following resolution:

"In order to put all Mizo tribes including those living in our neighbourhood under one set up of administration, the house consider lasting peace and tranquility and statehood as of imperative necessity and decided to bring this to the notice of the Centre Government as soon as possible".

The District Council delegation consisting of C. Chhunga, CEM, Zalawma, Dy. CEM, K.Thansiama, MDC and Lalbuaia, MDC, met the Prime Minister, Mrs Indira Gandhi, in mid-May, 1971 and placed their demand for a full-fledged Mizoram state. And on July 17, 1971, S.J. Das, I.A.S., Commissioner for Cachar and Mizo District and Central Liaison Officer, came to Aizawl with a proposal of the Centre Government to confer the status of Union Territory on Mizoram. After a series of discussions held at the residence of the Deputy Commissioner of Mizo District on the evening of July 17, 1971, seventeen representatives of the UMPP agreed to appreciate the Centre Government's proposal and submit the following memorandum,

"The proposal (dated Aizawl the 17th July, 1971) of Union Territory status for Mizoram District was discussed. In view of the present circumstances prevailing in this part of the country, it was felt by leaders that the decision of the Government of India in granting the Union Territory status to Mizo Hills was a reasonable proposal for the Centre Government to make. The political leaders, however, felt that clarification on certain points was required. For this purpose it was imperative that a delegation consisting of about ten members should go to Delhi. It was further suggested that the Minister of State, Home Affairs, Government of India, should visit the District to get first hand knowledge".

Zakhi Hlychho, CEM Pawi-Lakher Regional Council, also expressed that there was no objection to this proposal provided that a separate autonomous District Council provision is being made for the Pawi and Lakher people. Christo Mohan Chakma, president of the Demagiri Congress Committee, welcomed the proposal on condition that a separate District Council for the Chakmas should be created. MDCC at the same time urged the Centre Government to have peaceful negotiation with the MNF before any political settlement is reached. The Youth Wing of the Mizo Union also submitted a memorandum which stated:

"The offer of Union Territory status to Mizoram is considered a sincere proposal by the Government of India for bringing in peace and normalcy. However, if s statehood is promised in principle at the outset there will be no objection to our acceptance of Union Territory status as an interim arrangement for a limited period".

The congress victory in 1970 was short lived as the Mizo Union made a landslide victory over the Congress in the first Assembly elections under Union Territory status in 1972. This had an end result in the merger of non-Unionist parties under Congress. The Mizo Union leaders realised the dwindling support they have under the new circumstances, and consequently also decided to merge with the Congress. Several oppositions were raised from different corners particularly from the Aizawl District Congress Committee. But the AICC leaders ultimately decided to accept the Mizo Union probably as a step toward final domination of Mizoram politics. This was, however, foiled by the emergence of a new political party, the People's Conference (PC) under the leadership of Brig. Thenphunga Sailo. The new party was able to gain support of the pro-MNF camp by creating image of Mizo identity in line with the MNF. As a consequence, PC emerged as the ruling party in both 1978 and 1979 Assembly elections. But the Congress again emerged as the ruling party defeating the PC in 1984 Assembly elections. The Congress was able to do this because it had the edge over other parties in bringing about peaceful solution to the ongoing peace talks between the MNF underground and the Government of India. During the 14 years of Union Territory status, the village council affairs have been taken over by the Local Administration Department as the Mizo District Council was abolished. Village council was like an unwanted child and nothing new has been introduced towards its improvement.

At the invitation of the Government of India, Laldenga arrived in New Delhi in the month of January, 1976 to have rounds of talks with Union Home Secretary, Mr S.L. Khurana. After one month's discussion, some understanding was reached on February 17, 1976. The terms of understanding was reviewed by the MNF leaders at the Calcutta Convention during March 24, 1976. The first step in peaceful agreement was reached on New Delhi when an official announcement was made to the effect that MNF had acknowledged that Mizoram was an integral part of India, and that the MNF had accepted the Constitution of India. Both the MNF and Government of India undertook to suspend violence and military operations. The MNF accepted to collect its underground personnel with arms at mutually agreed camp. But before the modality for actual settlement regarding 'mutually agreed camp' could be worked out, the Government at the Centre changed. The Janata Government came to power in 1977 and the peace talks with Laldenga was not resumed. The dialogue was totally broken off by March 20, 1978. Laldenga was arrested on July 28, 1978 and held in Tihar jail. He was bailed out in October, 1978 and was allowed to leave India.

The peace talks were resumed soon after Mrs Indira Gandhi returned to power in January, 1980. On July 30, 1980, the then Home Minister, Mr Jail Singh, announced yet another accord following which cease fire was announced. However, Brig. Sailo's People's Conference hostile relations with the MNF resulted in deadlock, and the talks broke down again in 1982. Brig. Sailo, the Chief Minister, refused to step down for Mr Laldenga. Mrs Gandhi also informed the Parliament that a duly elected government could not be thrown out. Laldenga and his family left for London in August, 1982.

In the 1984 elections the Congress (I) defeated the People's Conference. Steps for resumption of talks were soon initiated, and on October 2, 1984, Laldenga was again summoned to resume talks. He was to meet the Prime Minister, Mrs Indira Gandhi, on October 31, 1984, but her assassination on that fateful day prevented the meeting. Talks were resumed only in March-April, 1985 under Mr Rajiv Gandhi's government, represented by Mr P.V. Narasimha Rao and Mr G. Parthasarathi, and some headway was soon made. The question again seems to be on political interim arrangement. Laldenga suddenly left for London on December 23, 1985, after meeting the Prime Minister. Laldenga was again invited to India in March, 1986, and the stage was opened for final settlement. The Centre was determined to arrive at the final accord during June, 1986. The Chief Minister, Lalthanhawla, was summoned to New Delhi on June 2, 1986 and the Chief Secretary, Mr Lalkhama, on June 4, 1986. Mr Laldenga was then summoned to a meeting with Mr Ram Niwas Mirdha, Union Minister of State for Home. This was followed by a meeting with Mr Arjun Singh, Congress (I) vice president, subsequently followed by a number of meetings with Mr R.D. Pradhan, Home Secretary and other Congress (I) leaders.

On June 21, 1986, the draft agreement for the Mizo Accord was finalised, followed by the signing of the political settlement on June 25, 1986 between Mr Laldenga and Mr Arjun Singh, providing coalition interim government between the MNF and the Congress (I). This was subsequently followed by the signing of the Mizo Accord on June 30, 1986 between the Union Home Secretary, Mr R.D. Pradhan, Mr Laldenga and Mr Lalkhama, Chief Secretary of Mizoram. The accord provided among other things full statehood for Mizoram with 40 members Legislative Assembly. Mizoram state was inaugurated on February 20, 1987, and the elections to the first 40 members Assembly were held on February 16, 1987 in which the MNF bagged 24 seats and emerged as the ruling party.

However, nothing concrete happen for the village councils during Laldenga's government and subsequent governments. There is no new legislation, no new Act. Members of Mizoram State Legislative Assembly seem to recognise the predicament and quandary of people in the country-side particularly village councils, but nothing tangible happen and no worthwhile step have been taken so far. The main deficit of the village council is its financial weakness as there is no permanent source of income. It is empowered to collect animal tax out of which fifty per cent goes to the State LAD department. This is awfully nominal amount in all the villages and in many instances cannot even match the expenditure required for visiting district headquarters once. Another handicap is that people cannot participate directly in the discussions of the village affairs as the Lushai Hills District (Village Council) Act, 1953, as amended up to date, Sub-section (3) of Section 13 reads, *'No person other than the member of the village council shall vote nor shall speak or take part in its deliberation and any person contravening this provision shall be punishable with fine not exceeding Rs 50 by the village courts'.* The Sub-section (1) of the Section 25 of the Act provides, *'The Governor, by public notification, order the dissolution of village council if in his opinion, the village council is too inefficient or is not able to carry on the village administration or is acting in manner prejudicial to the interest of the State or for any other reasons sufficient for such dissolution'.*

The autonomy of village council as local self-government is exceedingly restricted by government intervention at every step.

The comparison between village councils in Mizoram and panchayati raj institutions elsewhere in India other than those specified not to be applied, made by Lalzawnga (2010) may be reproduced below:

- The PRIs has root in the Constitution of India whereas village councils has not such (PRIs now constitutional bodies).
- Unlike two or three tiers of PRIs there is only one tier in village council.
- Absence of seat reservation for women.
- While the duration of panchayat is five years, village councils term is only three years.
- Election to the panchayats is vested in the hands of state election commissions whereas the elections of the village councils are conducted by the state local administration department.(This has so far been taken over by the Mizoram state election commission).
- Gram sabha provides a platform for public grievances and exchange of ideas whereas, public participation in village councils is restricted.
- Power, authority and responsibilities of panchayats to prepare plan for economic development and social justice and the implementation of such schemes (including the matters listed in the Eleventh Schedule) are not comparable to village councils.
- The representation of different level of panchayats from local to district level is not comparable with village councils in Mizoram.

As far as participation of women considered to be the weaker section of the society, out of 2,071 elected candidates in 2009, only 31 women were included against 2,040 men. In Aizawl district 22 women were elected, six in Lunglei district, and one each in Serchhip, Kolasib, and Mamit district and no woman was elected in Champhai district. In 2012, Aizawl Urban areas under Aizawl municipalities had its first general election to 82 local councils in which 529 were elected as council members of which only 26 women were elected. In the 2012, village council elections conducted by the Mizoram state election commission, out of a total of 2,055 village council members elected, only 17 women were included.

In compliance to the 73rd constitutional amendment, many states have enacted Panchayati Raj Acts and readily created rural level institutions which have been superimposed on the existing administrative hierarchy at the district level. The administrative frame consisting of the field establishments of line departments, Deputy Commissioner, and Block Development Officers remain intact and continue handling all the regulatory, development and remaining functions of the government. Today the entire rural India is delimited into CD Block which are about 5,000 in numbers.' We have yet to see the implementation of the recommendations of the State Finance Commission which is to be ready by later part of 2014. We shall know by then the genuineness of those occupying offices of responsibility and representing people in the urban and rural areas.

2.6 Constitution of Mizoram Finance Commission

Mizoram Finance Commission has been constituted by an Order of the Governor, Vakkom Purushothaman, on September 30, 2011, in pursuance of sub-section (1) of section 3 of the Mizoram Finance Commission Act, 2010 consisting of Pu Van Hela Pachuau, Chief Secretary to the Government of Mizoram as the Chairman (Part-time) and Pu Lalthansanga, Secretary to the Government of Mizoram, Finance Department as Member Secretary (part-time). They were to assume Office in the first week of November, 2011, and shall make its report available by the 30th day of November, 2012 covering the period of five years commencing on the 1st day of April, 2013. However, the services of Pu Van Hela Pachuau and Pu Lalthansanga have been extended by the Government of Mizoram and were unable to assume Office as stipulated. Subsequent Notification dated August 30, 2012 stated,'in pursuance of sub-section (1) of Section 3 of the Mizoram Finance Commission Act, 2010 (Act No 17 of 2010), the Governor of Mizoram is pleased to order that Pu Van Hela Pachuau, IAS and Pu Lalthansanga, MF and AS shall be full time Chairman and Member-Secretary respectively of the Mizoram Finance Commission from the date immediately following the date on which they finally leave service, i.e., 31.8.2012' and that the Commission shall make available its report latest by the 31st day of October, 2014 covering a period of five years commencing on 1.4.2015.

The Terms of Reference (ToR) on which the Commission shall make the recommendations consist of the following matters:

"3(1) the principles which should govern—

(i) The distribution between the state and the village councils, Aizawl Municipal Council and the Autonomous District Councils of the net proceeds of the taxes, duties, tolls, and fees leviable by the state, which may be divided between them to enable these bodies to perform the functions assigned, and which may be assigned to it under any laws in force or orders, and the allocation between the village councils, Aizawl Municipal Council and the Autonomous District Councils at all levels of their respective shares of such proceeds;

(ii) The determination of the taxes, duties, tolls and fees which may be assigned to, or appropriated by, the village councils, Aizawl Municipal Council and the Autonomous District Councils;

(iii) The grant-in-aid to the village councils, Aizawl Municipal Council and the Autonomous District Councils from the Consolidated Fund of Mizoram;

(2) the measures needed to improve the financial position of the village councils, Aizawl Municipal Council and the Autonomous District Councils;

4. In making its recommendations, the Commission shall have regard, among other considerations, to–

(i) the resources of the state government, for five years commencing on 1st April, 2015, on the basis of levels of taxation and non-tax revenues likely to be reached at the end of 2014-15;

(ii) the demands on the resources of the state government, in particular, on account of civil administration, keeping of law and order, debt servicing and other committed expenditure and liabilities;

(iii) The objectives of State's fiscal consolidation roadmap recommended by the Thirteenth Finance Commission, which bind the management of public finance in Mizoram;

(iv) The functions which may be transferred to the village councils, Aizawl Municipal Council and the Autonomous District Councils for the coming five years with effect from 1st April, 2015; and the manner in which the existing functionaries of the state government, who are at the time of making recommendations are performing the functions recommended for transfer to the local bodies, shall be transferred to the village councils, Aizawl Municipal Council and the Autonomous District Councils;

(v) The taxation efforts of the state government in relation to levy of all types of property tax by the local bodies for additional resource mobilisation to enhance the financial independence and capacity of the local bodies to perform the functions assigned to them;

(vi) The need to enhance disaster management at the local levels so as to avoid minor disasters such as landslips, etc. at the local levels;

(vii) The need to manage ecology, environment and climate change as the local levels;

(viii) The need to improve the quality of public expenditure to obtain better outputs and outcomes through innovative monitoring and appraisal system at the local levels;

5. In making its recommendations on various matters, the Commission shall take the base of population figures as of 2001, in all such cases where population is a factor for determination of devolution of taxes and duties and grants-in-aids.

6. The commission shall indicate the basis on which it has arrived at its findings and make available the estimates of receipts and expenditures of the state government and each of the local bodies.

7. The Commission shall make its report available by the 30th day of October, 2014, covering the period of five years commencing on the 1st day of April, 2015.

The 73rd and constitutional amendments and attendant Part IX which provided democratic decentralisation in rural India exempted Mizoram and other hilly states such as Meghalaya and Nagaland in the North-east from its purview. Nonetheless, the Government of Mizoram is on the path to democratic governance and decentralisation as manifested in the Introduction to the Mizoram Finance Commission Act, 2010, which reads, *'it is expedient to constitute a single State Finance Commission for all the local bodies which will also be suitable to local bodies exempted by the afore mentioned provisions of the Constitution on the basis of the existing administrative arrangements to enable all the local bodies to have financial autonomy to perform functions analogous to the functions of other local bodies constituted under Constitution Part IX and Part IX-A while retaining the distinctive tribal identity protected by the Sixth Schedule to the Constitution of India which is foundational to the local bodies of the State'.*

According to the Second Administrative Reforms Commission, the tradition of the Centre Government in accepting the devolution package of the Central Finance Commission without deviation has not been established in the states. As such, state government do not commit adequate resources for the local government. This is an unfortunate situation, The healthy precedence established by the Union Government in accepting devolution proposals made by Union Finance Commission should be followed by state government. With this, the task of State Finance Commission, pointed by the Commission, is to assess the resource gap in case of all urban and rural local bodies and services provided. Lack of data in many states on various aspects of local governance makes the task difficult. Resource gap is to be estimated and recommend devolution of funds accordingly. The resource gap of any local body can never be measured in unqualified manner as the resource gap is a function of a variety of factors such as the level and quality of civic amenities provided, the efficiency of local body in raising resources, the quantum of service charges levied by the local body, etc.

The Terms of Reference (ToR) is very clear. The resources that can be raised by the village councils from own source will remain to be highly unsatisfactory as it is in other States. The recommendations of the State Finance Commission are expected to lay sound foundation for the local finance and promote effective decentralisation. However, the state governments failed to adopt distinct policies on allocation of funds to the local governments. Mizoram state so far has not even done meaningful exercise on this line. It will be a welcome gesture if the Union Government make it mandatory for the States to frame legislation in this regard clarifying an explicit procedure for such devolution.

As far as transfer and posting of administrative staff, it seem that some state governments have difficulty in placing the services of the concerned staff to the local governments consequent upon the devolution of certain activities and institutions. It will be easier for the state governments to take appropriate actions if there is 'enabling provision in the constitution' permitting the state legislature to make, by law, such provisions to enable the state governments to depute such staff to the local governments and to enable the local governments to exercise full power of administrative and functional control over such staff.

3

Local Government in India

3.1 Evolution of Local Government in India

It is widely known that self-governing bodies had existed in India from the earliest times. There is also evidence available of the existence of village sabhas (village assemblies) and *gramins* (senior persons of the village) until about 600 B.C. These village bodies were the lines of contact with higher authorities on matters affecting the villages (ISS, 1994). In course of time these village bodies took the form of panchayats(an assembly of five persons) which looked after the affairs of the village. Besides the village panchayats, there were also caste panchayats, to ensure that persons belonging to a particular caste adhered to its code of social conduct and ethics. After British rule, these bodies were replaced by formally constituted institutions of village administration. It is a historical fact that local self-government in India, in the sense of an accountable representative institution, was the creation of the British.

Lord Ripon was instrumental in the structural evolution of local government in India. Under his viceroyalty, the government resolution of 18th May, 1882 provided the creation of local boards consisting of a large majority of elected non-official members and presided over by a non-official chairperson. This is considered to be the *Magna Carta* of local democracy in India. It resulted in the establishment of local rural boards, in which two-thirds of the membership was composed of elected representatives. As a result of this resolution, the term self-government gained popularity. Thus, in 1906, the Congress, under the presidency of Dadabhai Naoroji, received self-government as the political goal for the country. And in 1907, the government constituted a Royal Commission on Decentralisation which further expanded and elaborated the principles expressed and articulated in the Ripon resolution. The Commission, consisting of five Englishmen and one Indian, Ramesh Chandra Dutt, recognised the importance of panchayats in the Indian context and recommended that *'it is most desirable, alike in the interests of decentralisation and in order to associate the people with the local tasks of administration, that an attempt should be made to constitute and develop village panchayats for the administration of local village affairs'* (Maviya, 1956).

The Congress in its twenty-fourth session at Lahore in 1909 also urged the government to take steps 'to make all local bodies from village panchayats upwards elective with elected non-official chairman and to support them with adequate financial aid'. However, Ripon resolution and the recommendations of the Royal Commission on Decentralisation were ineffective and remained largely on paper, the fact underscored by the Congress in a resolution adopted in its twenty-eight session in December, 1913. Annie Besant, in her presidential address at the Congress session in Calcutta in 1917 blamed the 'inefficient bureaucracy' for not taking action on what was suggested in the report of the Royal Commission on Decentralisation.

In 1919, Montagu-Chelmsford Reforms suggested that local self-government should be brought under the domain of Indian ministers in the provinces. The reforms had suggested that *'there should be, as far as possible, complete popular control in local bodies and the largest possible independence for them to outside control'*. However, in spite of the reforms objective, a truly democratic institution did not evolve. By 1925, eight provinces such as Madras (Panchayat Act of 1920), Bombay (Village Panchayat Act of 1920), Bengal (Self-government Act of 1919), Bihar (Self-government Act of 1919), Central Provinces and Berar (Panchayat Act of 1920), Uttar Pradesh (Village Panchayat Act of 1920), Punjab (Panchayat Act of 1922) and Assam (Self-government Act of 1925) passed acts for the establishment of village panchayats.

The Government of India Act, 1935, and the declaration of provincial autonomy in the Act marked another significant development in the emergence of panchayats in the country. With elected popular governments in the provinces, provincial administration enacted legislations for further democratisation of local self-government institutions including village panchayats. This had been the position regarding local self-government when India attained independence in 1947. Village panchayats had been central to the psyche of India's national movement. This was partly because of the influence of Mahatma Gandhi who categorically stated his vision of village panchayats as *'My idea of village Swaraj is that it is a complete republic independent of its neighbours for its own vital wants and yet interdependent for many others in which dependence is a necessity... The government of the village will be conducted by the Panchayat of five persons annually elected by the adult villagers, males and females, possessing minimum prescribed qualifications. These will have all the authority and jurisdiction required. Since there will be no system of punishment in the accepted sense, the Panchayat will be the legislature, judiciary and executive combined to operate its year of office. Any village can become such a republic today without much interference even from the present government whose sole effective connection with the villages is the execution of the village revenue... Here there is perfect democracy based upon individual freedom. The individual is the architect of his own Government'* (Gandhi, 1942).

Despite the historical commitment to democratic decentralisation, nationalist movement's commitment to panchayat and Mahatma Gandhi's strong propagation of democratic government at the village level, the first draft of Indian constitution, as pointed out earlier, did not include any provision for panchayats. When Mahatma Gandhi learnt about this, he called for immediate attention. It is to be noted here also that Ambedkar was against panchayats in the Constituent Assembly. Reacting to Ambedkar on the issue, Madhava Rau of Mysore said, *'It is true, some villages are chronically faction-ridden and indulge in petty tyrannies, or remain the strongholds of untouchability. A considerable number are pathetic or even moribund'* (Venkatarangaiya, 1969). But he insisted that even if 30 per cent could be classed as good, they could not be ignored. The argument of those who pleaded for the inclusion of village panchayats in the constitution finally prevailed. They managed to get a provision included in Part IV of the Constitution in the Directive Principles of State Policy. Article 40 reads, "The State should take steps to organise village panchayats and endow them with such power and authority as may be necessary to enable them to function as units of self-government." Ambedkar's objection was not the concept of democratic decentralisation *per se,* but he was speaking from his own experience of what a caste-ridden village society of India had meant to him. However, Gandhians believed panchayats as both means and end in democratic decentralisation and for devolving power to the people.

The basic conviction that village panchayat could play an important role in implementation of development programmes could not be ignored. But why is it not given the constitutional status and recognition it deserved? The answer as given in the Introduction of the Status of Panchayati Raj in the States of India, 1994, is that the urban and rural elites, their representatives in politics (from the time of the national freedom movement onwards), and a bureaucracy conditioned by its class character, had a disdain for panchayat and this has ever since remained intact. Whatever genuine attempt were made for the evolution of power, these interests saw to it that the attempts did not succeed. The story of panchayat institution since independence is no different.

Soon after Independence, Community Development Projects were launched as a model for rural development. But it soon found out that it was a failure without effective channel for people's participation. In order to boost participation in both Community Development and National Extension Services Programmes, the committee on plan projects in 1957 constituted a team for the study of the two programmes. The team was headed by Balwantrai Mehta, a member of Parliament. The team's recommendations favoured democratic decentralisation through the setting up of panchayati raj institutions. Without an agency at the village level to represents the entire village community, and to assume responsibility and provide necessary leadership for implementation, real progress in rural development could not be achieved, noted the team. National Development Council also subsequently reaffirmed the basic principles of democratic decentralisation expressed in Balwantrai Mehta recommendations, and left it to the states to work out arrangements suitable to each state. Panchayati raj refers to a system linking people from the gram sabha to the Lok Sabha. The term was probably coined by Jawaharlal Nehru, and it is distinct from the term, panchayat, which connotes a local body limited to a geographical area.

Rajasthan was the first state to install panchayati raj after Balwantrai Mehta study team's report. Prime Minister Jawaharlal Nehru inaugurated the first panchayati raj on 2 October, 1959 at Nagpur. Nehru felt that democracy at the top would not succeed unless it was built from below, and expressed the system as 'the most revolutionary and historical step in the context of new India'. By 1959, all the states had passed panchayat acts, and by mid-1960s, panchayats had reached all parts of the country, and more than 217,300 village panchayats covering over 96 per cent of the 579,000 inhabited villages and 92 per cent of the rural population had been established (ISS, 1994). It was generally felt that the establishment of panchayati raj enhanced the appearance of local leadership by creating new seats of power for democratic elections. A study team under the Association of Voluntary Agencies for Rural Development (AVARD) in 1962 evaluated the working of the panchayati raj in Rajasthan and observed, *'It was reported that the people felt that they had sufficient powers to enable them to mould their future... They are fully conscious of the fact that such privileges and favours which were formerly under the control of the BDO are now under their control. In this sense full advantage of democratic decentralisation has been secured'* (AVARD, 1962).

Soon after this, five States-Andhra Pradesh, Karnataka, Maharashtra, Rajasthan and Uttar Pradesh had constituted committees to study and assess the working of panchayati raj and suggest measures for improvement. The general findings, however, indicated that panchayati raj system was moving downhill. The critical problem was the domination of panchayati raj institutions by the economically and socially powerful castes and classes. In many cases, elections were not held regularly. Thus, G.V.K. Rao committee, appointed by the Planning Commission, observed, *'Apart from inadequate resources, elections to these bodies have not been held rergularly. In fact, elections have become overdue for one or more tiers of the panchayati raj institutions in eleven States, and in eight States even elections to Gram Panchayats are overdue. Elections have been put off on one pretext or another.... And the term of the existing bodies have been extended or the bodies have been superseded'* (CAARD, 1985). Evidence suggests that there was a deliberate plan by the bureaucracy, local vested interests and their elected representatives in the state legislature and in the Parliament to cripple and eventually discard panchayati raj because its ascendancy was feared (ISS, 1994). The ISS volume further states that the root of this hidden agenda could be traced to 1960 when the government launched an intensive agricultural district programme by-passing the Community Development Programmes.

Jayprakash Narayan committee of 1961 detected contrary positions developing within the government in the creation of an independent intensive programme. The Community Development Ministry was tensed with the launching of the intensive agricultural district programme. Nonetheless, schemes like Small farmers Development Agency (SFDA), Drought Prone Areas Programme (DPAP), Intensive Tribal Development Programme (ITDP) have been introduced outside the purview of local governments. In 1966-67, the Ministry of Community Development was reduced to a department status under the Ministry of Food and Agriculture. And in 1971, the very title of 'Community Development' was ultimately dropped and replaced by 'Rural Development'. L.C. Jain (1985) observes, that this marked the end of 'community' and 'panchayats' as agents of change and agencies of development. All development programmes became bureaucracy-centred with hardly any participation of the people. In this way, panchayati raj became part of the Ministry of Rural Development at the centre. Thus, the bureaucratic role in bringing panchayati raj to its present plight has been brought out by Asoka Mehta committee: *'The bureaucracy had probably its own role in dissociating the PRIs from the development process. Several factors seem to have conditioned their perception. The system of line hierarchy would find favour with them as an organisational principle. The officers would feel that they are primarily accountable for results and financial proprieties to the state government. The officials knew no better than to trust their own fraternity. They would, on the one hand, therefore be averse to the PRIs being entrusted with additional functions and, on the other, would not easily get adjusted to working under the supervision of elected representatives'* (Mehta Committee, 1977).

This has always been the condition during the British period and Independent India. The All India Congress Committee (AICC, 1954) expressed the main reason for the disintegration of village panchayats during British period as that of *'the inordinate greed of the East India Company caused slow but steady disintegration of these village panchayats... The excessive centralisation of the executive and judicial powers in the hands of the government officials deprived the village functionaries of their age long powers and influence'*. In the face of this, the Indian Statutory Commission of 1929 stated that Lord Ripon's reforms in the sphere of local self-government were not free from official control and no real attempt was made to inaugurate a system amenable to the will of the local inhabitants(Shukla, 1964). Thus, it was a combination of bureaucracy, commercial interest, the professional middle class, the police and the political elite against democratic decentralisation. In this situation, Rajni Kothari observes, *'We have ended up creating an impregnable alliance of urban officialdom and the rural rich, and have excluded the rural poor from it'* (Jain, 1985).

However, the appointment of Asoka Mehta committee in 1977 characterised a turning point in the concepts and practice of panchayati raj. It was set up to enquire into the working of the panchayati raj institutions, and to recommend measures for strengthening them to enable an effective decentralised system of planning and development. The report was submitted in 1978 which seeks to make panchayats an integral part of our democratic process. West Bengal, Karnataka, Andhra Pradesh, and Jammu and Kashmir either passed new acts or revised their existing panchayat acts, accepting the Asoka Mehta Committee report. The emphasis shifted from the bureaucracy to the political elements. The Balwantrai Mehta committee made development central to the panchayat system, and Asoka Mehta Committee attempts to make panchayats into genuine political institutions. Both the committees recognised the need for constitutional support and legislative measures to bring about social change. One can argue that there never was constitutional mandate for self-government below the state level till April,

1993. But political will and people's political awareness are crucial for bringing about democratic decentralisation (local self-government) below the state level. Constitutional support and legislative measures can only create necessary conditions. Therefore, a three dimensional approach–political will, people's awareness, and constitutional and legislative measures–is a crucial requisite for far-reaching positive changes to be brought about in our society. The weakening of any of these three requisites will bring the process to slow down.

The Asoka Mehta committee has been the first to make official recommendation for inclusion of panchayati raj in the constitution emphasising that panchayati raj should be considered political rather than mere developmental institutions. The predominant views on the issue of panchayati raj in the mid-eighties can be summarised below (ISS, 1994):

1. The Constitutional amendment to guarantee elections to local bodies at the expiry of their term is a sufficient condition for bringing life into the local bodies.
2. The Constitutional guarantee of elections is not a sufficient condition but only a necessary condition. What is really needed is a 'quantum jump" in political democracy providing for a three or four-tier government that is, the centre, state, district and village governments.
3. Local self-governments must be strengthened, but not through rigid and uniform constitutional provisions. Freedom at the state and regional levels for experimenting and evolving suitable systems is a must.
4. A "marriage" of district governments and panchayati raj is possible. The concept of people's participation must be considered an ideological commitment and, therefore, the need is to take up legislative and structural measures to give legitimacy to people's participation.

3.2. The 73rd and 74th Constitutional Amendment and Decentralisation

By the end of 1988, a sub-committee of parliament under P.K. Thangon made suggestions for strengthening the panchayati raj system, particularly proposing that panchayati raj should be constitutionally recognised.. It was then that on 15 May, 1989 the Constitution (64th Amendment) Bill was introduced in Parliament. The Bill in principle was welcomed but there was objections on two basic grounds–(a) the bill overlooked the states and was seen as an instrument of the centre to deal directly with the panchayati raj institutions; and (b) that it was imposing a uniform pattern throughout the country instead of permitting individual states to legislate the details, keeping in mind the local circumstances. Against this backdrop, the combined opposition under National Front appointed a committee headed by S.R. Bommai to prepare an alternative legislation. The report of this committee formed the subsequent bills on panchayats introduced in the Parliament.

The Constitution (64th Amendment) Bill was passed in the Lok Sabha by a two-third majority, but in the Rajya Sabha in 15 October, 1989, it failed to get the mandatory requirement by two votes. The National Front government introduced the 74th Amendment Bill on 7 September, 1990, but it was never taken up for discussion. In September, 1991, the Congress under Narasimha Rao introduced the 72nd (Panchayats) and 73rd (Nagarpalika) constitutional amendment bills. They were referred to a Joint Select Committee of Parliament. The Lok Sabha passed the Bill on 22 December, 1992, while the Rajya Sabha passed the following day. Following its ratification by more than half the state assemblies, the president gave his assent on 20 April 1993, and the act was brought into force by a government notification on 24 April 1993 as the 1992 Constitution (73rd Amendment) Act.

The 73rd constitutional amendment has been a new chapter in the process of democratic decentralisation in India. The responsibility for taking decisions affecting the people at the grass roots level now rest upon the elected members of the people themselves. The local level institutions have been given entities of self-government with a specific role in planning for economic development and social justice in rural areas. The intention is to assign a position of command to them in the democratic framework of the country. Local government, however, is a state subject under Schedule VII, and the implementation is dependent upon the intention of the state panchayati raj/local government enactment. The challenge is to ensure evolution of state law which is entirely in harmony with the spirit of the 73rd and 74th constitutional amendment.

The principles governing democratic decentralisation are the same for both rural and urban areas. The 73rd and 74th amendments of the constitution were passed in 1992 and came into effect in 1993with great anticipation. Panchayats, nagarpalikas, and municipalities have come into existence. But in many instances this has not always transform itself into actual decentralisation of power. The constitution has given this responsibility of empowerment and devolution to State Legislature.

In many states, panchayati raj institutions follow three-tier system. At the village level, three institutions–Gram sabha, Gram panchayat, and Nyaya panchayat- are functioning. The gram sabha is the general assembly of all the adult people and assigns functions such as–(i) to consider annual budget of gram panchayat; (ii) to examine audit report of the gram panchayat; (iii) to review report of gram panchayat; (iv) to approve the income and the expenditure estimates for the year; (v) to consider new taxes which the gram panchayat would like to levy; and (vi)to select schemes, beneficiaries and locations, etc. Gram panchayat is the executive committee of the gram sabha and has a tenure of five years. Seats are reserved for Scheduled Castes and Scheduled Tribes and one third of total seats are reserved for women. The chairman and vice chairman are elected by the gram sabha. The functions of gram panchayat include provision of drinking water, village roads and those 29 subjects listed in the Eleventh Schedule devolved by the Stare government. Nyaya panchayat deals with administration of Justice which includes minor criminal and civil cases. It can impose a fine up to rupees one thousand. Panchayat Samiti (Block Level) is the second intermediate tier. It consists of all the sarpanchs (chairman) of the Gram panchayats within the Block, the MPs and MLAs of the area. The second Administrative Reforms Commission, however, recommends to remove MPs and MLAs as members of any local bodies. The functions include control of the BDO for implementing resolutions of the samiti, agriculture, animal husbandry, cottage industries, fisheries, health, communications etc., and to help the villagers in the services of these sectors. At the apex is Zila Parishad (District Level). The main functions include: (i) to examine and approve the budget of panchayat samiti; (ii) to supervise the activities of the samiti; (iii) to advice the state government on all matters relating to development activities of the district; (iv) distribute funds allocated by the government to the samities; (v) exercise such powers and functions as may be assigned to it by the state government. The zila parishad functioning are through the operation of good number of standing committees like– Planning and Finance, Production Programme, Social Amenities, Welfare of Weaker Section of Society and so on.

However, in spite of constitutional provisions and observations made by various expert groups and Parliamentary Committees, devolution and empowerment of local governments in real term has not taken place. It, therefore, becomes the responsibility of the Union Government to ensure that the 73rd and 74th constitutional amendments are implemented both in letter and spirit. This is particularly necessary as major development schemes funded largely by the Union Government are being implemented by the local governments. The important issue, therefore, is the manner in which the Union Government intervenes in ensuring that local governments are appropriately empowered by the States. Article 40 of the Constitution states, "the states shall take steps to organise panchayats and vest them with such powers and authority as may be necessary to enable them to function as units of self-government". Article 243G widely empowers these bodies to enjoy devolution of powers and responsibilities with regard to (i) preparation of plans for economic development and social justice (ii) implementation of schemes for the above relating to matters listed in Eleventh Schedule. The implicit prerequisite is that most of the functions/activities now being performed by the state government agencies at the local level have to be withdrawn and handed over to the panchayats/local governments together with functional autonomy and adequate resources in discharging those activities. But there is a tendency to consider panchayats as extension of the field machinery of the state government. village councils in Mizoram remained to be considered not even as field machinery of the state government, but purely as agents of the state government in development.

The experiences gained from almost twenty years of performance of PRIs in many states can be a guide for the North-eastern states particularly those where 73rd constitutional amendment is not in operation. There is no uniform local government system in Nagaland, Meghalaya and Mizoram. In the pre-insurgent epoch of 1966, village councils in Mizoram enjoyed autonomy in judicial and administrative functions while development functions, except sanitation, were not given to them. However, in the post-1966 period, especially after North-east reorganisation and attainment of UT and statehood in 1971 and 1987 respectively, the relative emphasis on development functions renders the role of village councils redundant and ambiguous. The following query may be worthwhile to take into consideration:

- What activities are required to enable local governments to really emerge as local government?
- Is it possible to identify functions and activities to be exclusive domain of local governments? Core subjects which may be entrusted to the local governments for effective decentralisation could include:
  (i) Elementary education, adult and non-formal education;
  (ii) Primary healthcare, drinking water and sanitation;
  (iii) Women and child development;
  (iv) Roads, culverts and bridges;
  (v) Rural infrastructure including rural electrification;
  (vi) Natural resource management;
  (vii) Livelihood for the poor: (a) Implementation of the poverty alleviation schemes such as MGNREGS (b)Targeted Public distribution system;
  (viii) Civic amenities.
- Local governments, apart from functions listed in the Eleventh Schedule, may be endowed with: (i) judicial functions, (ii) some legislative functions, (iii) police functions/local crime control, (iv) enforcing provisions of some regulatory laws, and (v) granting licenses.
- It is also important to identify functional areas where the state government and local governments should work as equal partners.
- The effective goals of decentralisation-service delivery, fair distribution of the fruits of development, accountability, participatory planning-must be ensured.

- Certain areas may be identified where local government institutions may act as agencies for implementing certain schemes sponsored by the state and Union Governments.

It is also to be noted that many States have transferred functions contained in Eleventh Schedule through executive instructions which is less effective. The Union Government must ensure that functions are transferred by an act of legislation, and state governments must follow Article 243B requiring the creation of three tier PRI system, which need to be reframed to accommodate North-eastern states by introducing flexibility and left to the prerogative of the states. Field investigation has gained enough evidence that all the institutions for delivery of services—Primary health centres, veterinary centres, primary schools, secondary schools, public libraries, *anganwadi* centres are controlled by the line department of the state government, Mizoram as it is to certain extent in other states. For effective decentralisation, these institutions and the staff attached to them may be transferred to the local governments.

3.3 Second Administrative Reforms Commission

The second Administrative Reforms Commission has examined local governance relating to rural and urban local governance in India with a focus on the need for real democratic decentralisation to bring home grass roots democracy in its sixth report. It says that a good governance has the following characteristics:

(1) ***Participation:*** All men and women should have a voice in decision-making, either directly or through legitimate institutions that represent their interests. There must be capacities to participate constructively.

(2) ***Rule of Law:*** Legal framework should be fair and applied impartially particularly laws on human rights.

(3) ***Transparency*:** Transparency is built on the free flow of information.

(4) ***Responsiveness*:** Institutions and processes try to serve all stakeholders.

(5) ***Consensus Orientation:*** Good governance reconcile diverse interests to reach a broad consensus in what is the best interests of the group.

(6) *Equity:* All men and women have opportunities to improve or maintain their well being.

(7) *Effectiveness and Efficiency:* Processes and institutions produce results that make the best use of resources.

(8) *Accountability:* Decision-makers in government, private sector and civil society organisations are accountable to the public, as well as the institutional stakeholders.

(9) *Strategic vision*: Leaders and public have a broad and long-term perspective on good governance and human development. There is also an understanding of the historical, cultural and social complexities in which that perspective is grounded.

Empowerment

Indian Constitution provides for democratic decentralisation through Directive Principles of State Policy to promote Panchayati Raj Institutions, and more specifically now through the 73rd and 74th constitutional amendments for institutional framework for grass roots democracy. Despite constitutional mandate, the growth of self-governing local bodies is very slow particularly in North-east India. The Second Administrative Reforms Commission, after holding two national level colloquiums separately for rural and urban governance, has considered the principles which may be followed in the reform of governance. The roles of Union and state government is clearly demarcated, the fact of the matter being that the constitutional changes very often favour greater empowerment of states. However, in many states the relationship between states and local government is still in its infancy and needs to be strengthened by empowering local governments. Recommendations of the commission include: application of the principle of subsidiarity in the context of decentralisation; delineation of functions of local governments *vis-à-vis* state government and among different tiers of local governments; effective devolution of functions and resources accompanied by capacity-building and accountability; integrated view of local services and development through convergence of programmes and agencies and above all 'citizen-centricity'.

The second Administrative Reforms Commission, after examining the functioning of local government in some states particularly in regard to empowerment, has made the following conclusion:

- Despite the mandatory constitutional injunctions, it took years, and in some cases a decade, to even constitute local governments and hold elections.
- Even when local governments are constituted and elections are held, states often postponed the subsequent elections on some pretext or other. Each time it is an uphill task to ensure compliance in some states, even with the mandatory provisions of the constitution.
- There has been no linear development or evolution in respect of democratic decentralisation.
- State governments, legislators and civil servants are in general reluctant to effectively empower local governments. Only the bare minimum required to implement the strict letter of the Constitution prevails in many States. What is implied by the spirit of the constitution and principles of democracy is often ignored.
- Even mandatory provisions like the constitution of District Planning Committees and Metropolitan Planning Committees have been ignored in many states.
- Where the panchayats have been constituted, and elections held regularly, they are still left at the mercy of state legislatures and state executive. Although local governments have a long tradition of autonomy, the fact that Uunion and state governments have an established tradition of centralisation for nearly four decades, means that strong vested interests have developed over time disallowing devolution of power.
- Some legislators at times tend to act as 'executives', intervening in transfers and postings, sanctioning of local bodies' contracts and tenders, crime investigation and prosecution–all of which are therefore often at the mercy of the local legislator. Given the compulsions of survival, the state government which depends on the goodwill and support of legislators, does not usually intervene except where the constitution specifically and unambiguously direct it.

The provision of Article 243G and 243W of the constitution in terms of power, authority and responsibilities of local bodies have been taken as merely advisory by many states. But the Commission observes that the statement of objects and reasons of the Constitution (73rd Amendment) Acts indicates: "*Though the panchayati raj institutions have been in existence for a long time, it has been observed that these institutions have not been able to acquire the status and dignity of viable and responsive people's bodies due to a number of reasons including absence of regular elections, prolonged supersessions, insufficient representation of weaker sections like the Scheduled Castes, Scheduled Tribes and women, inadequate devolution of powers and lack of financial resources Article 40 of the Constitution which enshrines one of the Directive Principles of State Policy lays down that the state shall take steps to organise village panchayats and endow them with such powers and authority as may be necessary to enable them to function as units of self-government. In the light of the experience in the last forty years and in view of the shortcomings which have been observed, it is considered that there is an imperative need to enshrine in the constitution certain basic and essential features of Panchayati Raj Institutions to impact certainty, continuity and strengthen them*".

The statement of objects and Rreasons of the constitution (74th Amendment) Act also says: "*In many states, local bodies have become weak and ineffective on account of a variety of reasons, including the failure to hold regular elections,, prolonged supersessions and inadequate devolution of powers and functions. As a result, urban local bodies are not able to perform effectively as vibrant democratic units of self-government*".

The drawback that can be observed in the actual functioning is that most states are still reluctant to provide devolution in real term and they are in favour of minimum local empowerment. In view of this, the commission desires a strong constitutional provision mandating effective empowerment of local governments. However, the autonomy of the States must be observed and that states are at different levels of development in the matter. The commission also observes that the Eleventh and Twelfth Schedules could not be fully handled by local government. There appear to be certain incongruities in the Twelfth Schedule and several matters listed in the Eleventh Schedule that ought to have been included, but omitted by accident. As such they may be considered only as illustrative and not exhaustive.

Eleventh and Twelfth Schedules

The Commission observes that "Agriculture, rural housing, watershed development, farm forestry, minor forest produce, rural electrification– all are functions which by their very nature belong to the rural local bodies. But non-conventional energy (source), poverty alleviation programme, education including primary and secondary education, adult education, technical training and vocational education, women and child welfare, family welfare, the public distribution system, even animal management and welfare (slightly different from husbandry in the traditional sense), libraries, cultural activities (which figure in the Eleventh Schedule but not in the Twelfth)– can surely be functions for municipalities, too. The Twelfth Schedule does cover a vast range of subjects– urban planning, land and building regulation, fire services, roads and bridges, urban poverty alleviation, slum improvement and up-gradation, provision of amenities, water supply, sanitation, public health, environment and so on. However, somewhat unexpectedly, "economic and social development" of urban citizens is restricted to only planning for them, and education covered only as "promotion of education... aspects. On the other hand, as mentioned above, various aspects of education figure prominently in the three functions listed in the Eleventh Schedule and are intended to be developed on rural local bodies."

In spite of this, the commission is of the view that the two Schedules need not be reviewed at this juncture, but that the lists are merely illustrative and not exhaustive should be recognised. In any case, functional delineation between the state government and local government in respect of most of these matters will have to be made, and a clear activity mapping is a must for them.

The National Commission to Review the Working of the Constitution also considered this matter and the commission was concerned about the poor devolution of functions, and made recommendation as follow: "*Article 243G along with the Eleventh Schedule indicates the kind of functions to be discharged by the panchayats. It does not guarantee assignments of a set of exclusive functions to the panchayats. Hence the kind of role they would be expected to play in governance depends on the regime that controls the government of a state. The commission, therefore, recommends that panchayats should be categorically declared to be "institutions of self-government" and exclusive functions should be assigned to them. For this purpose, Article 243G should be amended to read as follows: 'Substitution of Article 243G- For Article 243G, the following Article shall be substituted, namely, Powers, authority and responsibility to the provisions of this constitution, the Legislature of a state shall, by law, vest the panchayats with such powers and authority as are necessary to enable them to function as institutions of self-government and such law shall contain provisions for the devolution of powers and responsibilities upon Panchayats at the appropriate level, subject to such conditions as shall be specified therein, with respect to– (a) preparation of plans for economic development and social justice; (b) the implementation of schemes for economic development and social justice as shall be entrusted to them including those in relation to the matters listed in the Eleventh Schedule"*. The Commission also recommends similar amendment to be made in Article 243W relating to the powers, authority and responsibilities of municipalities.

The second Administrative Reforms Commission carefully examined the reports, came to the view that while Article 243G and 243W need to be strengthened, it is desirable to lay down general principles of empowerment without undue restriction to the states' freedom of action. In particular, they would favour, two principles which need to be stated in the constitution so that the state legislatures can make laws based on these governing principles. First, devolution should be based on the broad principle of subsidiarity, and local governments at the appropriate level should be vested with adequate powers and authority to enable them to function as institution of self-government in respect of functions that can be performed by the local level. Second, as matters listed in Eleventh Schedule are not intended to be wholly transferred to local governments, the empowerment of local governments should be limited to specific functions, which can be performed at the local level. It, thus, recommends that:

(a) *Article 243G should be amended as follows: "Subject to the provisions of this constitution, the legislature of a state shall, by law, vest a panchayat at the appropriate level with such powers and authority as are necessary to enable them to function as institutions of self-government in respect of all functions which can be performed at the local level including the functions in respect of the matters listed in the Eleventh Schedule" (b) Article 243W should be similarly amended to empower urban local bodies".*

The commission also bear in mind the voices from different parts of the country seeking more flexibility to states in designing the panchayat structure suitable to local requirements. The commission examined three issues: (1) Number of tiers (2) Composition of local bodies and mode of elections, and (3) Urban rural divide at the district level.

Number of Tiers

Article 243B makes it mandatory for every states with a population exceeding 20 lakhs to have three tiers of panchayats at the village, intermediate and district levels. It is not feasible to prescribe nationally any specific pattern of local governments. The states must have freedom to experiment and improve the design. The commission is of the considered view that while the states should constitute the panchayats, the tiers of local government should be left for the state legislatures to decide. Article 243B should be amended to constitute in every State Panchayats at the appropriate levels instead of specifying mandatory creation of village, intermediary and district panchayats.

Composition of Local Bodies and Mode of Elections

Until 1993, states had their own models of panchayats. In most states, the village panchayat head was the ex-officio head of the intermediate panchayat and the head of intermediate panchayat was the member of district panchayat. But Article 243C of the constitution makes it mandatory for all the seats in a panchayat (at every level) to be 'filled by person chosen by direct election from territorial constituencies in the panchayat area'. There is also a growing demand in favour of each panchayat being directly elected by the people, instead of a series of indirect elections. Article 243C(3) and (d) stipulates that the state legislature may, by law, provide for the representation of the members of parliament and state legislature of the state at level other than the village level. The commission is, however, of the view that the imposing presence of members of Parliament and the state legislature in the panchayats would subdue the emergence of local leadership which is a *sine qua non* for development of vibrant local governments. Therefore, members of parliament and state legislature, the commission desires, should not become members of local bodies. This would endow the local bodies with decision-making capabilities.

District Council

The commission observes that the isolation of rural local governments from urban local governments has resulted in several unhappy consequences. First, there is an artificial divide between rural and urban populations even in matters relating to common needs such as healthcare and education which are basic public services that should be available to all categories everywhere.

Second, in rapidly urbanising society, the boundaries between rural and urban territories keep shifting. Population served by rural local governments may shrink, and the peri-urban areas around fast growing urban areas have hybrid characteristics of both village and town and their special needs must be addressed in an integrated manner. Moreover, the need for coordination between rural and urban local governments at the district level has given rise to replicated institutions like District Planning Boards and District Development Review Committee in the pre-1993 period. This is now replaced in the Constitution by the formation of DPCs under Article 243 ZD.

The DPCs prescribed in Article 243ZD are too weak and ineffective in many states. The commission is of the view that there must be a single elected district council with representatives from all rural and urban areas. That will function as a true local government for the entire district. The district council will be responsible for all the local functions including those listed for them in the Eleventh and Twelfth Schedules. Planning for the whole district– urban and rural– will become an integral part of the district council's responsibility.

The commission, thus, recommends the followings as far as the structure is concerned:

(a) Article 243B(1) should be amended to read as follows: "There shall be constituted in every state, as the state legislature may, by law, provide panchayats at appropriate levels in accordance with the provisions of this part".

(b) The constitutional provisions relating to reservation of seats (Article 243D) must be retained in the current form to ensure adequate representation to the under-privileged sections and women.

(c) Members of parliament and state legislature should not become members of local bodies.

(d) Article 243 C(1) should be retained.

(e) Article 243C (2 and 3) should be repealed and supplanted by Article 243C (2) as follows: 243C (2) Subject to the provisions of this part, the legislature of a state may, by law, make provisions with respect to composition of Panchayats and the manner of elections provided that in any tier there shall be direct election of at least one of the two offices of chairperson or members.

    Provided that in case of direct elections of members in any tier, the ratio between the population of the territorial area of a panchayat at any level and the number of seats in such panchayat to be filled by election shall, so far as practicable, be the same throughout the state. Also, each panchayat area shall be divided into territorial constituencies in such manner that the ratio between the population of each constituency and the number of seats allotted to it shall, so far as practicable, be the same throughout the panchayat area.

(f) There shall be a district council in every district with representation from both urban and rural areas.

(g) 243B (2) should be substituted by: "There shall be constituted in every district, a district council representing all rural and urban areas in the district and exercising powers and functions in accordance with the provisions of Articles 243G and 243W of the constitution.

The creation of district council as recommended here may not be to the best interest of small states like Mizoram where state revenue is very precarious. The existing district council in the Sixth Scheduled areas– Mara ADC, Lai ADC and Chakma ADC can be cited as illustrative model. The cost of infrastructure and administrative build-up are so great that developmental functions seem to take a back seat. It should be a glaring fact that if all the eight districts have district council of their own, the administrative expenditure shall be so immense that development functions and activities will be weakened, and will create unnecessary avenues for misappropriation and corruptive practices. It is, therefore, desirable that in small States such as Mizoram Block level elected local governments may cater to the needs of the village councils. If need be for purpose of uniform planning process, a District Planning Committee consisting of non-elected members, can be organised. This is for optimum result in view of the dismal state revenue.

State Election Commission

The commission also makes certain observations and recommendations as to the provisions, power of delimitation, notification of an election, reservation of seats of the state election commission as follows:

(a) The task of delimitation and reservation of constituencies should be entrusted to the state election commission.

(b) Local government laws in all states should provide for adoption of the assembly electoral rolls for local governments without any revision of names by SECs. For such a process to be effective it is necessary to ensure that the voter registration and preparation of electoral rolls by election commission of India is based on geographic contiguity. Similarly, the electoral divisions for elections to local bodies should follow the Building Blocks approach.

(c) The Registration of Electors Rules, 1960, should be amended to define a 'Part' as a compact geographical unit.

(d) In order to achieve convergence between census data and electoral rolls, the boundaries of a 'Part' and an Enumeration Block' should coincide.

(e) Reservation of seats should follow any one of the two principles mentioned below: (i) In case of single-member constituencies, the rotation can be after at least two terms of five years each so that there is possibility of longevity of leadership and nurturing of constituencies. (ii) Instead of single-member constituencies, elections can be held to multiple-member constituencies by the List System, ensuring the reservation of seats. This will obviate the need for rotation thus guaranteeing allocation of seats for the reserved categories.

(f) The conduct of elections for the elected members of District and Metropolitan Planning Committee should be entrusted to the state election commission.

Functions of Local Government

Article 243G and 243W, the 73rd and 74th constitution amendments empowered state legislature to endow by law:

- Such powers and authority as may be necessary to enable them to function as institutions of self-government.
- Such law may contain provisions for devolution of powers and responsibilities, subject to conditions specified therein, with respect to: (a) the preparation of plans for economic development and social justice, and (b) implementation of schemes for economic development and social justice as may be entrusted to them (Article 243G/performance of functions and implementation of schemes as may be entrusted to them (Article 243W) including those in relation to the matters listed in the Eleventh Schedule (Panchayats) and the Twelfth Schedule (Municipalities) respectively.

The supreme purpose of these is that powers and authority may be devolved to enable the panchayats and municipalities to function as institutions of self-government. This will also entail preparation of local plans for economic development and social justice and implement schemes including those listed in the relevant Schedules.

Based on the survey of the present status of devolution of powers and responsibilities to local governments at various levels the commission reveals the followings:

(a) Devolution has been sought to be done in most of the States by omnibus legislations regarding panchayats/ municipalities and municipal corporations in which the 'matters' listed in the Eleventh and Twelfth Schedules are just repeated.

(b) The number of 'subjects' said to have been transferred varies from a few in number in some states to the entire list as given in the Schedules in some others. However, in all cases the progress in delineation of functions of the different tiers of local governments in a given subject matter has been very slow.

(c) Due to the persistent efforts of the Ministry of Panchayati Raj in the last three years, detailed "activity mapping" of different tiers of local governments have been undertaken in all the states.

(d) However, the exercise continues to be partial and prolonged. The draft activity mapping lists have not been approved by the state governments in some cases.

(e) Even where activity mapping has been approved, parallel action to enable local governments to exercise the functions has not been taken. The existing government departments with their executive orders and instructions, parallel government bodies like DRDAs and the continuation of statutory bodies (as regards water, electricity, etc.) without any change, prevent the local governments from exercising the so called transferred functions.

(f) In some cases, even those activities that can be undertaken by local governments within the existing arrangements are got done by encouraging and financing the formation of a number of parallel community organisations of stakeholders and entrusting the activities exclusively to them, instead of working out a synergic relationship between them and the local governments.

The commission observes that there are confusion, unnecessary duplication, inefficiency, wastage of funds, poor outputs and outcomes are the result of this. The Standing Committee on Urban and Rural Development, 2004, also noted the failure of implementing the provisions of the constitution. It observed, "*The overall aim of Part IX is to endow the Panchayats with such powers and responsibilities as may be necessary to enable them to function successfully as institutions of self-government, as per Article 243G of the constitution. State legislatures have been empowered to endow panchayats by law with such powers and authority as may be necessary to enable them to prepare plans for economic development and social justice and implement schemes for economic development and social justice, including those in relation to the matters contained in the Eleventh Schedule. The committee are, however, constrained to note that although more than nine years have passed since the constitution (73rd Amendment) Act was enacted, very few states seem to be serious about the implementation of said provision of Part IX. They further find that endowing panchayats with certain functions is fruitful only if the panchayats are equipped with the trained functionaries and adequate finances are also made available to them. Thus, they note that panchayats can fulfill their responsibility as institutions of self-government only if devolution is patterned on a nexus between the three Fs, i.e., functions, functionaries and finances. The committee is unhappy to note that very few states have linked the very important devolution of functions to the means of actualising such devolution through the devolution of functionaries and funds for all the 29 subjects enlisted in the Eleventh Schedule".*

Article 243N and 243ZF mandate that all laws which are "inconsistent' with the provisions of Part IX and X of the constitution shall continue to be in force until such laws are suitably amended to bring them in conformity with the constitution or repealed, or until the expiration of one year from the dates of the 73rd and 74th constitutional amendments coming into effect. The 73rd and 74th constitutional amendments came into effect on 24 April, 1993 and 1 June, 1993 respectively, and despite the passage of more than 15 years since then, most states have not even identified all the statutes which are inconsistent with the Parts IX and X of the constitution. Kerala is quoted as significant exception where dozens of laws have been identified and amended. The commission recommends the followings:

(a) There should be clear delineation of functions for each level of local government in the case of each subject matter law. This is not one-time exercise and has to be done continuously while working out locally relevant socio-economic programmes, restructuring organisations and framing subject-matter laws.

(b) Each subject-matter law, which has functional elements that are best attended to at local levels, should have provision for appropriate devolution to such levels– either in the law or in subordinate legislation. All the relevant union and state laws to be reviewed urgently and suitably amended.

(c) In the case of new laws, it will be advisable to add a 'local government memorandum' (on the analogy of financial memorandum and memorandum of subordinate legislation) indicating whether any functions to be attended to by local governments are involved and if so, whether this has been provided for in the law.

(d) In case of urban local bodies, in addition to the functions listed in the Twelfth Schedule, the following should be devolved to urban local bodies:

- School education;
- Public health, including community health centres/ area hospitals;
- Traffic management and civic policing activities;
- Urban environment management and heritage;
- Land management, including registration.

These are only illustrative additional functions and more functions could be devolved by the respective states.

Framework Law for Local Governments

Article 243(d) of the constitution defines a panchayat as an 'institution of self-government' for the rural areas, and Article 243G expresses the intention that while framing laws on panchayats, state legislature should endow these institutions 'with such power and authority as may be necessary to enable them to function as institutions of self-government'. This means that they should have an autonomous jurisdiction of their own. Thus, it cannot be too small to make the concept of self-governing institutions at the local level meaningless. Creating an autonomous jurisdiction is based on the constitutional mandate for effective decentralisation of governmental power as opposed to mere administrative de-concentration. The Eleventh Schedule gives a list of 29 functions, intended to be transferred to the local governments, which covers a wide range of development activities ranging from activities in the social and economic sectors (education, health, women and child development, social security, farm and non-farm economic activities, etc.) to the development of infrastructure and institutions needed for social and economic development. The thrust is, therefore, on development.

In the urban sector, Article 243P (c) describes a Municipality as an institutions of self-government. Article 243W proposes that state legislature may, by law, endow, "the municipalities with such powers and authority as may be necessary to enable them to function as institutions of self-government and such law contain provision for the devolution of powers and responsibilities upon municipalities". The National Commission to Review the Working of the Constitution (NCRWC) also recommended certain changes in the constitution as follow: "*The commission, therefore, recommends that the Eleventh and Twelfth Schedules should be restructured in a manner that creates a separate fiscal domain for panchayats and municipalities. Accordingly, Articles 243H and 243X should be amended making it mandatory for the legislature of the state to make laws devolving powers to the panchayats and municipalities.*"

The Commission, thus, recommends the followings: "*(a) Government of India should draft and place before parliament, a framework law for local governments. The framework law could be enacted under Article 252 of the constitution on the lines of the South African Act (Cooperative model of government) for the states to adopt. This Law should lay down the broad principles of devolution of powers, responsibilities and functions to the local governments and communities, based on the following:*

- *Principle of Subsidiarity,*
- *Democratic Decentralisation,*
- *Delineation of Functions,*
- *Devolution in Real Terms,*
- *Convergence,*
- *Citizen Centricity.*

Devolution of Funds

Despite the importance of local bodies in the democratic process, the financial resources generated by them fall far short of their requirements. The local governments have to depend heavily on state governments for financial help because taxes like state excise, VAT and Motor Vehicles Tax, part of state consolidated fund are not available to them. Articles 243H and 243X make it obligatory for the state government to authorise the local governments, by law, to impose taxes, duties and assign to them taxes/duties collected by the state government, also provision for grants-in-aid to the local bodies from the consolidated fund of the state. The devolution of financial resources has been ensured through the constitution of state Finance Commission that are to make recommendations. Similar to the role of Finance Commission in recommending devolution of funds from the Union to the states, the State Finance Commission also make recommendations regarding the principle that should govern the distribution of taxes between the State and local governments. The commission noted the experiences of State Finance Commission in India which is reproduced as follows:

(1) There has not been genuine efforts by the states to make clear expenditure assignments to the local governments and corresponding restructuring of state's set-up;

(2) The state government staff transfers to the local governments have not been accompanied by revenue source transfers;

(3) The SFCs waste much of their time to collect routine financial data from the local governments that the states should have collected in a routine manner; collection of qualitative data for policy purposes e.g., fiscal autonomy/ revenue dependency, expenditure/revenue decentralisation, is not attempted;

(4) There is inadequate realisation that the SFCs are supposed to recommend fiscal transfers in aid of local revenue and not finance for creating local infrastructure;

(5) The SFCs have paid much attention to improve fiscal administration of the local bodies, which might be more important than fiscal transfer *per se*;

(6) The SFCs are not required to cover issues of local taxation or borrowings, in case some of these are required to be examined 'in the interest of sound finance' these should be specifically included in their terms of reference;

(7) The SFCs do not start their work after first reviewing state finances, nor did they suggest significant transfer of, or surcharging on, the state taxes;

(8) Inadequate attention is given by the SFCs to the adverse consequences of grants on local revenue efforts and local fiscal autonomy;

(9) The state governments treat the SFCs with scant respect, partly due to their membership composition that includes serving civil servants: and

(10) The state governments generally take a long time to accept and act on the SFCs recommendation.

(*Source:* "The National Finance Commission and Fiscal Devolution to Local Bodies" by Shri Abhijit Datta, 'Municipal Finance in India' IIPA (Data compiled by the NIRD (SFC cell) Hyderabad and NIUA, New Delhi).

4

Review of Status of Decentralised Governance and Devolution of Functions in Mizoram

4.1 Functional Devolution and Activity Mapping

There are certain reasons for uninspiring performance of village councils, Autonomous District Councils and even local councils and Aizawl Municipal Council. Why do they fail to deliver services? The main reasons could perhaps be functional overlap in ADC areas, functional ambiguity and vagueness in village councils or inadequate finance and technical staff in the case of Aizawl Municipal Council. In this section, we shall try to see functional devolution in regard to Autonomous District Councils, Aizawl Municipal Council in a cursory way, and in greater details as far as the village councils are concerned.

Autonomous District Council Areas

The Sixth Schedule has vested certain powers and functions as organs of self-government to Autonomous District Councils and shall have power to make laws with respect to:

(1) Allotment, occupation and use, or setting apart of land other than the reserved forest, for the purpose of agriculture or grasing or residential or any other purpose;

(2) Management of forest not being a reserved forests;

(3) Use of canal or any water-course for agriculture purpose;

(4) Regulation of the practices of *Jhum* or any other forms of shifting cultivation;

(5) Establishment of village or town committees or councils and their powers;

(6) Any other matters relating to village or town administration, including village or town police and public health and sanitation;

(7) Appointment of succession of chiefs or headmen;

(8) Inheritance of property, marriage and divorce;

(9) Social customs and regulation and control of money lending and trading by non-tribals.

Apart from these legislative provisions, the Government of Mizoram have also entrusted some subjects to the three Autonomous District Councils through Executive Orders and Notifications. On the 20th August, 1986 a Notification issued by Secretary to the Government of Mizoram, District Council Affairs Department, K.N. Srivastava, vide Notification No. DCA/E-212/83/52 in accordance with sub-paragraph (2) of paragraph 6 of the Sixth Schedule to the Constitution of India, conveyed that the Government of Mizoram entrusted functions in relation to *Agriculture, Animal Husbandry, Community Project, Social Welfare* and *Village Planning*, to the District Councils with effect from 1 September, 1986. The Notification contained eleven clear instructions, some of which may be pointed out: (a) The District Council shall prepare detailed schemes and submit to the Government; (b) On approval of schemes submitted, provisions of fund will be made in Mizoram Budget; (c) There must be competent technical personnel to execute the schemes; (d) The District Council shall not entertain new staff out of the fund placed at their disposal without approval of Government of Mizoram.

Again on the 22 September, 1993, a fresh Notification No. B.17012/3/92-DCA was issued by Dr H.C. Thanhranga, Secretary to the Government of Mizoram (Gazatted on Monday, 27 September, 1993) entrusting various subjects under different Departments and in modification of earlier Notification of

20 August, 1986, to the three Autonomous District Councils, on the same terms and conditions as in the Notification dated 20.8.1986, with effect from Financial Year 1994-1995. The list of subjects include:

***(1) Agriculture and Horticulture*:**

- (i) Agriculture Link Road;
- (ii) Distribution of planting material/certified seeds;
- (iii) Procurement of machineries for 50 per cent subsidy;
- (iv) Implements and Tools;
- (v) Water Pumping Machineries;
- (vi) Land Development by manuals;
- (vii) Minor Irrigation Construction of field channels.

***(2) Fisheries Department*:**

- (i) Grant-in-aid to individual fish farmers for fish pond development.

***(3) Public Health Engineering Department*:**

- (i) Rural Sanitation,
- (ii) Spring Source Development,
- (iii) Public Latrine/Urinal (Rural Sanitation).

***(4) Industry Department*:**

- (i) Handloom and Handicraft,
- (ii) Grant-in-aid to individuals for supply of tools and implements,
- (iii) Selection of SEEYOU Loanees.

***(5) Sericulture Department*:**

- (i) Grant-in-aid to Private Rearers under Promotion Scheme,
- (ii) Marketing-selling of cocoon to state government.

(6) A.H. and Vety. Department:

- (i) Subsidy Scheme on–
  Cattle Development,
  Piggery Development,
  Poultry Development,
  Dispensary.

(7) ***Arts and Culture Department***:

(i) Grant-in-aid to promotion of Arts and Culture,

(ii) District Library,

(iv) District Museum,

(iv) Assistance for Publication.

(8) ***Social Welfare Department***:

(i) Old Age Pension (Plan and Non-Plan),

(ii) Assistance to Voluntary Organisations,

(iii) Pre-school,

(iv) Welfare of Handicap,

(v) Welfare of Poor and Destitutes.

(9) ***Soil Conservation Department***:

(i) Implementation of Terracing,

(ii) Plantation Subsidy Scheme,

(iii) Village Grassing Ground.

(10) ***Local Administration Department:***

(i) Urban Development,

(ii) All minor works of the department such as construction of steps/culverts/retaining wall etc.

(11) ***Forest Department***: All the projects taken by Forest Department within Council areas can be handed over to the District Council concerned including all the assets and liabilities, if any. National Park at Phawngpui and sanctuary at Ngengpui under centrally sponsored schemes will be looked after by the Forest Department of Government of Mizoram.

(12) ***Transport Department***: It is agreed that separate Transport Department may be created by each District Council w.e.f 1994-95 Financial Year. It is further decided that cost Transport Department of Mizoram may set aside the cost One Bus for each District Council including maintenance charges. It is also agreed and decided that the Government of Mizoram should try to obtain the procedure followed by the District Council of Assam etc. regarding the collection of Road Tax, Goods and Passenger tax, etc.

(13) ***Sports and Youth Services Department*:** It is agreed that the council may create Sports and Youth Services Department and requirement of fund for the purpose may be provided within their budget. Sports and Youth Services Department will provide requirement of fund.

(14) ***Cooperation Department*:** It is agreed that the Council may create cooperative Department as one of the Department but technical subjects will be considered later.

(15) ***Public Works Department*:** Creation/opening of District Council Public Works Department is agreed. The District Councils will, however, have to strengthen their technical hands to cope with the works in accordance with PWD norms. The following works will be entrusted to the councils:

   (i) Inter-village approach road to link up with the PWD roads;

   (ii) Maintenance and improvement of satellite towns and village roads.

(16) ***Education Department:***

   (i) *Primary School:* As for Primary School, it is decided that from 1994-95 onwards, the budget provision will be reflected in District Council budget and Education Department will no longer include the same in the State budget;

   (ii) Adult Education will be handed over to District Council;

   (iii) *Middle School:* Handing over of Middle School to District Council is agreed. However, Examination will be continued under the Examination Board of the State.

(17) ***Rural Development Department*:**

   (i) Rural Communication;

   (ii) Construction of Community Hall;

   (iii) Rural Housing.

(18) ***Relief and Rehabilitation Department*:** It is agreed that Rs 1 lakh each be provided by the respective council for 1994-95 under non-plan. It is further agreed that Finance Department should set aside fund for this purpose.

(19) ***DRDA and ICDS*****:** Regarding the handing over of DRDA (including CD Block) and ICDS, the Hon'ble Minister in charge District Council Affairs Department informed that the government will seek clarification/permission from Centre Government whether these two Agencies can be handed over to District Councils since they are centre sponsored programmes.

(20) ***Water Ways (Inland Water Transport)*****:** The need to have separate allocation of fund under Water Ways (Inland water transport) for the three District Councils is considered really important by the Committee. The District Council Headquarters are disconnected by Road Transport in rainy season. The only way foodstuff and other essential commodities can be sent to the District Council Headquarters is through Water Way Transport. Since there is no budget provision under State Budget the District Council may provide budget provision for this also from 1994-95. Government of Mizoram may provide separate fund for this to the three District Councils.

Further, the Government of Mizoram, by a Notification No. C.13016/3/2010-DCA dated 29 August, 2011, in exercise of powers under Paragraph 6(2) and 20 BB of the Sixth Schedule, once again entrusted the following functions to the Autonomous District Councils of LAI, MARA and CHAKMA:

(1) Agriculture (Crop Husbandry) Department– with seven identified activity areas-same as in 1986.

(2) Animal Husbandry and Veterinary Department– with two specified activity areas.

(3) Art and Culture Department–with specified four activity areas-same as 1986.

(4) Cooperation Department– containing three specified areas (new).

(5) Disaster Management, Relief and Rehabilitation Department– creation of corpus fund- (new).

(6) Fisheries Department– Grant-in-aid and development of pisciculture– same as in 1986.

(7) Horticulture Department– with eight activity areas specified.

(8) Industries Department– with three specified areas.

(9) *Local Administration Department–* with three activity areas.

(10) *Minor Irrigation Department–* construction of field channels.

(11) *Public Works Department–* two selected activity.

(12) *Public Health Engineering Department–* with three selected activity areas.

(13) *Rural Development Department–* four selected activity areas.

(14) *Social Welfare Department–* three areas- same as in 1986.

(15) *Soil Conservation Department–* two areas.

(16) *Sports and Youth Services Department–* all schemes.

(17) *Sericulture Department–* same as 1986- two activity areas.

(18) *Transport Department–* almost same as 1986.

(19) *Urban Development and Poverty Alleviation Department–* new.

The notification specifically mentioned that, 'the concerned Administrative Department shall oversee and ensure that these functions are not again undertaken by their offices in the Autonomous District Council areas and only some skeleton staff are retained there for the purpose of statistical requirements and coordination'. However, the desire to eliminate duplication of functions is not easy. Even though many subjects and functional items have been entrusted by the state government, to the three Autonomous District Councils, majority of the entrusted items have continued to be performed by the line and administrative offices in Council areas. There continue to be a dichotomy in the approach toward district development between the state government and the Councils. The state government continues to undertake works in respect of the devolved functions without consulting the District Councils. Separate DRDA continue to exist in both districts. MGNREGS is also being implemented outside the Councils. As such, CEM, R.T. Zachono of Mara ADC, stated that the District Council do not play major functional role even in the execution of centrally sponsored schemes such as MGNREGS, IAY, BRGF, and DADP. It is, therefore, very difficult to identify which functions are devolved in the true sense of the term.

Many items and subjects have been entrusted to the three ADCs without accompanying devolution of functions and finances, making the ADCs a duplication of the State Departments.This resulted simply in the increase of administrative personnel and staff without attendant delivery of services. Devolution of the three Fs (Functions, Functionaries and Finance) is yet to take a proper shape. Since most of the functional activities continue to be performed by the State departmental offices in the Council Areas till the field-work was conducted recently, in spite of instruction contained in Notification No.C.13016/3/2010-DCA dated 29th August, 2011, functionaries at the Autonomous District Councils do not seem to be taking serious note of the terms and conditions requiring them to prepare detailed schemes in consonant with available competent technical personnel, and also seem to violate condition not to entertain new staff out of the fund placed at their disposal. Absence of detailed good schemes entails absence of adequate financial devolution as stated by senior State Planning official. The key is to operationalise these orders by backing them up with the devolution of funds and the dismantling of parallel structures that exist.

Table 4.1: Detailed Statement of Fund Transferred to Autonomous District Councils (in lakh)

Mara Autonomous District Council							
2009-2010			*2010-2011*			*2011-2012*	
Plan	*NP*	*Total*	*Plan*	*NP*	*Total*	*Plan*	*NP*
1450	3381	4,831	1782	4390	6,172	2193	4928
Lai Autonomous District Council							
2009-2010			*2010-2011*			*2011-2012*	
Plan	*NP*	*Total*	*Plan*	*NP*	*Total*	*Plan*	*NP*
1557	3492	5,049	2327	4890	7,217	2341	5183
Chakma Autonomous District Council							
2009-2010			*2010-2011*			*2011-2012*	
Plan	*NP*	*Total*	*Plan*	*NP*	*Total*	*Plan*	*NP*
1698	1491	3,189	1778	2186	3,964	1479	2657

Source: *State Planning Board and Finance Department.*

There is, however, differences between this record and the record kept in respective Autonomous District Council Accounts Departments. For example, the total amount of financial devolution to Mara ADC as recorded by them is– Rs 5024.71 during 2009-2010, Rs 6402.74 during 2010-2011, Rs 7381.67 duting 2011-2012 and Rs 9,106.33 during 2012-2013. For Lai Autonomous District Council, the sanctioned amount during 2009-2010 according to their record is Rs 5049.56, Rs 7,277 during 2010-2011, Rs 7399 during 2011-2012 and Rs 10,395 during 2012-2013.

As far as Chakma Autonomous District Council is concerned, the fund transferred during 2009-2010 in their own record indicates Rs 3,187.25, Rs 3,964 during 2010-2011, Rs 4,136 during 2011-2012 and Rs 5,797 against State record of Rs 6,613. What is reflected here is the inadequacy of finances devolved coupled with State intrusion in many departments. The total fund devolved to the three Autonomous District Councils in 2012-2013 amounts to Rs 278.18 crores.

Village Councils in the Autonomous District Council areas more or less function in the same capacity as those in the non-Autonomous area. village council in Mizoram was a creation of Mizo District Council through the Lushai Hills District (Village Councils) Act, 1953. Without much modification in its important contents, this has been adopted through legislation wherever necessary in the Council Areas, stated by CEMs. Altogether six village councils– Thingkah, Chawntlangpui, Maubawk Zero, Saihatlangkawn (Siahatla) I, II, III have been visited and discussed in details their problems and functional activities. The VC members feel that their position in terms of authority, functional clarity and financial power is simply inadequate in order to carry out the massive service delivery expected of them. Following is a quick summary observations:

Table 4.2: Village Councils Selected for Field-study in Council Area

Village	*Distance from District Hqrs.*	*Number of Households*	*Population*
Thingkah	5 kms	258	1219
Chawntlangpui	24 kms	107	597
Maubawk Zero	27 kms	149	726
Siahatla I	3 kms	257	1328
Siahatla II	3 kms	255	1375
Siahatla III	3 kms	202	897

Source: *Field source.*

All the villages, except Chawntlangpui, a small village, do not have adequate drinking water supply. VC Court, except in the cases of the three village councils of Saihatlangkawn I,II, and III where one or two cases have been settled amicably recently in each case, is almost a non-functional entity in the other villages. All the village councils have their respective sanitation committee headed by the VCP to oversee the village cleaning drive and sanitation related activities in the villages. However, in the absence of fund, nothing much can really be achieved. Whatever a meager annual fund given has been controlled by the health workers. There is also Health Sub-Centre in the bigger villages of Thingkah and Saihatlangkawn with health workers, majority of which are untrained. Health workers are under the guidance of Supervisor from the Chief Medical Officer of Lawngtlai Civil Hospital. The village councils nor the District Councils have any authority in the matter, and as such monitoring of the functions of Health Sub-centre is very unreliable and irregular.

The performance of rural housing programme under IAY is left to a Committee headed by the VCP and other VC members consisting of representatives of NGOs at the village level. This Committee initially prepared Wait List of beneficiaries as per the requisite number prepared by BDO. The village level Wait List is then sent to the BDO. Selection of beneficiary list is finalised at the DRDA office in which the original list prepared by the village level committee stands almost cancelled or modified tremendously. In the process, political influence of District Council Members, particularly Executive Members, and of ruling party unit as well as bureaucratic involvement, is extensive.

As far as selection of items for BRGF (Border Region Grant Fund) is concerned, 40 per cent is supposed to be reserved for the village council, but empirical evidence shows that not even 1 per cent is given to them. Work proposals were prepared by the village councils and NGOs, but these proposals have not been accepted, as a general rule, in the District level committee. The District level Joint village council is also helpless to bring this issue to the CEM or any other Officers of the District Council as the village council can always be dissolved by the Executive Committee of the District Councils. State ministers are also stated to be involved in this and as such contractors are almost always from Aizawl.

Primary Schools and Middle Schools are under the authority of the District Councils whereas High School and Secondary Schools are managed by the State Education Department. In Thingkah, some teachers of the Middle schools and Primary Schools habitually engaged themselves in card games during class hours and indulge in alcoholic drinks during duty hours. VC members feel helpless to do anything except report the matters to the authority where no action was taken. Similar lapses in the educational institutions can be reported from other villages. The point here is that elected representatives at the local level simply have no control, no authority in this matter in their own jurisdiction.

In terms of Finance, village councils simply do not have own source of finance. Unlike other parts of Mizoram, they do not collect animal tax or collect fees as a result of animal control. However, they receive as in other parts of Mizoram, TFC grants and MGNREGS. Apart from this, a small fund may be reserved and set aside for village level development items from District Councils fund which, of course, is at the disposal of the Officers of the District Council and selection of contractors is made by them. Since the village councils are not involved, performance is below average standard.

VC members feel that they cannot take any major steps towards stable and better water supply, and other developmental works and deliver better services to the people due to lack of power, authority, and the needed finance and infrastructure. They feel that change is very much needed.

Village Councils in Non-council Areas

As pointed out earlier, village council system was a creation of Lushai Hills (Village Councils) Act, 1953 which received the assent of the Governor of Assam on 19th November, 1953 and published as such in Assam Gazette on 9 December, 1953.. The Act stipulates the function of the village council to include- (1) allotment of jhum land within the village jurisdiction and distribution of jhum plots; (2) power to enforce *'hnatlang'* in the interest of the public whenever occasion so demands; (3) Each village council shall be responsible for the sanitation of the village. A sanitation committee shall be appointed by the village council if necessary. In addition, the Act empower the village council to make rules which may prescribe:

(1) Control, preservation and use of timbers and other forest products except of the reserved forests, ordinarily utilised for building purposes such as canes, sungrass, siallu, thilthek, laisawral, etc.

(2) Maintenance, preservation and improvement of good water supply;

(3) Control of stray animals within its jurisdiction and at night within the Village Ram;

(4) Prevention and control of fire within the Village and the Village Ram;

(5) Ngawidawh;

(6) Sanitation and cleanliness of the village;

(7) Extraction of Khamkhuai.

The village councils have been careful in enforcing the legislation regarding preservation of forests and forest products. In Lallen, Vaitin and other villages visited, the village council have strictly prohibited wanton destruction of forests, and the use of forest products except for building purposes as they also realise the depleting forests results in diminished water supply in the village. Thus, they slowly comprehend the environmental consequences of devastation of forest. In some villages such as Ngur, the Mizo Upa Pawl (Mizo Senior Citizens' Association) and other NGOs are taking active part in the preservation of forests.However, some of these provisions such as Ngawidawh, Extraction of Khamkhuai, may not be relevant today. But village councils are actively engaging themselves in thecontrol of fire within the Village Ram, control of stray animals, sanitation and cleanliness of the villages. However, the efforts that they have render for the welfare of the village, they feel, is ineffective because of the absence of devolution of funds, functions and functionaries. The allotment of jhum land and distribution of jhum plots have lost its traditional importance. Many families are now engaging themselves in occupations other than jhum cultivation as the main source of family livelihood. This is partly due to the dwindling yield of *jhum* cultivation and the growing diversification of occupation. The power to enforce *'hnatlang'* also have lost its traditional significance in many contemporary villages. Although many village councils continue to enforce 'hnatlang' (community work), this is mainly done in connection with MGNREGS related works, and not in its traditional standingas means of community welfare. The following village councils have been visited and painstaking, thorough and fruitful discussions on the kind of problems they face and the functions entrusted to them have been highlighted.The discussions were held in formal as well as informal style, and the members of the village council openly and freely discussed their problems and their aspirations. They were most concerned about the ambiguous and indistinct role they play in connection with development functions. During 2013, all the village councils visited have vehemently complained about the introduction of Village Employment Council (VEC) to take over the responsibility of implementing MGNREGS programmes from the village councils. They strongly felt that this has sidelined and further marginalised them and rendered village council as ineffectual and incompetent self-government institution.

Table 2.6 describes the village councils selected in non-council areas, their distance from respective district headquarters, number of households and population and the size of the village councils.This has covered more or less the entire Mizoram and its representativeness should not be an issue.

Table 4.3: List of Village Councils Selected for Field-study in Non-Council Areas

Village	*District*	*Distance from District Hqrs*	*House-hold*
Sakawrdai	Aizawl	170 kms	541
Zohmun	Aizawl	180 kms	275
Muthi	Aizawl	12 kms	175
Vaitin	Aizawl	173 kms	245
Sailutar	Aizawl	136 kms	104
Chamring	Aizawl	54 kms	55
Muallungthu	Aizawl	17 kms	270
Sumsuih	Aizawl	48 kms	166
Samlukhai	Aizawl	60 kms	237
Thuampui	Lunglei	17 kms	104

Village	*District*	*Distance from District Hqrs*	*House-hold*
Luangmual	Lunglei	09 kms	405
Zote	Champhai	05 kms	311
Ngur	Champhai	18 kms	360
W.Phaileng	Mamit	40 kms	430
N.W.Phaileng	Mamit	44 kms	377
Damparengpui	Mamit	74 kms	468
New Mamit	Mamit	01 kms	435
Lallen	Mamit	60 kms	164
Rawpuichhip	Mamit	45 kms	326
Thingdawl	Kolasib	07 kms	655
Nisapui	Kolasib	79 kms	180
Bukpui	Kolasib	88 kms	241
Lungdai	Kolasib	56 kms	530
Chhiahtlang	Serchhip	12 kms	730

(**Note:** 2012 VC elections could not be held in Sakawrdai, Zohmun and Vaitin resulting in the extension of the term of previous and existing VC till August 2013. State election commission announced election of 15 village councils in this area on 23 July, 2013 and elections were held after a gap of almost one and a half year.)

Table 2.7 indicates some selected functions of the selected village councils such as functioning of the VC Court, the nature of allotment of *jhum* land, enforcement of *'hnatlang'* (public works), functional role in activities concerning education in the village, sanitation, selection of beneficiaries as highlighted in the operation of NLUP, and functional role in MGNREGS.

Table 4.4: Some Functional Activities of Village Councils

Name of VC	*VC Court*	*Allotment of Jhum land*	*Hna (pub*
Sakawrdai	No case/suit	No allotment this year, but about 300 families engage in jhumming	occa
Zohmun	Two cases of land & garden disputes; arrived at amicable solution	Allotment to 78 families, others are doing jhumming in their own land	Occ
Muth	No case	Allotment with proper guidelines for jhum and horticulture	occa

Name of VC	*VC Court*	*Allotment of Jhum land*	*Hnatlang (public works)*	*Education*	*Sanitation*	*NLUP*	*MGNREGS*
Vaitin	Cases of divorce and custody of children was settled amicably	Allotted to 50 families. VC also allotted land for NLUP	occasional	VEC is doing midday meal and disciplinary actions if needed	The committee functions, but not satisfactorily as there is no fund.	VLIC is simply controlled by the ruling party workers.	Good performance in both the schemes
Sailutar	No case	Allotted to 15 families- those without NLUP private land	occasional	VEC is involved in midday meal only	Satisfactory performance. Received Rs.50,000 for cleanliness drive	Initial selection was on party line, but later includes others	Material component done by VC, and wage component by VEC
Chamring	No case	Allotted to 17 families. Private land owners do jhum cultivation on their own land	occasional	VEC is involved in midday meal and do supervision and take disciplinary actions when necessary	The Committee functions satisfactory given the limited finance and space	Selection of beneficiaries is done by party unit alone	Satisfactory performance
Muallungthu	No case	No one depends on jhumming. Only 13 families have been allotted	occasional	VEC is non-functional In any disciplinary action , VEC or VC is not involved.	The Committee is non-functional. Health Worker is taking all the decisions.	Party unit role in the selection of beneficiaries is very prominent	Good performance. But Monitoring Committee is dismantled by the BDO.

Name of VC	*VC Court*	*Allotment of jhum land*	*Hnatlang (public works)*	*Education*	*Sanitation*	*NLUP*	*MGNREGS*
Sumsuih	There are cases which involve imposition of fines in which the party fined would say "I shall not give such fines" implying the degrading status of VC	Out of 182 families 150 households are still engaging in jhum cultivation. *Ramtheh Board* is doing the allotment	occasional	VEC is involved in the appointment of cooks but not in the day to day activities of the school	The Committee is taking steps to improve drinking water supply, but no tangible result as there is no fund.	Selection of beneficiaries is done by party unit	Good performance. They do not seem to have any problem
Samlukhai	No case during the present VC term	*Ramtheh Board* is doing the allotment. About 80 families engage in Jhumming, 30 families in WRC, others engage in vegetable gardens,etc.	occasional	VEC is functioning satisfactory	There are Village Health & Sanitation Committee and Local Sanitation Committee. Local level committee is doing better.	Selection of beneficiaries and even monitoring is done by party unit. VC has little functional role to play	Wage component is performed good. But the bulk of material component done by BDO and not satisfactory

Name of VC	*VC Court*	*Allotment of jhum land*	*Hnatlang (public works)*	*Education*	*Sanitation*	*NLUP*	*MGNREGS*
Thuampui	VC members vaguely recollect cases brought to VC many years back	It continues as before as most of the villagers are still engaging in it	Not regular as it was before	VEC was formed earlier, but not in the present VC term. VC is not involved.	Village Health & Sanitation Committee, but nothing to do. Health sub-centre and 3 Health workers staying at Lunglei only come occasionally. VC has no control	Selection of beneficiaries is done by Village Level Implementing Committee	Performance is good. Monitoring by the Village Level Monitoring Committee. But VLA stays at Lunglei and visit only occasionally
Luangmual	There were cases before 2006 and were settled, no case now	Not any more	Not any more	VEC is formed but in reality it is non-functional.	Health sub-centre sine 1997 which functions 3 days a week. Sanitation Committee is formed, but no role, no control over health workers.	Village Level Implementing Committee is involved in selection of beneficiaries, but party influence is very strong	Performance isa good. Monitoring Committee is formed, but actual monitoring is done by line departments.

Name of VC	*VC Court*	*Allotment of jhum land*	*Hnatlang (public works)*	*Education*	*Sanitation*	*NLUP*	*MGNREGS*
Zote	It is not functioning any more for the last 20 years	Only few families now depend on jhum cultivation for livelihood	occasional	VEC is formed to act as central Committee over various school managing committees. It is yet to take effective functional role	There is Water and Sanitation Committee ,but main concern is on water supply. VC is working on what they call 'gravitation water supply'	Decisions according to proposal made by Village Level Implementing Committee	CSS programme-s are performed well. The main complaint is that they were handicapped to make grass roots planning
Ngur	During the last 4 years, 8 cases were brought to VC Court on disputes over land, animals and property. All were settled amicably	Many villagers are now no longer depend on jhum cultivation	occasional	VEC is formed to function as coordinating body for various school managing committees, but really functions as advisory in midday meal and monitoring	There is Water &Sanitation Committee to oversee drainage and cleanliness. But no control on health workers.	Proposal for list of beneficiaries is prepared by VLIC	Normal performance

Name of VC	*VC Court*	*Allotment of jhum land*	*Hnatlang(public works)*	*Education*	*Sanitation*	*NLUP*	*MGNREGS*
W.Phaileng	No case or suit during the present term	Major part of the village land belong to individual families during earlier NLUP. As such VC is not doing any allotment although 250 families still depend on it. No proper control of fire	occasional	VEC is formed. Functions include demand for Higher Secondary School as there is none in Phaileng Block area. They are not involved in monitoring	They formed the committee and function s as nodal for certain committed activities	VLIC is formed and has its own list of beneficiaries. Party unit also has its own list which always take prior importance over the list prepared by VLIC.	Performance is good. The only problem they have is that during the very recent past, the material component portion is entirely controlled by the BDO and VC has no share
N.W.Phaileng	VC Court is not functioning for the last 5 years due the fact that VC has no control over allotment of house sites.	As the village was entirely covered by earlier NLUP and allotment of land to individual families, there is no need for fresh allotment	occasional	VEC is formed which involved in only midday meal. No inspection and no monitoring of school.	Normal Village level Committee, but no liaison with Health Sub-centre, but concern itself with village sanitation such as pit latrine. But entrusted the work to MUP.	Selection of beneficiaries is done by party unit without the knowledge of VLIC and VC resulting in the replacement of the existing VCP who indulge in this activity.	TFC grant & MGNREGS on wage component have been performed satisfactory. But material component is now entirely at the disposal of BDO. VC has no part in its operation now.

Name of VC	*VC Court*	*Allotment of jhum land*	*Hnatlan (public works)*	*Education*	*Sanitation*	*NLUP*	*MGNREGS*
Dampa-rengpui	Below VC Court there are six choudhirys (Bru Court).Cases which cannot be settled in these courts go to VC Court	VC is making allotment	Not regular	The Committee Is involved In midday meal, but no other function	Main function include looking after cleanliness of street. No control On functioning of Health workers	In selection of beneficiaries, Party involvement Is very real	TFC & NREGS wage component have been performed well. But material component has been taken away by BDO for private contractors and party workers.
New Mamit	No case during the present tenure	NLUP directs Allotment must stop. But allotted to 75 families (non-NLUP Recipients	Regularly for local level public works apart from NREGS Related works	VEC works in relation to Govt. school. Involves in repair works, midday meal & other routine functions	Committee existed earlier but no commendable work. VC is now doing hygiene & cleaning drive in the absence of Such Committee	VC members were involved in the initial phase but the role of VC become ambiguous now. It is almost taken over by party workers	TFC grants and MGNREGS wage component are properly managed. But material component of NREGS has not been received regularly due to political interference and involvement

Name of VC	VC Court	Allotment of jhum land	Hnatlang (public works0·	Education	Sanitation	NLUP	MGNERGS
Lallen	Continue to function, but the number of cases suits reduced considerably.	They continue this. During 2013 they allotted jhum plot to 30 families. Number is decreasing	Occasional	VEC is looking after midday meal in primary and middle school. But it has no authority over High School	The concerned committee is doing well. They in fact received reward for achievement in every family having proper toilet	VLIC recommended 40 beneficiaries but party unit replaced 19 of them. Beneficiaries with with good start in life are doing well, for others it is a complete failure	Both TFC grants and wage component have been performed well. But the share of VC has been waived by BDO and taken control of entire scheme. Presence of Village Employme-nt Council is hindrance
Rawpui-chhip	VC Court considered many cases & agreements reached in the past. But such suits and cases are very rare now	Allotment continues. But the number of families decreased very fast. During 2012 only six families had been allotted.	This continues whenever needed, and the response is still very good	VEC is very active in 1)midday meal 2)Any work items for school whenever fund is there 3)Appointment of local teachers under SSA scheme	Village Committee is active in cleanliness, awareness campaign in schools etc. Awarded Presidential prize of Rs.1,00,000 for modern latrine in public & private	All selected beneficiaries are members of ruling party. VC has no involvement in real term.	Achievement is good. They utilized fund fruitfully in both TFC grants & NREGS wage component. They receive nothing from material component

Name of VC	*VC Court*	*Allotment of jhum land*	*Hnatlang (public works)*	*Education*	*Sanitation*	*NLUP*	*MGNREGS*
Thingdawl	VC Court is active. During the past few months there are 10 cases involving land disputes and addiction. All the cases were settled	Not any more. It is no longer possible as private land ownership is very common now	They do enforce and respond from the people is very good	Any problem in the different schools managing committees will be brought to VEC	The Village Level committee functional role includes: cleanliness drive, awareness campaign in drug abuse, alcohol etc. together with Health Deptt.	Initial list was prepared by VC. But party unit prepared another list which prevailed. Now the list is made purely by party uniy.VMC is formed, but monitoring is done by departments. Mis-management is common	TFC grants& MGNREGS grants used to be at the hand of VC, and achievement was good. But now the Village Employment Council is taking over the roles and marginalizes VC functions
Nisapui	No case any more	Majority of villagers no longer engage in jhumming In 2013 only 9 families were allotted Jhum land	occasional	VEC is performing normal function as per guidelines	Sanitation Committee is also performing its formal duties	Initial selection was by VLIC. But later party unit has its own list which ultimately formed the final selected list of beneficiaries	The TFC grants have been performed satisfactorily. No problem with the VEC. They have good working relationship. Work profit may go to VC fund without objection from VEC

Name of VC	*VC Court*	*Allotment of jhum land*	*Hnatlang (public works)*	*Education*	*Sanitation*	*NLUP*	*MGNREGS*
Bukpui	No more case	Out 160 families, only 30 came forward for jhum allotment, but only 20 families did actually engage in jhumming	occasional	VEC involvement includes midday meal and SSA teachers appointment	Sanitation Committee looks after Health sub-centre, do repair work from sanitation grant of Rs.10,000 annually- also do street cleaning, drainage with YMA	VLIC is formed, but the role of party unit in selection of beneficiaries is real.	TFC grants performance is good. They also receive MGNREGS grants regularly and seem to be doing well also
Lungdai	During 2 years, three cases involving house sites, land boundaries, water pipes disputes have been considered and settled peacefully	There are hardly any families in jhum cultivation. As such, Allotment is not continued	Not any more	VEC functions include visiting & inspecting schools, take needed actions when necessary. It also include midday meal. Inspection is actually done only when needed.	Village level Sanitation Committee is doing well in collaboration with Primary and Sub-Health Centres	Present VC members have no role in the selection of beneficiaries. Previous VCs are involved. Beneficiaries are doing well. This is the few places where VC members are happy with the NLUP programme	They used to perform both TFC and MGNREGS grants fairly good. But now Village Employment Council taking over the role of VC and they are not at all happy with this arrangement.

Name of VC	*VC Court*	*Allotment of jhum land*	*Hnatlang (public works)*	*Education*	*Sanitation*	*NLUP*	*MGNREGS*
Chhiah-tlang	As in the past, VC court is vibrant	No more allotment as people engaged in jhumming has been reduce d tremendoulsy	occasional	VEC is formed and functions as per the guidelines	The village is divided into six sanitation areas. Each of these has been led by VC members and very active since 1988. It was malaria infected area and it is now relieved of it.	Selection is done by VLIC which is normally changed as in other places. Beneficiaries have been doing well.	VC members take care to see that the programme perform well. They go the work places and social audit every six month. But a parger share of material component goes to BDO/TA
Khawlai-lung	Three normal cases and 5 petty disputes have been tried, and decisions are respected by the aggrieved parties	No free land for allotment due to NLUP for gardening works. Each family do jhumming in their private land	occasional	VEC is active. Besides Midday meal, they do regular inspection They even take disciplinary actions to many teachers whenever needed	They Village Health, Sanitation & Nutrition Committee They have good working relation with Primary Health Centre and the villagers	VLIC prepares list of beneficiaries in consultation with ruling party unit There seem to be problem here	TFC grants and wage component of NREGS have been performed well. But in material component major portion (60%) is taken over by the BDO. They feel deprived.

Name of VC	*VC Court*	*Allotment of Jhum land*	*Hnatlang (public works)*	*Education*	*Sanitation*	*NLUP*	*MGNREGS*
Keitum	No more cases	Many families with private land. Only 50 families came forward and allotment made to them. VC convened a meeting which decides the method of allotment	Occasional	VEC is involve es in midday meal and SSA school and teachers. Day to day activities are left to respective school committee But if need be, they feel they can take disciplinary action.	Two committees. Health & Sanitation and Water & Sanitation committees. Both function well and they have enough water supply	VLIC is formed. But it is ruling party which prepares list of beneficiaries. They then request the VLIC to accept and sign. VC is not doing any monitoring but ruling party is doing supervision and monitoring	They receive TFC grants regularly and become main source for VC fund from the profit. In material component, VC is receiving less proportion and Technical Assistant (BDO) is getting more
New Serchhip	No more case	Jhumming is only subsidiary income source now. Private land ownership makes allotment difficult and it is abolished in the village	occasional	VEC is not at all active here	The village is divided into 4 squads, each with a local committee headed by VC member. The local committee will report matters to the Village Level Committee and VC will see that actions are taken	VLIC prepares list of beneficiaries. There was no addition from other sources. There seems to be less political and bureaucratic encroachment in the process of final selection	Performance of TFC and MGNREGS grants are normal but not outstanding

Source: Field notes and data.

The functional activities included here are not exhaustive. But these are reflective of the functional devolution at the village council level. It can be summarised as follow:

(a) Village Council Court

In the majority of the sampled villages, there simply is no case or suit in the village. Whatever minor conflicts, discords, frictions and dissensions have been, very often, informally settled by the village council members. In some villages the decision reached by the VC Court is appreciated by the villagers. But in few villages, the decisions of the court have been scorned and ridiculed, and the fine imposed looked upon with contempt and disapproval, and refused to comply with. In such a situation the VC members expressed their helplessness as they have no authority to enforce the police power.

Improvement of the quality and status of the village council Court will definitely enhance the power and authority of the VC and shall be in line with transfer of

appropriate functional subjects. The Mizoram Finance Commission Act states, '*..to enable all the local bodies to have financial autonomy to perform functions analogous to the functions of other local bodies constituted under Constitution Part IX and Part IX-A while retaining the distinctive tribal identity protected by the Sixth Schedule to the Constitution of India which is foundational to the local bodies of the State*'. Augmentation of village council Court and its power and muscle will help in achieving this objective goal. There cannot be divergent views regarding the need to make the village council the nodal authority at the village level for decentralised planning and implementation.

(b) Allotment of Jhum Land

In many villages, the number of households depending on jhum cultivation is decreasing tremendously in the past few years. Nonetheless, there are sizeable families still depending on jhumming as a source of livelihood in quite a few villages. As such, VCs continue to allot *jhum* land to those who express their requirement. In few villages, the actual allotment is left to the public assembly convened by the village council for the purpose, and the method of allotment to be worked out on the spot. Occupational adjustment,mobility and transformation is so enormous that in many villages nobody come forward for *jhum* allotment. This is partly true due to the fact that many families have their own private land as a result of "Jhum Control" scheme initiated by Pu Laldenga, and the introduction of NLUP by the Congress Government. Many families are doing jhum cultivation in their own private plot. It may be noted here that the village RAM which used to be the communal land of the villagers has undergone colossal transformation and VCs are in fact, perplexed and mystified about the actual legal ownership of the village land. Government departments have encroached upon village land without consulting the village authority. VCs are now bewildered about the real authority of the village–Village Council or NGOs–YMA, MHIP, MUP. In many instances where the state government is taking certain initiatives, the NGOs may be consulted or informed whereas the village council is kept uninformed or badly inappropriately informed. This only shows that functional relationship between the state government and local government is very pitiable and unfortunate.

(c) Enforcement of 'Hnatlang'

Enforcement of *'hnatlang'* is the prerogative of the village council as mandated under section 8(2) of the Lushai Hills District (Village Councils) Acts, 1953 wherein it says, *"the village council shall have powers to enforce 'Hnatlang' in the interest of the public whenever occasion so demands"*. Any person who does not comply with the order of *hnatlang* shall be subject to 'Run' either in kind or in cash.. unless he has been exempted from hnatlang under section 9(1) or has obtained commutation under section 9(3). The provision of 'enforcement of hnatlang' was thus taken seriously. However, occupational diversity and transformation of life-style in the rural areas make it redundant, and becomes almost outmoded and disused. Lungdai and Luangmual(Lunglei) completely stopped enforcing 'Hnatlang'. It is continued in Thingdawl, Rawpuichhip and New Mamit and the response is still very good. But in others, it is an occasional occurrence, and people do not seem to give serious and sober thought about it.

(d) Sanitation

Section 11 of the Lushai Hills District (Village Councils) Acts, 1953 states, *'Each village council shall be responsible for the sanitation of the Village. A Sanitation Committee shall be appointed by the village council if necessary'*. In almost all the villages, Village Health and

Sanitation Committee has been appointed. In some villages, they also have Village Water and Sanitation Committee, and in Samlukhai, VC appointed Local Sanitation Committee which is relatively more active. Sanitation Committee is exceptionally doing well in Chhiahtlang, but in other villages the main functional activities remain to be normal cleaning drive. Without allocated fund, they feel they cannot achieve much.

(e) Animal Control

With the passing of Mizoram Animal(Control and Taxation) Act, 1980 and the Mizoram Animal (Control and Taxation) Rules, 1982, VCs have taken care to see that Section 3(2) *'No owner of animal shall allow his animal to trespass upon any land or property whether private or public'* is strictly adhered to. Animal tax is supposed to form local source of fund for VCs. But with the strict adherent observation to Animal Control Act and Rules, the number of animals in the villages shrinks, and do not bring any substantial amount to local fund.

(*f*) Village Education Committee

Village Education Committee is appointed in every village visited to look after, monitor, and coordinate activities of the educational institutions in the village, particularly the lower level of educational institutions. Some village councils, such as Rawpuichhip, have done commendable work in supervising and monitoring the functioning of educational institutions. But in many villages the functional role of the VEC remain to be appointment of cooks for the midday meal where they have normally no control for the routine daily activities of the schools, and have no control over the annual maintenance fund sanctioned by the Government. Some VC members express confidence in their role to enforce disciplinary actions against the teachers whenever necessary. But such action is rare, indeed quite uncommon. As it is the case in Thingkah, some teachers indulging in card games during teaching hours and who came to schools in an inebriated conditionwhich is becoming habitual. VC members reported to the school authority, but nothing happen, and almost parallel situation like this can be found in other parts of Mizoram. This may be the reason why 80.58 per cent of the respondents selected from VCP and VC Secretary suggested transfer of Primary School to village council.

(g) Centrally Sponsored Schemes and VEC

We have grants from Thirteenth Finance Commission and Mahatma Gandhi National Rural Employment Generation Scheme

(MGNREGS).TFC grant is assigned to the village council category-wise based on the size of the village council. It is provided directly to the village council for pre-selected items of developmental work. It is supervised and monitored almost entirely by the village council members according to visited the sites of the work in many villages and the work engaged and completed are satisfactory. The MGNREGS is replacing many other centrally sponsored schemes in villages in Mizoram. The scheme is operated by DRDA through BDO office. The style of functioning of the scheme is that the wage component(100 days employment) encompass 60 per cent of the entire MGNREGS budget. This is properly managed and people are happy. The remaining 40 per cent is reserved for the material component which is supposed to work out 50-50 between village council and line department. The fact of the matter is that there are village councils which have been receiving nothing at all from material component in the past two years.. Others receive but less than 50 per cent, to the extent of 20-40 per cent. When the work is performed by Technical Assistant from BDO office or party workers, VC has no control over monitoring of the work, and the quality of the work is relatively substandard and inferior compared to the work performed by the VC. I personally visited work sites and see empirical evidence to this.

Village Employment Council has been constituted vide Notification No. B.110118/23/2005-RD(NREGP) dated 28 April, 2009 creating the Mizoram Rural Employment Guarantee Scheme, 2009, Section 7A of which contain Village Employment Council which is amended vide Notification No. F23012/7/09-RD (NREGS) dated 20.8.2010. The Government of Mizoram again issued official letter No. F.13013/1/12-RD(NREGS) dated 5th November, 2012 on the subject 'Establishment/Introduction of VEC under MGNREGS' to all District Programme Coordinators (MGNREGS) stating that, *'in accordance with the Mizoram Rural Employment Guarantee Scheme, 2009, the Village Employment Council (VEC) has been invested with the responsibility of the Gram Panchayat and that all references to the Gram Panchayat in the MGNREGS Act/ operational Guidelines shall imply the Village Employment Council, as duly constituted by the State'*. Henceforward, the VEC has been taking over matters relating to MGNREGS and VC has been, to a certain extent, side-lined and marginalised in the situation. This has created a lot of displeasure and restlessness among VC members throughout Mizoram. The discontentment was reflected in the decision taken by Serchhip Town Joint village council on May 20, 2013 where they have expressed the view that VEC is the source of discord and tension in the localities, and therefore, decided to do away with it.

This only echoes and exposes the ground reality of village councils in Mizoram.

Village Council Acts, 1953 created in 1953 and practically effective from 1954 has undergone modest amendments and adjustments, but the structure of the original Acts has not been altered. In many areas we have already duplicated and reproduced provisions contained in Panchayati Raj system provided in the 73rd constitutional amendment such as Gram Sabha and social audit. The present system of village council is outmoded to cater to the needs of the rising people's aspirations.The information collected through questionnaire from 102 village council Presidents and VC Secretaries from the eight districts of Mizoram reveals the following:

Table 4.5: Functional Items Suggested to be Transferred to Village Council

Items	*Response*
Perception of present status in terms of powers and authority	Good : 11 respondents
	Depraved: 91 respondents
Subjects and functional items suggested to be transferred to Village Councils.	*Drinking water*:90 respondents *Road/Culvertetc.* : 86 respondents *Public Health & Sanitation* : 86 responde *Rural Housing* : 79 responder *Primary Education*:79 respondents *Agriculture* : 78 responden *Minor irrigation*: 77 responden *Social Welfare* : 68 responde *Family Welfare*: 67 responder *Markets & Fairs*:61 responden *Rural Electrification*:61 respondents
Record keeping of VC Accounts & Files	Good: 11 respondents
	Need upgrading: 91 responde

Source: Field Questionnaire.

Perception of 150 village council Members from the 31 village councils(including those in the Autonomous District Council Areas i.e., Mara ADC, Lai ADC and Chakma ADC) selected for field studypertaining to roadmap for change has been delineated. Due to practical and physical difficulties in visiting the area, villages in the Chakma ADC area has not been included. But the 31 village councils visited should be considered representative of the entire Mizoram. Villages have been selected from the eastern-most district of Champhai, western-most district of Mamit, southern-most district of Saiha, northern-most villages (Sakawrdai, Zohmun, Vaitin) of Hmar People's Convention (HPC) dominated area of Aizawl district. This may be compared with the perception of the people of Mizoram appeared in Table 4.7. Survey questionnaire has been conducted among the selected people of Mizoram consisting of 2,400 male respondents and 1,060 female respondents taken from all the eight districts of Mizoram. The picture that emerges from the insight and observation of the VC members and the the people of Mizoram can be compared and contrasted.

Table 4.6: Perceptions of Elected Village Council Members

Questions	*Response*
Have the VC ever been consulted in matters of rural Development?	Yes : 30 respondents
	No : 120 respondents
How do you perceive the functional authority vested in VC in rural development Programmes/schemes?	Adequate: 14 respondents
	Inadequate: 136 respondents
Who has the final authority in the selection of NLUP beneficiaries?	VLIC (VC): 61 respondents
	Pol. Party : 89 respondents
Would you favour introduction of 73rd Amendment(Panchayati Raj System)?	Yes: 139 respondents
	No : 11 respondents
How would you like transfer of 29 subject enumerated in Eleventh Schedule to Village Council	Yes : 142 respondents
	No : 8 respondents
Would you like reservation of seats for women?	Yes : 40 respondents
	No : 110 respondents

Source: Field Questionnaire.

As for the introduction of Panchayati Raj system as provided in the 73rd constitutional amendment Act, 1992, those who say 'yes' from among the VC members is very high (139 out of 150 respondents or 92.66 per cent) while the response from the people indicates appositive 'yes' is somewhat high, but not very high (1,479 out of 2460 respondents or 60.1 per cent). The aspiration of the VC members to have a genuine, powerful local government is unambiguous and unmistakable. However, the perception of the people as to the introduction of Panchayati Raj system is not as overwhelming as that of the VC members, but 60.1 per cent is very conspicuous and eye-catching and cannot be ignored. However, the contrasting picture can be observed on the issue of reservation of seats for women. The people of Mizoram is now ready for constitutional mandate of seat reservation for women (1,502 out of 2,460 respondents or 61 per cent) while the response from the VC members for the same issue very depressing at 26.66 per cent only. This is in contradiction to the high per centage in favour of introduction of Panchayati Raj Institution as provided in the Constitution. VC members and the people of Mizoram have one voice in supporting more powerful village council as implied from their overall responses.

Table 4.7: Opinions of the People of Mizoram on Certain Selected Items (2,460 Respondents)

Sl. No.	*Subject items*	*Male respondents (1400)*		*Female R (1060)*
01	**Opinion on the performance of VC/LC on the following subjects/functions**	**Good/ Yes**	**Not good/ No**	**Good/Ye**
(1)	Sanitation and health	817 (58.3)	583 (41.7)	659 (62.1)
(2)	Control of animals	756 (54)	644 (46)	506 (47.7)
(3)	Control of fire within the village 'RAM'	948 (67.7)	452 (32.3)	784 (73.9)
(4)	Allotment of jhum land	1,022 (73)	378 (27)	752 (70.9)
(5)	Preservation and upholding of forests	938 (67)	462 (33)	864 (81.5)
(6)	Community Work	1,120 (80)	280 (20)	882 (83.2)

Sl. No.	*Subject items*	*Male respondents (1400)*		*Female F (1060)*
02	**Conferring more powers to VC/LC**	924 (66)	476 (34)	686 (64.7)
03	**Adoption of Panchayati Raj system**	794 (56.7)	606 (43.3)	685 (64.6)
04	**Reservation of seats fpr women**	770 (55)	630 (45)	732 (69)
05	**Transfer of the following subjects/functions to VC/LC**			
(1)	Primary School	641 (45.7)	759 (53.3)	637 (60)
(2)	ME School	618 (44.1)	782 (53.9)	505 (47.6)
(3)	Primary Health Centres	737 (52.6)	663 (47.4)	629 (59.3)
(4)	Public Libraries	785 (56)	615 (44)	534 50.3)
(5)	Anganwadi Centres	845 (60.3)	555 39.7)	542 (51.1)

Source: Field Survey Questionnaire.

Aizawl Municipal Council

As per theprovisions of 74th constitutional amendment Act, 1992, Mizoram Municipalities Act, 2007 was passed by Mizoram State Assembly on 16 April, 2007 and appeared in Mizoram Gazette on 24 April, 2007. Accordingly Aizawl Municipal Council was established on the First of July, 2008. The Government of Mizoram set up a Committee to review and look into the details of the Act, and came out with the Mizoram Municipalities (Amendment), 2009, and on 29 October, 2009 the Mizoram Assembly passed the Amendment with reservation of one-thirds of the total seats for women. Accordingly, the first ever election to the Aizawl Municipal Council was held on 11 November, 2010 with 19 elected councilors including six women. For better local level administration, revocation of village councils within the Aizawl urban areas have been replaced by local councils as per the provision of The Mizoram Municipalities (Ward Committee and Local Council) Rules, 2010 which appeared in Mizoram Gazette 4 November, 2010. There are 82 local councils in the last elections to the local council in 2012.

The Mizoram Municipalities Act, 2007 (as amended in 2009) classified municipalities into three categories, namely—a Municipal Board for a specified transitional area, a Municipal Council for a smalle urban area, and a Muncipal Corporation for a larger urban area. The number of wards in any municipal area may be decided by the state govarment having regard to population, dwelling pattern, geographical condition and economic considerations of the area, and the number of wards in any municipal area shall be:

(a) in the case of a Municipal Board, not less than five but not more than nine;

(b) in the case of a Municipal Council, not less than elevemn but not more than twenty three; and

(c) in the case of Municipal Corporation, not less than fifteen but not more than thirty-one.

As already stated, The Mizoram Municipalities (Ward Committee and Local Council) Rules, 2010, makes provision for local council in a cursory and superficial way replacing the previous village councils. Aizawl Municipal Council has nineteen Wards and 82 local councils. They are yet to take functional role. Many Wards are yet to conduct their formal meetings, and under the current tentative and indecisive situation of municipal functioning, the position of the local councils is vague, unspecified, uncertain and wavering.

There are 18 functional subjects to be transferred to Municipal Council as provided in the Constitution of India Article 243W which are:

(1) Urban Planning including town planning.

(2) Regulation of land use and construction of buildings.

(3) Planning for economic and social development.

(4) Roads and bridges.

(5) Water supply for domestic, industrial and commercial purposes.

(6) Public health, sanitation conservancy and solid waste management.

(7) Fire Services.

(8) Urban forestry, protection of the environment and promotion of ecological aspects.

(9) Safeguarding the interests of weaker sections of society, including the handicapped and mentally retarded.

(10) Slum improvement and upgradation.

(11) Urban Poverty Alleviation.

(12) Provision of urban amenities and facilities such as parks, gardens, playgrounds.

(13) Promotion of cultural, educational, and aesthetic aspects.

(14) Burials and burial grounds; cremations, cremation grounds and electric crematoriums.

(15) Cattle ponds, prevention of cruelty to animals.

(16) Vital statistics including registration of births and dates.

(17) Public amenities including street lighting, parking lots, bus stops and public conveniences.

(18) Regulation of slaughter houses and tanneries.

The Government of Mizoram has successfully devolves and transfers only four such functional items such as—(1) solid waste management; (2) Cemetery and burial ground; (3) Parking Lots; and (4) Street Lighting and High Mast. The Aizawl Municipal Council has also been entrusted with collection of land revenue and house taxes. The revenue proceeds, however, go to the Land Revenue and Settlement Department, and not retained yet by AMC. The assistants in the accounts department of AMC reiterated that had the land and house revenue collected by them been retained, the financial position of the AMC would have been very much improved.

To see the functional level of local councils, activities in which they are empirically involved or uninvolved, few local councils have been visited as follows:

Table 4.8: Some Functions of Local Councils

Local Council	*Street Light*	*Water Supply*	*Sanitation*	*Education*	*NLUP*
Tanhril	Previous year AMC provided them with six boxes of street light and Rs.2,000 for fitting charges. This is simply not enough. The LC plays supervisory no role but no final authority	Drinking water supply is inadequate and it is within LC purview. But without financial power the final decision is with the PHE	Solid waste disposal is the responsibility of the LC where 90% of transport charge is borne by AMC, and 10% is collected from the people.LC also supervise public toilet and latrine, but its role is suggestive and no decision making role	VEC is formed with LC chairman as President of the VEC. But apart from signature for drawing fund, VEC do not play ant significant role	Local Level Implementing Committee is formed and prepared beneficiary list, but actual selection is done by ruling party unit

Local Council	*Street Light*	*Water Supply*	*Sanitation*	*Education*	*NLUP*
Hunthara	The Local Council is very much concerned with this function. But final decision is the AMC and line departments.	Drinking water supply is inadequate. But without financial power, LC do not have control on any work	Solid waste disposal is the same as in Tanhril. But when local collection is more than the required 10% then it become the source of LC fund	VEC is formed, but it has not played any significant role till now	Local Level Implementing Committee is formed, but ruling party unit is controlling the final selection procedure
Armed Vang	They know their responsibility, but were unable to do effective work due to lack of fund. What AMC supply was simply not enough	Drinking water supply is not adequate. PHE do not seem to trust present set-up and do not entrust any function	For solid waste disposal, AMC sanction normal charges. They collect Rs.20 from every household for local burden	Local Council do not play any functional role on education	LC plays no signioficant role They feel their position is pathetic and they occupy, they feel, a status lower than NGOs-YMA,MHIP,MUP
College Veng	They have to purchase, repair and install new street lights from the public contribution. What they receive from the AMC is not enough.	They have no serious water problem	For solid waste disposal one trip to the dumping ground at Tuirial costs Rs.1,800 of which 90% is borne by AMC. They collect Rs.20 from each household for 10% local share. They can make small balance to enable them to distribute polythene	Local Council do not play any significant role in the functioning of educational institutions.	Selection of beneficiartiesd is done by ruling party and not by the Local Level Implementing Committee

Local Council	*Street Light*	*Water Supply*	*Sanitation*	*Education*	*NLUP*
Tlangruam	They receive as in other cases 6 sets of street lights, but they have about 100 points. This the responsibility, the feel, they cannot fulfill at present. Without financial power	They have taken steps to improve water supply to be implemented by PHE. As there is no fund with them, they cannot really take initiative other than this	They have Sanitation & Disaster Committees. But these are non-functional. As for solid waste disposal AMC insists on local contribution as in other cases.	VEC is formed, but so far has no real involvement in the functioning of educational institutions in the area	Local Level Implementing Committee has been formed But selection of beneficiaries has been done ruling party unit
Selesih	They also received 6 sets of street Light which is not enough	Local Council here is unable to play significant important role. They would rather wish, if possible, to remain a village council so that they can enjoy the benefits of MGNREGS as well as TFC grants	There are only 130 households. It is therefore difficult for them to raise the local percentage share of solid waste disposal.	Do not any significant role in education. There are officers and employees of the Veterinary University, who are staying in the locality. But they do not take interest in local affairs nor do they participate in local affairs. hey are simply indifference toward local affairs making it difficult for LC to have impact on any local affairs	Local Council is simply not involved in the selection of beneficiaries

Source: Field Notes.

We can see that the condition of local council is well below normal standard, worst than the position of village council. Members of local councils expressed their feelings that unless there is some kind of improvement and positive çhange undertakenwe may not have anyone to contest the next elections to local councils.

Table 4.9: Opinions of people within Aizawl Municipal Council Area on selected items

Sl. No	*Subject Items*	*Mipa respondents (500)*		*Hmeichhe responc (500)*	
		Tha	*Tha lo*	*Tha*	*Tha*
01	**Assessment of the performance of VC/LC in the following subject**				
(1)	Sanitation and Health	227(45.4)	273(54.6)	225(45.0)	275(
(2)	Control of animals	238(47.6)	262(52.4)	201(40.2)	299(
(3)	Control of fire within the village 'RAM'	379(75.8)	121(24.2)	433(86.6)	67(1
(4)	Allotment of jhum land	353(70.6)	147(29.4)	367(73.4)	133(
(5)	Preservation of forests	317(63.4)	183(36.6)	339(67.8)	161(
(6)	Community Work	380(76.0)	120(24.0)	419(83.8)	81(1
02	**Devolve more powers to VC/LC**	368(73.6)	132(26.4)	414(82.8)	86(1
03	**Adoption of Panchayati Raj system**	273(54.6)	227(45.4)	343(68.6)	157(
04	**Reservation of seats for women**	259(51.8)	241(48.2)	309(61.8)	191(
05	**Transfer of the following subjects to VC/LC**				
(1)	Primary Education	370(74.0)	230(26.0)	272(54.4)	228(

Source: Field Survey Questionnaire.

It is to be noted that the perception of people in the Municipal area in regard to introduction of Panchayati Raj system (which is 61.6 per cent) and reservation of seats for women (which is 56.8 per cent) and the people at large throughout Mizoram is almost parallel.

Activity Mapping

Activity Mapping must be delineated clearly spelling out activities with respect to each devolved functions which are to be attributed to each level of local bodies so that there is no ambiguity at any level *vis-a-vis* the functions entrusted to them. Activity mapping is to spark off devolution of not only functions, but finances and functionaries. Sikkim's activity mapping includes detailed assignment of funds to local bodies as well as clear-cut details of the officials who will be attached to each local government for performance of devolved functional activities. Based on Activity Map and in conformity with the pattern of devolution of functions, state government will need to accurately identify budgetary items that will go to the village councils and other local bodies. Such funds should be earmarked through a Village Council/Aizawl Municipal Council/District Council sector in the budgets of the State to ensure smooth flow of funds for undertaking devolved activities. Activity Mapping discussed and projected here will focused particularly on devolution of functions to village councils.

Strengthening democratic functioning of the village councils in both the District Council areas and non-council areas is crucial. We also need to have agenda for improving core civic services by the local bodies which may include drinking water supply and sanitation, public health, universal literacy and elementary education, sports and culture, road connectivity, transport, drainage, housing, marketing and other facilities. Augmentation of local bodies' finance and improving financial management is also vital, including budgetary control and improvement of accounting practices and computerisation of accounts. This will entails functionaries of the local bodies and building their capacities- both functionaries and elected representatives. Activity Mapping must propose roles and responsibilities of the local bodies to reach the goals and the steps government should take for effecting the changes. It charts the future path of decentralisation agenda for local government in Mizoram.

Improving accountability is essential for better functioning of the local bodies. This is attempted by calling all the voters to attend Gram Sabha every six months for receiving suggestions of the people. Social audit of all important programmes is to be made a regular activity.

Clarity on the role and responsibilities of different local bodies is to be provided which will become an important steps in devolution of functions. It may also be noted that Activity Mapping does not necessarily imply that the subjects are devolved wholesale. Activity Mapping would take into consideration where competence, authority and accountability lie. The most extraordinary example is Kerala's decentralisation process which abandoned gradualism and took to a big bang approach. Devolution of functions, funds and functionaries in a single step is the best way to carry decentralised democracy forward. The Union Ministry of Panchayati Raj at that time in 2008 appreciated this and has announced its readiness to support a big bang devolution in other states by making available additional funds for building capacity and formal training. Kerala was in fact considered to be the only state that has initiated measures towards decentralised planning. In Karnataka and Kerala, Activity Mapping for all 29 functions had been done and all activities devolved to PRIs, but in Uttar Pradesh, only 16 subjects related to 12 departments had been devolved, and Gujarat devolved 14 functions are completely devolved and five are partially devolved. In Karnataka, each Gram Panchayat receives Rs 25 lakh a year for development work.

Autonomous District Council

The philosophy of the Sixth Schedule of the Constitution is aimed at protection of tribal areas and interests by constitutionally mandating district council. This institution is entrusted with the twin tasks of protecting tribal culture and customs and undertake development tasks for them. On paper, the impression may be that such councils are well equipped with a wide degree of autonomy. But the actual ground situation varies from state to state. As such, there is significant degree of variation in the functions devolved to Autonomous District Council.

In Mizoram, the three Autonomous District Councils have been entrusted with numerous subjects as already highlighted. The Revised Note on Decentralised Governance in North-eastern States by the Ministry of Panchayati Raj, 19 March, 2010 recommended enlargement of the legislative powers of the three District Councils of Mizoram to bring at par with Councils in North Cachar and Karbi Anglong as per Para 3A provision of the Sixth Schedule.

Under Para 6(1) of the Sixth Schedule, District Councils have powers to establish, construct and manage primary schools, dispensaries, markets, cattle ponds, ferries, fisheries, roads, road transport and water ways. The councils also have the power to assess, levy and collect revenue in respect of land and buildings, taxes on professions, trades callings and employments, animals, vehicles and boats, toll on passengers and goods carried in ferries, and taxes on the maintenance of schools, dispensaries, or roads as listed in paragraph 8 of the Sixth Schedule.

The Executive functions have already been given in details as per the Notification orders, particularly of dated 22 September, 1993 and 29 August, 2011 containing 21 functional subjects and activity mapping for each subject. The Finance Commission may see that these functional activity mapping may be strictly adhered to as far as the Autonomous District Councils are concerned. The Functional subjects and functional activities are listed below:

Table 4.10: Functional Subjects and Activities for Devolution to Autonomous District Councils

Sl. No.	*Subject (Department)*	*A*
1	Agriculture and Horticulture	(a) Agriculture Li (b) Distribution c certified seec (c) Procurement per cent subs (d) Procurement agriculture in distribute at s (e) Procurement water pumpir subsidised ra (f) Procurement manure and rate

contd...

Sl.No.	*Subject (Department)*	*Activities*
2	**Fisheries**	Grant-in-aid to indivi pond development a development of pisc
3	**Public Health Engineering**	(a) Sewerage and S Sanitation (b) Cons and urinals under F (c) Spring water s storage of water
4	**Industries Department**	(a)Development of I (b)Procurement of t distribution to artis Promotional assistai
5	**Sericulture**	(a) Grant-in-aid to pı Promotional Schem(Assistance for mark(
6	**Anumal Husbandry and Veterinary Department**	(a) Maintenance of ' by the MADC, an(respectively; (b) I Poultry, Piggery aı duly approved Rules
7	**Arts and Culture**	Grants-in-aid for pro under duly approve condition that the entitled to the State-
8	**Social Welfare**	(a) Old age pensior beneficiaries and dı of Pension; (b) A

Sl.No	*Subject (Department)*	*Activities*
12	**Transport**	Collection of Road Tax Tax for the vehicles Autonomous District C amendment of the releva
13	**Sports and Youth Services**	All schemes for promoti Services.
14	**Co-operation**	(a) Cooperation Departm Autonomous District Co the provisions of Si Constitution (b)Registrati Dissolution of Cooperati Council area in accordar Mizoram Cooperative S Financial Assistance to subject to the condition tl not be entitled to any su the state government unc
15	**Public Works Department**	(a) Construction and ma roads to link up with PWI (b) Maintenance and ir satellite towns and Villag
16	**Education**	(a) Primary School: It is c 95 budget provision will b Council budget and Educ longer include the same i education will be handed

Source: Field Information.

Operationalisation and actual devolution of the entrusted subjects and activities may be recommended. The administrative machinery is broadly of two wing–a Council Secretariat wing, very similar to State legislative wing, and an Executive wing. The Council Secretariat wing is headed by the Chairman of the Council, assisted by Secretary and other officials and staff. The executive functions are vested in the Executive Committee headed by Chief Executive Member (CEM). Each member of the Executive Committee is entrusted subject matters by the CEM. Executive Committee is assisted by the Executive Secretary, Deputy Secretary, Under Secretaries and other officials and staff with prior approval of the Governor. All the Three Councils have official employees the number of which is not less than 2,000, which may be considered *over-staff*. When the Expert Committee for the Planning for the Sixth Schedule Areas and those areas not covered by Parts IX and IX-A of the Constitution visited Mizoram in 2007, the then Chief Secretary stated that posts were often filled up by the Councils without state government sanctions and matching fund allocations. *Downsising* to the appropriate level may be recommended.

At the same time parallel administrative hierarchical functioning in the ADC areas– one headed by the Council and the other coordinated by the Deputy Commissioner (DC), who operate through separate agencies such as DRDA and state level line departments. Thus, state government continues to undertake works in respect of the same devolved functions without seeking advice from the Councils. All the centrally sponsored schemes have been operationalised by DRDA through Block Development Officers (BDO). This may be stopped and entrusted for implementation to District Councils. The instructions contained in the Notification of the Government of Mizoram, dated 29 August, 2011 which states, "*Administrative departments shall oversee and ensure that these entrusted functions are not again undertaken by their offices in the Autonomous District Council areas and only some skeleton staff are retained there...*". This has not been effectively implemented till now. The Government must ensure that it is implemented. Village councils in the ADC areas also need to be strengthend, and a new legislative guideline may be provided.

Village Councils in non-ADC Areas

Perceptions of 150 village council leaders (Table 2.3) confirms that 92.66 per cent would like to go for Panchayati Raj System of local government provided in the 73rd constitutional amendment, and 94.66 per cent would like to see more subjects (29 subjects in the Eleventh Schedule) devolved to village councils. In Mizoram, the gram sabha provided in Article 243A and stipulating to exercise such powers and perform such functions at the village level as the legislature of a State may, by law, provide, is already viable and active in every village. This entails democracy at the grassroots facilitating participation in planning and implementation of development programme and ensuring accountability of elected village council members. But the Gram Sabha has been introduced in relation to centrally sponsored schemes of MGNREGS. In panchayat system, Article 243G of the constitution stipulates the state legislative to endow the panchayats, by law, such powers and authority as may be required to enable them to function as institutions of self-government. Such laws may also provide for the devolution of powers and responsibilities upon panchayats for the preparation and implementation of plans for economic development and social justice, and may be entrusted to them, including those in relation to the 29 matters listed in the Eleventh Schedule.

Thus, therefore, in consonant with the above, the legislature of the state may come out with provision in accordance with 73rd constitutional amendment or else may, by law, endow the village councils with such powers and authority as may be necessary to enable them to function as institutions of self-government and such law may contain provisions for the devolution of powers and responsibilities upon village councils at the appropriate level, subject to such condition as may be specified there in, with respect to:

(a) The preparation of plans for economic development and social justice,

(b) The implementation of schemes for economic development and social justice as may be entrusted to them including those in relation to the subjects listed in Table 4.1 or more.

Devolution, in the context of village councils, would mean which authority in respect of specific activity is transferred from the state to the local governments, the latter should have the prerogative of making decisions in respect of planning and implementation of such activity.

- For effective implementation of their decisions, village councils need staff support and resources along with transfer of functions

- In fact, functions, funds and functionaries are complementary to one another in the process of devolution of responsibilities, power upon village councils.

Activity Mapping involves the following:

- Identification of activities related to devolved functions.
- Attribution of appropriate activity to a village council level, based on the principle that each activity must be undertaken at the lowest level that it can be undertaken.
- Activity Mapping is to activate fiscal decentralisation.

Now, therefore, in order to enable the village councils in Mizoram to function as democratic institution of self-government, the following subjects and functional activities may be devolved based on the findings of field-work questionnaire information from 102 local leaders, which is presented below:

Table 4.11: Activity Mapping of Subjects for Proposed Devolution Suggested by VC Members

Subjects	*Percentage of respondents*	*Proposed Fun Devolution*
Drinking water supply	91.80%	(a) Developme system includir (b) Monitoring I Schemes; (c) Maintenanc system.
Roads, Culverts, Bridges, etc.	87.72%	(a) Developme and accessibili (b) Improveme existing roads/
Public Health and Sanitation	87.72%	(a) Healthcare Workers. (b) Sewerage a
Primary Education	80.58%	(a) Expansion (b) Identifying a whenever neec (c) Monitoring t
Rural Housing	80.58%	(a) Approval of (b) Supervision
Agriculture	78.54%	(a) Increasing a (b) Agriculture (c) Credit Supp (d) Extension S (e) Soil Testing (f) Post Harves

contd...

Subjects	*Percentage of respondents*	*Proposed Fun Devolution*
Family Welfare	66.30%	Maternal and C
Markets and Fairs	62.22%	Identification of Development c
Rural Electrification	62.22%	(a) Expansion ((b) Monitoring (
Public Distribution System	51%	(a) Availability (Commodities a Assessment; (b) Transport, S System; (c) Linking PDS Programme su
Animal Husbandry, Dairying and Poultry	51%	(a) Developme (b) Veterinary S (c) Feeding an((d) Dairy Devel (e) Poultry Dev
Fisheries	51%	(a) Developing (b) Developme Marketing/proc Infrastructure.

Source: Based on Field Information.

After delineating subjects and functions within the subjects proposed to devolve, the activities to be devolved at the Block Development Council level and village council levelmay kindly be seen from Table 4.6. These constitute tentative activities proposed to be devolved at the Block and village level. Since rural development through Local Bodies will be the new largest Public Intervention Programme of the State in terms of reach, size of financial involvement and the number of public functionaries associated with its implementation, strengthening of the policy makers and programme implementors is necessary. Therefore, capacity building initiatives will have to be vigorously undertaken by both Rural Development Department, which will have to be bolstered, and the Local Administration Department. State Institute of Rural Development (SIRD) has to be extended to provide Extension Training Centre in some important places to undertake massive capacity building of members of elected Local Bodies and officials.

In order to make the Block Administration more responsible and stronger, the post of BDO as Executive Officer, may be upgraded and Assistant BDO posted. And in order to strengthen village council Administration and more accountable and responsive, an Executive Officer of the rank of Assistant Grade may be posted to look after bigger village councils of 301 housholds or more, and a cluster of two or more village councils in other cases. The VLAs/VLWs shall be posted in smaller villages.

Table 4.12: Item-wise Functional Activities Proposed for Devolution

Subjects	*Distribution of Func*	
	Block Development Council	
Drinking Water Supply	**Development of Water**	
	(a)Identifying and prioritizing of villages for drinking water scheme; (b)Formulating projects and seeking technical approval; (c)Collection of water sample and tested; (d)Construction of schemes within the prescribed cost limits for Village Councils.	(a) Ide locatic formu Gram (b) Cc and vi schen (c) Pe open and ei distrib house
	Monitoring Rural Water Supply Schem	
	(a)Monitoring and supervision of progress and quality of works	(a) Re monit of sch
	Maintenance of Water Supply System	
	(a)Maintenance of schemes, collection of water charges through VCs.	(a) Ma water impler
Roads, Culverts and Bridges	**Development of Road Network and Ac**	
	(a) Survey of technical feasibility, sanction of funds for	(a) As constr

Subjects	*Distribution of Functions*	
Roads, Culverts and Bridges	**Improvement and Maintenance o Roads/Culverts/Bridges**	
	(a) Convert existing roads into black topped roads; (b)Undertake annual repairs and maintenance of roads, culverts and bridges; (c) Approve, allocate and sanction funds for improvement and maintenance of roads (d) Monitor and supervise quality of works; (e) Execute works for providing rural link roads.	(a) A impr annu roads (b)Ra gove and c Sabh (c) E provi
Public Health and Sanitation	**Health Care and Qualified Health**	
	(a) Organise Health and family Welfare camps and conduct demonstration Programmes on Health, Family Welfare and Sanitation; (b) Coordinate communicable diseases Programmes with the State, (c) Supervise hospitals and	(a) M peop welfa (b) P progr (c) C Com quali poste

Subject	*Distribution of Functions*	
	Repair and maintenance of Existi	
Rural Housing	**Approval of Plan and Sanction**	
	(a) Execution of Housing Projects; (b) Procure and supply building materials; (c) Assist Village Council for execution of housing projects.	(a) Ide (b) As distrib house (c) Co Comm (d) Pr distrib materi
	Supervision and Monitoring	
	(a) Supervise in construction of Rural Housing Scheme.	(a) Su quality report
Agriculture	**Increasing Agriculture Productic**	
	(a) Help in crop yielding estimation through link with various agencies; (b) Coordinate activities of field level extension workers and officials; (c) Advise suitable,cropping system based on location specific characteristics.	(a) Es mainta (b) As crop p about activiti divers
	Agriculture Link Roads	
	(a) Assist in survey work; (b) Coordinate activities and assist in finance.	(a) Ide (b) As work;

Subject	*Distribution of Functions*	
Agriculture (cont.)	**Soil Testing**	
	(a) Monitoring Soil Testing work; (b)Help in identifying soil testing work; (c) Help farmers for improvement of soil fertility as per the soil testing results.	(a) Assist t conducting Help in ens soil testing
	Post-harvest Management	
	(a) Maintenance of godowns; (b) Regulate market charges and ensure correct weights and measures; (c) Ensure quick sale of produce and payment to farmers; (e) Help in minimizes dominance of private traders.	(a) Organis bulk; (b) Assist i about bette seeds and
Social Welfare	**Welfare of Disabled and Aged**	
	(a) Coordinating the Programme; (b) Identify the destitute and aged and help them in talking shelter in voluntary organisations receiving grant-in-aids from the Ministry of Welfare/ State Governments for old age pension etc.	(a) Ass the age coordir their m old age
	Drug Use Prevention	
	(a) Monitoring and Supervision.	(a) Imp help of
	Assistance to Voluntary Organisatio	
	(a) Assist in financial provision,	(a) Nee fund/in organi
	(a) Enforce fair trade practices and maintain quality of commodities; (b) Assist the maintenance of statistics on prices and commodities traded; (c) Maintain statistics on prices and commodities.	(a) Ass fair/tra of stati comm

Subject	*Distribution of Function*	
Family Welfare	**Maternal and Child Care/Health Cent**	
	(a) Create awareness about maternal and child care immunisation; (b) Coordinate and assist in monitoring and supervision of family welfare services; (c) Distribute materials, medicines and equipments to ICDS to promote school health programmes; (d) Assist beneficiaries, mothers and children; (e) Assist in Maternal and Child Health Centres; (f) Train ANMs and other workers.	(a) Ass materi Immun (b) Sup ANMs; (c) Invi Panch meetin follow- family
Markets and Fairs	**Identification of location and Develo Complex**	
	(a)Development and maintenance of places for	(a) Ow market

Subject	*Distribution of Functions*	
Rural Electrification	**Expansion of Electrification**	
	(a) Ensuring expansion of those villages not reached by rural electric supply.	(a) As progr
	Monitoring of Power Supply	
	(a) Monitoring Power Supply to rural areas within the Block.	
Public Distribution System	**Availability of Essential Commodit Assessment**	
	(a) Review if beneficiary list, distribution of cards and elimination of bogus cards.	(a) Ru distrib where (b) Id benef PDS (c) As of rati bogus elimin
	Transport, Storage and Delivery Sy	
	(a) Ensure improvement in Transport and storage of food grains & other food items.	(a) Er food g food i
	Linking PDS with Poverty Alleviati MGNREGS	

Subject	*Distribution of Functions*	
Fisheries (cont.)	**Development of Marketing/Proce**	
	(a) Organising training of Fishermen/ fish farmers in processing, packaging and preservation of fish products; (b) Developing tag-up arrangement between fishermen and the processing unit; (c) Assistance in establishing market infrastructure.	
Animal Husbandry, Dairying and Poultry	**Development of Livestock**	
	(a) Distribution of quality breed to beneficiaries; (b) Propagating improved breed of livestock among farmers.	(a) A: bene (b) M maint mode maint
	Veterinary Services	
	(a) Supervising the functioning of veterinary services in the Block; (b) Maintaining mobile veterinary units to provide veterinary care and control of diseases and epidemics.	(a) S functi Veter (b) R disea
	Feeding and Fodder	
	(a) Organise Cooperatives	(a) H

Source: Based on field data.

Activity Mapping should also specify the basic principle to devolve funds to match the functions. While devolving funds, the untied nature of funds, predictability, certainty, and zero discretion must be ensured. The local governments know well in advance how much resources they are going to get as reflected in the state government budget wherein each local government's share will be included. This cannot be changed through an executive decision and hence the certainty and zero discretion. The state will follow a formula based devolution which will prevent patronage and leads to fairness and equity. The funds thus devolved are pure ensuring quality of funds transferred. The followings may also guide financial devolution:

- Village Council, Urban Local Government and District Councils will have the powers to collect taxes.
- The entire plan grant will not include staff salaries or other administrative cost unless otherwise mentioned.
- About 90 per cent of the plan fund may be given in untied form to enable local government to prepare their own schemes and implement them with certain broad policy framework stipulating(as in the case of Kerala) that at least 40 per cent (10 per cent in urban areas) of the funds invested in productive sectors, not more than 30 per cent (50 per cent in urban areas) should be invested on roads.
- Fund transferred to local bodies are to be based on a transparent comprehensive formula which prevents any scope for patronage or partisanship in allocation of resources to local governments
- It will be the village councils which will be getting the major share of the grants with nearly 705 of the rural share going to them and Block Committee getting 30 per cent.

Sources of Funds of village councils and Urban Council can be of the following nature:

- ***Own Tax:*** Taxes which are statutorily assigned to the local bodies and levied by them; and income from building tax, professional tax, entertainment tax and advertisement tax.
- ***Assigned Taxes (Statutory Grants):*** Taxes which are

statutorily assigned to local bodies but collected by state government and made over to local governments; and income from Land revenue, Surcharge on Stamp Duty on transfer of immovable property etc.

- ***Shared Taxes*:** Taxes which are assigned to the state government and collected by them; but a share of the proceeds is disbursed among local governments; and Income from motor vehicles' Tax etc.
- ***Non-tax Revenue*:** Income from rents and other properties with local governments like markets, bus stands, shopping complex etc. license fees, fines, income from rivers by sale of sand etc.
- ***Grants*:** From state government for various specified purposes, either tied or untied; and Grants from Centre Government (TFC and Centrally Sponsored Schemes).
- ***Loans and Advances*:** From government and other financial institutions for specific purposes.

The work and the workers should go together should be the principle. The functionaries for specific tasks at various levels will have to be attached to the corresponding local governments to whom the functions have been transferred. This includes professionals, technical people, and ministerial staff of the transferred institutions. Salaries of the transferred staff are paid by the respective departments under the state government. Local governments may also keep its own office and staff, the salaries of which, as far as possible, are borne by local governments themselves. Issues of dual control may be solved by specifying that state departments have a say in matters of professional and technical nature and the local self-governments have their say base don the devolved functions and responsibilities.

Items in Table 2.7are subjects highly recommended by the leaders who are selected as respondents.. But there are other functions which are becoming almost indispensable now in the current circumstances such as Disaster Management, Relief and rehabilitation and Environmental Management. These two constitute the focal point of the Finance Commission's Term of

Reference (ToR), and should eventually be included in the Activity Mapping. The following chart (Table 4.7) shows the status of devolution of funds, functions and functionaries to the Panchayati Raj Institutions in major states in India. The overall weaknesses of the process of devolution identified in most States seem to be the following:

- Lack of Political will of political parties for decentralisation,
- Lack of public awareness and vigilance,
- Lack of orientation of officials for working with Local Governments,
- Elite capture in highly unequal and stratified societies,
- Bureaucracies have not learnt to work with the elected Local Government,
- Downward accountable mechanism not yet developed,
- Decision-making not yet broad-based,
- Rules and Procedures not adequately framed.

We believe that we can overcome the above hurdles in Mizoram once we establish Political Will and Public Awareness, and once we have adequate Rules and Procedures to follow.

Table 4.13: Status of Devolution of Departments/Subjects with Funds, Functions, and Functionaries

Sl.No	*State*	*Number and Names of Depar Transferred to Panchayats witl*	
		Funds	*Function*
1.	W. Bengal	GPs can impose and realize taxes .Untied funds are allocated under the TFC grant as well as SRC grant. 5 departments have opened Panchayat Window in their budgets	State Governn agrees w transfer subjects. departm have so issued m GOs trar 27 subje

Sl.No.	State	Number and Names of Departme Panchaya With respec	
		Funds	Functions
2	Tripura	Part funds related to PWD Department, Primary Schools and Social Welfare and Social Education department and pension funds have been transferred.Untied funds are also transferred	So far GOs h been issued devolving irrigation schemes, primary schc and adult anc non-formal educational activities,wor and child development social welfare
3.	Uttarakhand	All three tiers have the power to collect taxes	16 subjects relating to 12 departments have been devolved to F
4.	Sikkim	PRIs do not collect taxes. Funds are being transferred by 17 departments. 10 per cent of total fund of each department is given to Panchayats. Untied fund are given to PRIs.	All 29 subjec are devolved per legislatioi Activity Map has been conducted fo subjects covering 16 departments
5.	Orissa	PRIs collect six types of taxes. There is no clear devolution of untied funds	11 Departme have devolve 21 subjects

Sl.No	State	Number and names of Departm Panchay With respe	
		Funds	Functions
10.	Chhatisgarh	GP is authorised to collect various types of taxes .Funds for 12 departments have been devolved	Activity Maŗ of 27 matte been under GOs is not
11.	Gujarat	Eight major taxes are collected by PRUIs. In 2008-09 13 departments allocated funds to PRIs	14 function: been compl devolved aı are partially devolved
12.	Rajasthan	Five departments have issued GOs transferring funds to PRIs up to district level. 10 per cent untied fund to PRIs	Five depart have transf all functions district leve PRIs. Fresh activity mar of above fiv department been done
13.	Manipur	Five departments have issued GOs transferring funds to PRIs	GOs have t issued dev functions re to 22 department
14.	Assam	PRIs are	Activity Maŗ

Sl. No.	State	Number and Names of Departmer Panchaya With respec	
		Funds	Function
17.	Bihar	No taxes are collected by PRIs but a proposal regarding the same is under consideration of State Government.	Activity mapp has been conducted. 2(departments l issued GOs
18.	Jharkhand	Elections to PRIs were held in Noverr first time since 73rd CAA came into fc not been done so far.	
19.	Haryana	GPs generate revenue from lease of Panchayat and, liquor cess and rental of Panchayat premises	Panchayati R. devolves 29 functions. GO have been iss for 10 departr
20.	Arunachal Pradesh	PRIs do not collect taxes. Transfer of funds by departments has not taken place.	29 subjects h been devolve GOs covering departments l been issued, not yet implemented.
21.	Himachal Pradesh	Only GP is empowered to levy taxes. Funds have	27 out of 29 subjects have devolved to P

Sl.No.	*State*	*Number and Names of Departn Panchay With respe*	
		Funds	*Funct.*
25.	Maharashtra	ZP and GP collect taxes. Grant for 11 departments are transferred to PRIs	11 Subje have bee devolved 18 subjec schemes implemer PRIs
26.	Andaman & Nicobar Islands	Grant-in-aid is released to PRIs to discharge their functions	All the fui (29 subje have bee transferre the PTIs
27.	Daman & Diu	Not available	12 subjec fully devc and 10 si are partia devolved
28.	Puducherry	Panchasyats collect taxes and receive funds from the State Budget under the Community development sector	22 functic have bee devolved PRIs
29.	Lakshadweep	Entire Plan & Non-Plan budget required for Schemes and Programmes being	All schen and programr being

(**Note:** Mizoram, Meghalaya, and Nagaland are exempt; Delhi has no Panchayat Information is not available for UT of Dadra and Nagar Haveli).

4.2 Style of Functioning or Manner in which Functions are Discharged

The style of functioning of the three administrative units viz, Autonomous District Councils, village councils, and Aizawl Municipal Council is not identical. Legal provision is less marked in the case of village council and more apparent in the context of Autonomous District Council which is under the provisions of the Sixth Schedule to the Constitution, and Aizawl Municipal Council which is guided by The Mizoram Municipalities Act, 2007 and amended in 2009.

In the context of the three Autonomous District Councils, the provision of the Sixth Schedule and the legislative capacity of the Council is clearly directed. However, in spite of clear instructions for financial management from the state government, poor management of allocated budget fund is evident. Apart from this, the duplicate and dual performance of functions by state government officials and the ADC officials may have slacken the manner in which functions are discharged in the Councils. Parts IX and IXA of the constitution has not been extended to these areas, but extension of Part IX and additional powers and subjects included in Eleventh Schedule to the constitution shall be welcome.

Village Councils in the non-council areas, that is the entire Mizoram, has a total number of 493 village councils and total number of 2,055 elected council members. The number of village councils and elected members will automatically increase with the proposed elections to 15 village councils in HPC dominated areas during July, 2013.

The style of functioning of the village councils in the six districts of Aizawl, Lunglei, Champhai, Sserchhip, Mamit and Kolasib, continues to be based on village council Acts, 1953 and Administration of Justice Rules, 1953 with occasional circulars, notifications and Rules framed by the state government. But there is no clarity in the functions assigned or deemed to be entrusted to them. In Sumsuih village, VC Court resolved to bring harmony and settled the case peacefully by imposing a penalty of fine on one party. But the perpetrator refused to honor the fine. The village council Rules has empower the Court a fine for any offence which may extend to Rupees Five hundred. But the village council do not have the power to compel the person by force. The village council chooses VC Secretary from among the villagers who is supposed to keep records of the proceedings, accounts and other VC records including TFC grant and MGNREGS etc. I have visited 31 village councils, and not a single village council has a proper record of acceptable standard. Many village council do not have a village council House where the VC members can have VC proceedings without disturb, where they can safely keep all the records. But there are quite a few VCs with VC House of adequate dimension, but these have not been given the significance and magnitude it should have mainly due to ambiguous functional activities and lack of resources. The villagers expect so much from the VC members in terms of financial help, village security, educational activities, cultural functions, sanitation, water supply, and so on. The VC members expressed their inability to fulfill people's aspirations which is very frustrating.

The style of functioning of the Aizawl Municipal Council is yet to take shape and stabilise. Because of financial constraint and initial set back in the beginning, they were unable to start with a bang. AMC has 19 Ward Committees headed by a Councillor and 82 local councils. The Ward Committee is to be convened every three month in order to discharge, among other things, the assigned functions of local councils and allocated fund and monitor and oversee the performance of local councils. But of the six local councils visited belonging to different Ward Committees, three are yet to convene a meeting of the Ward Committee, and the other three had one meeting each of their respective Ward Committee in which no important transaction has been deliberated. Of the 18 subjects to be transferred to AMC, the Government of Mizoram has so far transferred four items—solid waste management, cemetery and burialground, Parking lots, street lighting and high mast. AMC is now almost ready to undertake some other functions. Land revenue and Zoram Tax have been entrusted to them by the Land Revenue and Settlement, but the revenue earnings have gone to the Revenue Department, and not retained by the AMC. This could be handed over to the AMC, and actual collection of taxes could be entrusted to the local councils with a share of certain per centage to them.

4.3 Role of Parastatals in the Functioning of Local Bodies

Role of parastatal organisations in the functioningof local bodies is of recent occurrence. It is a consequence of mandatory conditions imposed by International Financial Institutions. Parastatals are semi-government organisations, companies or agencies owned or controlled wholly or partly by government which have their own governing boards. The need for parastatal or other agencies stems from the requirement to provide the local bodies with expertise in different spheres, technical data and support to elected representatives to enable them to take proper and fitting policy decisions.

In Karnataka, most of the reforms to bring in good governance measures are mandatory conditions to loans provided by International Financial Institutions. According to the World Bank good governance needs good institutions, and the Bank has hard-pressed for the creation of parastatals. The real intent of creating multiple parastatals by the International Financial Institutions is to keep at bay "unwanted politicians' interference" which is in fact undermining the very basis of democracy. In this way, outsourcing of governance functions happens in a variety of ways. Functions such as planning, a task used to be done by State Planning Board, has been done by Price-Waterhouse-Coopers, in Karnataka. There has been an increase in the number of parastatals along with an increase in outsourcing of government activities to the private sector. Even in the implementation of Jawharlal Nehru National Urban Renewal Mission(JNNURM), the role of the Urban Local Bodies in planning for their cities is minimal. A National Steering Group, a Technical Advisory Group(TAG), appraisal agencies such as the National Institute of Urban Affairs (NIUA), and independent consultants are appraising city plans.

In this way, elected representatives or councils have no role in these. The provisions of 74th amendment such as District Planning Committee or Metropolitan Planning Committee comprising elected representatives, which is to consolidate grassroots plan, have not been set up or are dysfunctional. It may be pointed out here that parastatals are not subject to government laws and that their accounts are audited only by private chartered accountants. Hence, the current slogan coined by activists is, *"Shut down parastatals, empower local governments"*.

Parastatals are created at the state level by people elected to high offices such as chief minister. But one need to ask whether parastatals have been set up to deliberately by-pass democratic and statutory institutions. Given the fact that democratic and statutory institutions have degenerated their functions. Policies and projects have not been discussed and debated by the municipal councils and legislators. There seem to be overall decline in the way elected institutions are functioning. It can be considered that Parastatals and IFIs are taking up contracts with the state government filling the vacuum and occupying the space vacated by the renunciation of responsibilities by the democratically elected representatives.

At the state level, outsourcing of functions to parastatal organisations of different kind have been a phenomenon which is becoming a recurrent episode now. A critical debate and deliberation both by the elected representatives and the public should be contemplated. At the council levels (Autonomous District Council, village councils, Aizawl Municipal Councils, this is probably less frequent. In Mizoram, the task of the Finance Commission should rightfully be to strengthen and uplift the position and role of democratically elected representatives, particularly at the village levels. The role of parastatals should be minimised. However, semi-government parastatal organisation such as District Rural Development Agency (DRDA), District Water and Sanitation Committee (DWSC) and District Health Society (DHS) continue to function effectively in many States. In addition to DRDA, feasibility of introducing DWSC and DHS may be exploredin Mizoram to initiate the Accelerated Rural Water Supply Programme (centrally sponsored scheme) and National Rural Health Mission (NRHM).

5

Assessment of the Physical Services Provided by Local Bodies

5.1 Estimate of Service Deficits with a Brief Account of Reasons

For the Deficits

Decentralisation has been understood as mechanism to transfer responsibilities and authority from higher political and administrative entity to the lower level of political and administrative entities. The key characteristics of decentralisation essentially involve changes in pattern of authority and in the status of local level institutions. There are three main dimensions of decentralisation that reflect increasing stages of progress in achieving the objectives of decentralisation, which are: (a) Administrative decentralisation (functional responsibility); (b) Financial decentralisation (access to resources); (c) Political decentralisation (accountability). The process of decentralisation, thus, involves power shift (role, authority, and responsibility)in the direction of:

(a) Vertical shift from centre to state;

(b) From state to districts downwards to the units of local self-governments leading ultimately to people's participation in self-management;

(c) Ahorizontal power shift from the appointed executives to the elected representatives of people.

This has not been happening in Mizoram. Decentralisation is yet to take place in Mizoram. Mizoram is a special category state, and is a recipient of predominant grant based on central support for its plan. In spite of this, the debt situation and revenue deficits seems to continue. Private health clinics are growing in urban areas reflecting to a certain extent the declining faith in government institutions as providers of satisfactory healthcare. In the case of roads, the quality of service rendered is very unfortunate. Drinking water is simply not adequate, not to speak of the quality, in quantity. Electric supply is very erratic in the major parts of the rural areas. Both maintenance and quality of supply in these basic services cause for an increasing concern in rural areas. With the level of administrative, political and financial decentralisation pitiable and no proper record-keeping in the village councils in the country-side, it is almost impossible to obtain quantitative estimate of service deficits. This can only be obtained from government offices operating in the rural areas which may not reflect empirical reality.

The reason(s) for the service deficits can be attributed to the fact that the prime concern of political executives at the state level as well as appointed executives is to manage jobs and favourable postings for their constituents. This means a high measure of centralisation at the state government entailing little accountability. Functions of government are vested in the state government and not to local bodies, and employees even at the lower level, especially those to be attached to the rural areas, are recruited and managed at the state level. In the situation, better service provision is not clearly a primary concern for these executive providers.

Clients, faced with this delivery structure, do not always seek improvement from the policy-making level. But clients see politicians primarily as patrons for jobs, contracts, and not as policy-makers elected to ensure better delivery of services. Therefore, those who can afford are choosing to exit the system for public provision of services especially in education and health sectors resulting in the growth of private schools and healthcare clinics and institutions. In case of water and electricity, there is a tendency to purchase better provision at the individual level through money and influence. The system of public provision of basic services is, therefore, becoming increasingly only a space for the 'game of patronage' at the expense of the poor who do not have the means to exit the system or secure better services through extraneous influence.

The omnibus character of state intervention inherent in the development model adopted in post-independence meant large-scale growth in government employment in every possible sphere. Liberal central funds often dispensed as central patronage, opened up the possibilities of funds being used as a source of patronage at state level. The centralised delivery structures at state level were convenient vehicle for dispensing patronage in various forms as employment or subsidy or contract. Specific purpose transfer and centrally sponsored schemes usually favoured capital expenditure rather than sustainable delivery of services. They were usually prescriptive in nature emphasising staff and structure regardless of their utility in the local context. Overall, the principles guiding the central fund flow overwhelmingly favour expenditure as a criterion and bred lack of accountability for fiscal extravagance. For politicians,winning favours as a patron dispensing instant gratification in the shape of jobs or subsidy is clearly easier than reaching out with the indirect and uncertain appeal of better services. The absence of effective fiscal constraint on this ability to dispense patronage obviously aided this predilection. Over time, any focus on developing social and physical infrastructure has become largely a chance to snatch for the provision of employment in government.

Therefore, the crucial requirement for better delivery of services is essentially one of finding a way to curtail the "patronage based incentives" and enhance the accountability of the delivery mechanism to the client. A better fiscal framework which is federal in nature, that is able to bring greater responsibility at state level to overcome fiscal profligacy and wastefulness is desirable. Opening up space for private sector may create scope for greater accountability. Encouraging civil society action in some spheres may perhaps, be useful. But a role for the state will, of course, extend beyond regulation wherever the market is unlikely to step in and this would specially be true in ensuring access to the poor in the case of basic services.

If the public provision of such services is to exhibit desired improvement, an alternate delivery structure is evidently needed. What we need is one that opens up the possibility of escape from the existing clutch of patronage and allow clients seeking better services and a more direct form of control over the delivery mechanism. Thus, devolution of appropriate functions, ability to appoint or hire functionaries and access to requisite funds for local bodies could create the space for such client control to be exercised. It would also enable a situation where a regulation as a function can be independent of the provider with the state level undertaking the former role and the local bodies being responsible for actual delivery. Therefore, if community interest and capacity were to be mobilised to a sufficient degree, sustainable delivery of basic services could become a reality.

5.2 An Inventory of Assets and Value

Except the Autonomous District Councils which have been established more than 40 years back and with due recognition in the Sixth Schedule provisions of the Constitution of India, the Aizawl Municipal Council has been effectively functioning only for the last four years, and village councils are yet to function under proper legislative provisions. Under the circumstances, list of assets is very simple and asset limited in the case of village councils. Assets consist mainly of VC building constructed mainly out of TFC grant, or NREGS and other centrally sponsored schemes. As such, the purposes for which some of the VC buildings are used are diverse and multi-purpose as indicated in the following Table 5.1.

Table 5.1: Availability of Assets, Current Use and Valuation

VC/LC/ADC/AMC	*Assets and Use*
Chhiahtlang VC	Double storied VC house(concrete) for regular VC Sitting/Meeting etc.
Keitum VC	VC house(concrete) for VC Sitting, and Job Card activities.
Khawlailung VC	VC house(concrete) for Meetinç Quarry
New Serchhip VC	VC house (concrete) for Meetin
Muallungthu VC	VC house (concrete) for VC Sittings and other social purpos
Samlukhai VC	VC house(semi-pucca) for VC Meetings Sheds for shop to be rent out
Sumsuih VC	VC house(Assam type) which i rarely used
Chamring VC	VC(VNR) house+ Hall etc. This for multi-purpose use
Vaitin VC	VC house (NREGS)(concrete) used for VC meetings and Job Card distribution
Zohmun VC	VC house(NREGS) (concrete) f Meetings and Job Card distribution
Skawrdai VC	VC house (concrete) for VC

VC/LC/ADC/AMC	*Assets and Use*
Thingdawl VC	VC house (concrete) Multi-purpos use
Lungdai VC	VC house (semi-pucca) for VC Meetings
Lallen VC	VC house (concrete) for VC Meetings and Job Card Old VC house (Assam type) rente out
Damparengpui VC	VC house and Hall-use for VC Meetings and other social events
New Mamit VC	No VC House Joint VC house (Assam type) for Meetings
Rawpuichhip VC	Double storied VC house(concrete) Use for VC and YMA Meetings
W.Phaileng VC	Nil
New W.Phaileng VC	VC house(concrete) VC Meeting and other purposes
Ngur VC	VC house(Assam type) rented ou NREGS house(concrete) for VC Meetings
Zote VC	Small VC house; various uses
Chawntlangpui VC	VC house inaugurated in June,2013 (concrete)
Tbhingkah VC	VC house-use for multi-purpose and Sittings
Zero Point VC	Nil
Saihatlangkawn VC	Nil
Tanhril LC	Nil
Tlangnuam LC	Small building for Meetings
Hunthar LC	Slaughter house(local) rented ou

(**Source:** *Field Notes and Information from AMC and Mara ADC*).
(**Note:** Information not available from Lai ADC and Chakma ADC).

5.3. Basic Services; Availability, Coverage, Access and Quality

Development is not merely new investments and programmes but it is also a means to deliver quality public services to citizens.The directive principle of state policy enshrined in Part IV of Indian Constitution says, " the State shall, within the limits of its economic capacity and development make effective provision for securing the right to work, to education and to public assistance in case of an unemployment, old age, sickness and disablement, and in other cases of deserved want". This means that service delivery has been a major focus in making government policies. It is not merely achievement of physical economic target or per capita income, but also in terms of enhancement of human well being. This will include not only an adequate level of consumption of food and other types of consumer goods, but also access to basic social services especially healthcare,education, drinking water, and basic sanitation. It will also include expansion of economic and social opportunities, reduction in disparities, and greater participation in decision-making. There is a great degree of consensus on the need to improve the quality of services provided to public, particularly the poor. The quality of services is mainly constrained by managerial inefficiency in other places of India, but in Mizoram it is also by lack of resources. Services can be broadly classified into the following categories:

- Civic services like water supply and sanitation;
- Social services like health and nutrition care, family welfare and primary/school education;
- Infrastructure e.g. construction of roads and culverts and rural electrification;
- Welfare services like social security, pensions and distribution of essential commodities;
- Extension services for conveying development messages to the stakeholders;
- Governance-related services like issue of certificates and licenses, providing information etc.

Under the present system of arrangement, village councils have no practical role in many of the activities. The most important steps towards achieving better public service delivery would be to ensure grass roots participation Thus, public services in rural and remote areas may include Education and Health Services apart from provision of foodstuff and agriculture related products. Provision of civic amenities such as drinking water and streetlights, sanitation and community toilets may constitute immediate essential services. Many Programmes such as *Jhum Control, NLUP*, have been introduced in Mizoram in order to enhance agriculture boom and bring about sufficiency in foodstuff. But these are more a political schema rather than actual adept and proficient economic and social programme. These have brought occupational shift and transformation, but the actual achievement in real term is yet to be seen. Service deficits are rampant and unchecked and it almost become epidemic. The following may form some basic services. (Services that are provided by the Aizawl Municipal Council and the three Autonomous District Councils are not included)

Healthcare

All the bigger villages surveyed have at least Health sub-centre, smaller villages with less than 150 houses such as Chawntlangpui, do not have Health sub-Centre, but ASHA is being posted to look after the needs of the village, particularly in relation to maternity services. The Health sub-Centres may have two or three health workers, some of which are trained, and definitely not all of them. One of the health workers is supposed to be the Secretary of the Village Health and Sanitation Committee in which the village council President is the Chairman. Overall observation is that in the majority of the villages surveyed, the working relationship of the Health workers and the village council suggests many things to be desired. The Health workers are not subject to the village leadership, and are not, in actual reality, accountable to the villagers. Moreover, the facilities currently provided is unquestionably insufficient. Health Care is very basic to human development and need better provisions in rural Mizoram. In terms of availability, Coverage, access and quality, we certainly need lot of work and improvement to do. This may call for a totally new policy to be at par with the rest of the country and the world. Though primary healthcare is a subject that could be entrusted to local governments, in order to give a special trust to this sector, the Union Government has been directly running a large number of centrally funded programmes across the country. These are implemented through bodies functioning at the State as well as at the district level. The village councils in Mizoram play no practical role in this area, and no power to set right anomalies, discrepancies, irregularities or non-availability of services either at the Sub-centre or at Primary Health Centre. We need to address the health issue to include preventive and promotional healthcare, drinking water, sanitation including environmental improvement and nutrition under local governments.

Integrated Child Development Scheme (ICDS) was launched in 1975, and today it is one of the largest global programmes covering early childhood development. The main objective is to improve nutrition and healthcare status of these children, to reduce incidents of mortality, malnutrition and school dropouts rate, and also enhance the capability of the mother and family. It is a departmentally run programme. Transferring of the responsibility of the local level activities and the management of the local institutions related to such components such as (Health sub-centres, anganwadi centres) to local bodies..

School Facilities

Access to schooling for primary school going children is not a big issue. Even smaller villages do have their own primary schools and Middle School. The key activities in the delivery of primary education, however, in rural Mizoram should include the following and steps must be taken to initiate them in a practical manner.

- Allocating funds;
- Setting standards such as curriculum designs and learning achievement levels;
- Planning for physical expansion and quality improvement of infrastructure;
- Creating assets-human, social and physical;
- Operation and maintenance of the assets thus created.

Enrollment of students and prevention of drop-outs, provision of text books and learning materials, hiring of teachers, their pre-service training, performance evaluation, in-service training, career prospects, setting school calendar, maintenance of school buildings and facilities, maintenance of discipline and monitoring of entire school processes are essential for delivery of quality service and delivery must be ensure.

The main problem seems to be at the Higher Secondary School level. There are certain areas such as West Phaileng Block Development area, where there is no single Higher Secondary School. For many of the people in the rural area, access to higher level of education is denied. District headquarters is not convenient for them financially, socially and physically because of the rural economic condition. Thus in terms of access and coverage, not to speak of quality, availability itself is questionable. Another pitiable situation is the functioning of Village Education Committee. In few bigger villages like Rawpuichhip, and smaller villages like Chamring, VEC headed by VCP is doing not only appointment of midday meal cook(s) (which seem to be the only function of many VEC), but involves itself in monitoring, physical inspection, and discipline wherever the situation demands, and with the limited financial power provided to them, they do commendable works. But in majority of villages, the situation is pathetic.

Sarva Siksha Abhiyan (SSA) addresses primary schools and non formal education centres in the villages. The ultimate objective is: (1) to meet the demand for quality basic education, (2) to ensure 100 per centcoverage of children for elementary schooling by 2010, and (3) to attain universal retention during this period. Local governments are expected to play significant roles. But they do not seem to be given any crucial responsibility in respect of management, monitoring and supervision of the school system. Integration of the SSA with the local governance system is needed for better outcomes and sustainability of the programme.

A Mid-day meal, the national programme of nutrition support to primary education was launched in 1995. The intended purpose is to support universalisation of primary education by increasing enrolment, and to improve nutritional status of children in primary schools. It has been observed in other parts of India that in the absence of participation of the Panchayats, the monitoring of this programme has remained weak. The welfare of children is one area where the community in the form of Gram Sabha, Ward Sabha, village council or local council will be willing to show maximum cooperation. The programme guidelines may be revised so as to bring it directly under Local Government monitoring.

Drinking Water

Quantitative information is not possible here. Village councils are hard pressed to give the villagers sufficient drinking water supply. Majority of the villages do not have enough drinking water, except may be perhaps Thingdawl village, and the VCs are doing in every possible way to get sufficient supply through piped water sources, construction of water points, etc. Due to the porous water holding capacity of the land in Mizoram, rain water harvesting may be exploited in a practical way. Drinking water supply is a subject that can be entrusted to the local government. Government of India is funding substantially for execution of programmes in this sector. But the guidelines for the implementation of the programmes under National Drinking Water Mission leave the selection of implementing agency to the state government. Careful selection of implementing agency and involvement of local level self-government must be ensure.

Mention may be made here of Accelerated Rural Water Supply Programme (ARWSP) started in 1972-73. The basic goal of the programme is to provide safe drinking water to people in all the rural areas in India. The intended outcomes are: (1) ensuring a better quality of life, (2) improvement in general health status, (3) reducing drudgery of women. The funding pattern is 50-50 sharing between the Union and the state government. The entire programme was given a Mission Mode in 1986 and brought under the Technology Mission on Drinking Water Management and was named as the Rajiv Gandhi National Drinking Water Mission (RGNDWM). In 1999, a separate Department of Drinking Water Supply was created in the Government of India. The role played by National Flagship programmes such as Sarva Shiksha Abhiyan (SSA) is well known in Mizoram and North-east India, but other such programmes, viz., National Rural Health Mission (NRHM) and National Rural Drinking Water Programme, although certainly taking foundation, have yet to catch up with the people.

Table 5.2: Major Transfers of Central Flagship Programmess, 2011-12, Mizoram (in crore)

Name of Department	*Name of Scheme/program*	*Implementin(Agency*
Mizoram State Health Society	National Rural Health Mission (NRHM)	Mizoram (Health Socie
State Water & Sanitary Mission	National Rural Drinking Water Program	State Wate Sanitary Mis:
State Project Office	Sarva Shiksha Abhiyan (SSA)	State Pr officer
State Project Office	Rashtriya Madhyamik Shiksha Abhiyan(RMSA)	State Pr Officer
SCERT	English Language Teaching Institute (ELTI)	SCERT

Source: Finance Accounts, Government of Mizoram, 2011-12.

The above figure appears in the Report of Comptroller and Auditor general of India for Government of Mizoram, 2011-12. The Centre Government has been transferring substantial amount of funds directly to implementing agencies under Social Sector to different Departments. The above includes major transfers of schemes such as National Rural Health Mission and National Rural Drinking Water Programme, but the village councils are not aware of these programmes/schemes. Not to speak of quality, rural population clearly do not have access to these basic services.

Other Services

Provisions of streetlights, access to public toilets and drains, household wastewater disposal are patchy, lacking and deficient.

Ensuring efficient delivery of services could be considered through enduring systems and wide reforms in the areas of food and civil supplies, agriculture, land registration, education, healthcare, rural development, transport and power. The quality of service delivery and accountability of delivery system needs to be ensured.We may have to focus on the following in all the three local governments, viz., village councils, Aizawl Municipal Councils, and Autonomous District Councils.

(1) Deepen democratic self-government and participatory development, ensuring decentralisation of responsibilities to elected local governments.

(2) Enhance the accountability of government and the responsiveness of the public- involving the local people in the planning and management of services. Transparency in the administrative system which enables the citizen to assert his right, and accountability which would ensure that in case of failure to deliver the services or delay in delivering, the concerned officials in the government will be brought to book and compensation awarded to the citizen.

(3) Empower citizens through capacity building programme for civil society organisations with Public-Private-People partnerships. This will entail involvement of voluntary associations, professional bodies, universities and other civil society groups in the monitoring of public services and performance review of government officials.

(4) There is a lot of confusion about the role and responsibilities of different functionaries at the level of the three local governments in Mizoram. Role clarity is what is needed. It is, therefore, very essential to fix the functions and job charts of functionaries without overlapping each other and without ambiguity to ensure effective delivery of basic services.

(5) Social Audit must be made more effective. Social Audit is an innovative mechanism which could enhance conditions for accountability. But in many instances, without the demanding civil society it could be difficult to make social audit really work at the field level. It is proposed as a supplemental to conventional audit to help public agencies to understand their performance as perceived by the stake-holders and improve performance.

(6) Rural decentralisation is an essential element which makes services work for the poor. The idea of decentralisation calls for empowerment of the people with the government directly involving the people in the management of the services they use. It should include devolving specific and substantial executive power in respect of the subjects, activity mapping of the functions devolved, and highlighting specific standards of delivery.

Rural service delivery is very crucial. Mere redistribution of resources across different tiers of government may not solve the problem of public accountability and service delivery. The basic services required could be identified and the standards of such services need to be specified. It may be desirable to delineate the desired service levels, defining procedures with proper authority and flexibility to shape implementation in a befitting manner with the local conditions.

To ensure the centrality of local governments in service delivery system, the following measures need to be taken:

- Unbundling the service into activities;
- Assign clear responsibilities for different aspects of service delivery to agencies including village councils ranging from planning to supervision and feedback;
- Placing resources required for service delivery, both human and financial with VCs;
- Prepare service delivery plans by local governments based on the standard set in respect of each service, in consultation with the stakeholders and in accordance with the resources and facilities available.
- Putting in place a community based monitoring system including user groups, civil society organisations to monitor the implementation of Service Delivery Plans and provide inputs for further improvement.

6

Assessment of Finances of Local Bodies

6.1. Own Sources of Fund

The magnitude of own sources of fund in Mizoram is generally unsteady and insecure. The local governments have not yet been assigned their proper stance as far as collection of taxes, fees and other possible sources of local fund is concern. Due to the lesser number of population and economically fragile situation, local source of fund, even if fully explored, could not possibly be comparable to other parts of India. Table 6.2 reflects sources of fund including own source of fund of village councils and Local councils.The figures in the table denote the shaky condition of local sources of fund and the current insignificant state fund transferred to local bodies signaling the bulk of rural finance coming largely from central fund.

There are two types of village councils-village councilsin the Autonomous District Council areas totaling 248 village councils (93 in MADC, 86 in LADC and 69 in CADC areas), and village councils in non-council areas of Mizoram totaling 508 village councils. village councils in the non-council areas are directly looked after by the state government while those in the Council areas are looked after by the respective District Council. In Council areas the Thirteenth Finance Commission (TFC) grants seem to be operated through the District Councils and the Mahatma Gandhi National Rural Employment Guarantee Scheme (MGNREGS) through the state government offices. As such the actual allotment of TFC grants to village councils rests with the respective District Council and seemed to plague with uncertainty and ambiguity as some village councils expressed having received small amounts of such grants while other expressed having received nothing at all. But the state government has definitely extended the TFC to Council areas and allotment made to the Councils, category-wise, at par with the rest of Mizoram as indicated below:

Table 6.1: TFC Grants allocation during 2012-2013 (Central Fund)

District	*Category-wise District-wise number of village counci*				
	I	*II*	*III*	*IV*	*V*
Aizawl	17	6	16	32	20
Lunglei	20	13	21	39	45
Champhai	21	11	19	32	23
Serchhip	13	03	05	12	11
Kolasib	15	04	09	11	06
Mamit	10	10	15	29	21
MADC	02	05	09	39	38
LADC	06	04	17	32	27
CADC	03	01	08	26	31
Total	**107**	**57**	**119**	**251**	**222**
DTE LAD					
Grant Total					

Source: Directorate of Local Administration Department.

Table 6.2: Different Sources of Funds for Local Bodies in Mizoram during 2012-2013

Name of VC/LC	*Sources of Funds*			
	Own Source	*Amount*	*State Source*	*Amount*
Chhiahtlang	Animal tax	1,700.00	Honorarium	42,000.00
Keitum	Animal tax Garden Pass	500.00 1,000.00	Honorarium	32,400.00
Khawlailung	Animal tax Forest fire Hnatlang run	800.00 300.00 500.00 25,000.00	Honorarium	42,000.00

Name of VC/LC	Sources of Funds			
	Own source	Amount	State Source	Amount
Samlukhai	Animal tax Bazaar shed	320.00 2,400.00	Honorarium	32,400.00
Sumsuih	Animal tax	260.00	Honorarium	22,800.00
Chamring	Animal tax	100.00	Honorarium	22,800.00
Sakawrdai	Animal tax Forest Fire	860.00 500.00	Honorarium	32,400.00
Vaitin	Animal tax	350.00	Honorarium	32,400.00

Name of VC/LC	*Sources of Funds*			
	Own source	*Amount*	*State source*	*Amount*
Rawpuichhip	Animal tax	800.00	Honorarium	32,400.00
W.Phaileng	Animal tax	900.00	Honorarium	32,400.00
N.W.Phaileng	Building in bazaar area	50,0000.00	Honorarium	32,400.00
Lallen	Animal tax Fee from timber	300.00 2,000.00	Honorarium	22,800.00
Damprengpui	Animal tax	1000.00	Honorarium	32,400.00

Name of VC/LC	Sourcesof Funds			
	Own source	Amount	State source	Amount
Bukpui	Animal tax Forest Fire	500.00 200.00	Honorarium	32,400.00
Thingdawl	No source	Nil	Honorarium	42,000.00
Ngur	Animal tax	1,000.00	Honorarium	32,400.00
Zote	Animal tax	350.00	Honorarium	22,80,000.00
Thuampui	No	Nil	Honorarium	22,800.00

Name of VC/LC	Sources of Funds			
	Own source	Amount	State Source	Amount
Tanhril LC	No source	Nil	Irregular	Nil
Hunthar LC	Meat shed Bazar shed	22,000.00 14,000.00	UD & PA control	5,00,000.0(
Tlangnuam LC	No source	Nil	UD & PA,AMC	Nil
Armed Vang LC	2 sheds in Bazar area	20,640.00	AMC,UD &PA	Nil
College Veng LC	Bazaar sheds	18,000.00	UD & PA	30,000.00

Source: Field Notes and Information.

The above Table highlights the insecure and unstable nature of funding in local governments in Mizoram. Local councils' own sources of fund largely centre around animal tax which the government of Mizoram allowed them to collect and retain 50 per cent of the proceeds. There are only few village councils which have additional sources of income like quarry (Khawlailung), building in bazaar area (N.W. Phaileng), *bazaar* sheds (Samlukhai, Armed Veng, College Veng, Hunthar), fees from forest timber (Lallen), fines for forest fire (Khawlailung, Bukpui, Sakawrdai), Garden pass fee (Keitum), and Hnatlang run (Khawlailung). Many villages do not have regular market and as such no market shed as a local source of fund. Lallen has a good village forest where timber may be collected for building construction purpose only for which a nominal fee has been collected. This cannot prolifically and effectively be harnessed in other villages. In many villages, village councils are hardly able to impose fine on the one responsible for forest fire due mainly because of the gradual departure and disappearance of traditional *jhum* cultivation, and the fact that the land is continuing to loss its communal nature as private ownership has been introduced.

6.2. Transfer from State Government

The magnitude of fund transferred from state government to local bodies is not easy to ascertain. This is mainly because of the fact that the village council members are not aware of receiving anything from the state government except the honorarium of the VC members (Table 6.2). Some of the VC members vaguely remember having received development fund from the state government through Local Administration Department in the earlier time, but definitely not during the existing VC term. However, the government of Mizoram has been contributing a matching share in the MGNREGA since 2007-2008, although the scheme was started in Mizoram during 2005-2006 as was notified on September 7, 2005. The aim of the Act is enhancing livelihood security in rural areas by providing 100 days of guaranteed wage employment in a financial year to every household. The central government will bear the entire cost of wages for unskilled manual workers, and 75 per cent of the cost of material including wages for skilled and semi-skilled workers and six per cent of the total cost for meeting expenditure under administration. Administration will include the salary and allowances of Programme Officers and their supporting staff and work site facilities. The state government will bear 25 per cent of the cost of material including wages for skilled and semi-skilled workers, unemployment allowances and administrative expenses of the State Employment Guarantee Council.

During 2005-2006, government of India (Ministry of Rural Development) released a sum of Rs 666.44 lakhs only for implementation of NREGA for two districts in the Sixth Schedule Area- Saiha and Lawngtlai districts. During 2006-2007, the implementation of the Programme was extended to Champhai and Lunglei districts. But during 2007-2008, the implementation was again extended to all the remaining districts, viz., Aizawl, Kolasib, Mamit and Serchhip districts. A total sum of Rs 3398.49 lakhs had been released by the central government, and the state government had released a sum of Rs 490.739 lakhs making the total fund for implementation of MGNREGA at Rs 3889.229 lakhs. The district-wise distribution was Rs 1247.611 lakhs for Champhai district, Rs 592.158 lakhs for Saiha, Rs 844.712 lakhs for Lawngtlai, Rs 978.748 lakhs for Lunglei and Rs 56.50 lakhs each for Aizawl, Kolasib, Mamit and Serchhip districts.

During 2008-2009, the Programme under MGNREGA for wage employment was extended to all the districts in the country including those in Mizoram. During the year the centre government released a sum of Rs 15,930.15 lakhs, and the state government also released a matching sum of Rs 1,533.75 lakhs. During 2009-2010, the centre government released a total sum of Rs 27,697.03 lakhs, and the matching share of the state government was Rs 2,885.197 out of which only Rs 965.114 lakhs was actually disbursed to the implementing agencies, thus leaving a liabilities for the year 2009-2010 against the central fund release was Rs 1,371.816 lakhs.

The inability of the state governemnt to fulfill its responsibility during 2009-2010 and in subsequent years has lessen the effectiveness of the programme in sustaining rural development. Many identified items of functional activities have to be sacrificed due to shortage of fund partculalry in the material component portion. As the village councils simply do not have worthwhile local source of fund, the profit accrued from the ensuing works used to be a good source of village council fund. But shortage of fund and now the introduction of Village Employment Council become encumbrance to rural development. As indicated in Table 6.2 in relation to the sources of funds for the Local Governments, the major bulk of the already fading material component grants have been detained by the BDOs. In at least one or two constituencies, it is the political intrusion and interference which disturbs the normal functioning of the programme. The BDOs act as agents in such incursion. In such a situation, developmental works go to either party workers or to individual contractors or to somebody in the technical department, stated the VC members. In such cases, the VCs are not taken into confidence in regard to monitoring and inspection of the works. They feel helpless as they watch the performance of the works which, according to them, are very pitiable and sometimes even unsafe and hazarduous. On top of this, the Village Employment Council (VEC) has taken over the responsibility of looking after this programme. By and large, the village council, in its present context, has not been regarded as local government in its own right.

During 2010-2011, the Ministry of Rural Development, Government of India, released Rs 26,866.03 lakhs. The state matching share was Rs 2,798.63. The state government released Rs 2,929.34 lakhs. But the outstanding balance for 2009-2010 remained to be Rs 1,371.816 lakhs. This had consequently resulted in a further liabilities of Rs 1,557.524 lakhs. There was another outstanding balance of State matching share of Rs 2,298.112 lakhs during 2011-2012 to be released during 2012-2013. Because of the unfulfilled responsibilities of the state government the material component of the MGNREGA had to suffer. The total fund released by the central government since inception till 2011-2012 amounts to Rs 1,04,036.560 lakhs. But the state government has not released the full amount of its matching share. The outstanding balance to be released by the state government till 2011-2012 was Rs 2,298.11 lakhs. This could entail proportionate deduction from the subsequent installment.

Thus, the state government, in terms of the current agreement as reflected in the Mizoream Rural Employmenrt Guaratee Scheme, 2009, failed to fulfill its responsibility by releasing the matching share and shortage in the district budget of MGNREGS ranging from Rs 214.116 to 364.599. This has repercussion on the irregular release of fund impending the performance of rural local governments and creating unnecessary space between village councils and bureaucrats. Thus, it is not easy to ascertain actual receipt of the grant at the intended destinations. The following Table 6.3 shows year-wise release of fund by the state government from inception till 2011-2012.

It may be mentioned here that the Guidelines for the National Rural Employment Guarantee Act clearly states that, "Where Part Nine of The Constitution does not apply, local councils/ Authorities as mandated by the state concerned will be invested with corresponding responsibilities". The Mizoram Rural Employment Guarantee Scheme, 2009 Paragraph seven states that, "Since Part IX of the Constitution does not apply to Mizoram, local councils/Authorities as detailed under shall be vested with corresponding responsibilities for the Mizoram Rural Employment Guarantee Scheme as under.." and put – A: Village Employment Council; B: Block Employment Council and C:District Employment Council. This means that the Scheme does not recognise village council as Local Authorities. When Mizoram became Union Territory in 1972 it was reiterated that

Table 6.3: District-wise and Year-wise fund released by state government : 2005-06 to 2011-12

Year	*Name of district rural development agency (Rs In lakhs)*								
	Aizawl	*Champhai*	*Saiha*	*Lawngtlai*	*Kolasib*	*Lunglei*	*Mamit*	*Serchhip*	*Total*
2005-06	-	-	-	-	-	-	-	-	-
2006-07	-	-	-	-	-	-	-	-	-
2007-08	-	112.101	72.158	227.912	-	78.568	-	-	490.739
2008-09	161.175	282.094	217.10	238.35	52.617	439.02	53.894	89.50	1533.75
2009-10	179.28	131.13	61.268	126.452	96.735	221.55	79.758	68.941	965.114
2010-11	527.12	416.344	261.40	303.691	337.894	538.093	286.763	258.035	2929,34
2011-12	282.683	324.192	197.983	492.051	187.715	512.581	301.162	113.502	2411.869
Total fund released by state	1150.258	1265.861	809.909	1388.456	674.961	1789.812	721.577	529.978	8330.812
Total fund released by Centre Government	15640.348	17258.241	10420.459	18106.996	9910.431	22733.192	10396.997	7800.708	112367.372
Outstanding balance of state share	334.684	357.871	158.651	314.221	276.086	364.599	277.884	214.116	2298.112

Source: Rural Development Department, Mizoram.

the present system of arrangement (which includes village council) to continue until alternative arrangement is made. Such alternative arrangement has not been made till date.

It is therefore, difficult to understand the creation of Village Employment Council bypassing and marginalising the village councils. It is, thus, not surprising to see strong negation and disapproval from village council members across Mizoram. The scheme for the creation of VEC has not been immediately implemented before official order was issued on July 7, 2012 and November 5, 2012 which states, 'the Village Employment Council (VEC) has been invested with the responsibility of the Gram Panchayat and that all references to the Gram Panchayat in the MGNREG Act/Operational Guidelines shall imply the Village Employment Council, as duly constituted by the State Government'. It must be repeated here that if any entity is to be taken as comparable and counterpart of Gram Panchayat, it has to be an elected body duly recognised by the state election commission, and that will have to be the village council and not the VEC elected by Gram Sabha without proper notification, and also heavily loaded with bureaucratic structure. I have field confirmation that election to Village Employment Council in villages where existing ruling party is not in control would be held at a very short notice and the attendance is usually very poor. In Muallungthu, VC members told me that the timing of election of VEC was fixed at 7:00 a.m. where non-Congress VC was in power, and at 10:00 a.m. where Congress is in power with information circulated the previous night. This become a political design to capture the village level power. Empirical field situation suggests it is detrimental to the cohesion of the village and would debilitate healthy developmental works. Therefore, a review of the position of the Village Employment Council in Mizoram may be made immediately as this has been introduced in spite the existence of democratically elected body and representatives of the people, the village council.

6.3. Transfer from Centre Government

Mahatma Gandhi once said, "In this structure composed of innumerable villages, there will be ever widening, never ascending circles. Life will not be a pyramid with the apex sustained by the bottom. But it will be an oceanic circle, whose centre will be the individual, always ready to perish for the village, the latter ready to perish for the circle of the villages, till at last the whole becomes one life composed of individuals, never aggrasive in their arrogance, but ever humble, sharing the majesty of the oceanic circle of which they are integrated units. Therefore, the outermost circumference will not wield power to crush the inner circle, burt will give strength to all within and will derive its own strength from it". In the foot step of Gandhi's vision of 'Poorna Swaraj' economic reforms and local government empowerment are the two great initiatives launched in 1990s, and devolution of funds, functions and functionaries is the crucial programme envisaged by the Union Government.

We have seen the relatively feeble nature of transfer of fund from state government to local governments. Transfer from the Centre Government is constant and durable, but the actual and physical transfer reaching the intended destination could not really be ascertained. This is mainly due to the casual and shoddy manner in which records are being kept in the villages where nothing really can be ascertained, except from the memory of the village council members. The TFC grant is operated through the Local Administration Department based on the projected amount of the Thirteenth Finance Commission. Mahatma Gandhi National Rural Employment Guarantee Act/ Scheme is operated though Rural Development Department, and the year-wise released of fund from Centre Government may be seen from Table 6.4.

As far as allocation of fund for TFC grants, village councils are divided into five categories on the basis of size of the villages in terms of number of households as in Table 6.5.

Table 6.4: District-wise and year-wise fund released from Centre Government, 2005-06 to 2011-12 (Rupees in lakhs)

Year	*Name of District Rural Development Agency*								
	Aizawl	*Champhai*	*Saiha*	*Lawngtlai*	*Kolasib*	*Lunglei*	*Mamit*	*Serchhip*	*Total*
2005-06	-	-	131.44	535.00	-	-	-	-	666.44
2006-07	-	228.00	628.08	1168.82	-	128.00	-	-	2125.90
2007-08	56.50	1135.51	520.00	616.80	56.50	900.18	56.50	56.50	3398.49
2008-09	1611.82	3078.01	1871.00	2724.68	526.21	4238.15	538.91	973.37	15562.15
2009-10	4969.71	2874.34	1580.52	2992.52	2364.47	3693.26	2332.79	1626.22	22433.83
2010-11	3561.12	3726.07	2453.74	3508.37	2711.11	5698.81	3188.24	2018.57	26866.03
2011-12	4290.94	4950.45	2525.77	5172.35	3577.18	6284.98	3558.98	2596.07	32956.72
Total	**14490.09**	**15992.38**	**9710.55**	**16718.54**	**9235.47**	**20943.38**	**9675.42**	**7270.73**	**104036.56**

Source: Rural Development Department, Mizoram.

Table 6.5: Classification of Village Council : Number of household-wise

Category of Village Council	*Number of households in the category*	*Tot eac*
Category I	401 households or more	107
Category II	301 to 400 households	57
Category III	201 to 300 households	11
Category IV	101 to 200 households	251
Category V	Less than 100 households	222
Total		**756**

Source: Local Administration Department, Govt. of Mizoram.

The 13th Finance Commission has given emphasis on performance and achievement and came out with Performance Grant as follow:

Table 6.6: Performance Grant from Centre Government (in Crores)

Year	*Amount Expected*	*Amount of Grant Received*
2010-2011	Nil	
2011-2012	7.44	1,16,96,000.00
2012-2013	17.46	
2013-2014	20.60	
2014-2015	50.75	

Source: Local Administration Department, Mizoram.

The LAD requested to identify their area of priority as soon as the 13th Finance Commission recommendations were received. The following schemes are accordingly selected for implementation on the basis of priority list submitted, which is as follow:

1. ***Core Services***: Construction of Community water storage tank/ rain water harvesting tank
2. ***Improvement of Operational Infrastructure***: This includes
   (1) Village Council House
   (2) Community Auditorium
   (3) Photo voltaic alternative energy system for street light
3. ***Civic Amenities (Improvement of Village Internal road):***
   (1) Construction of foot-path, retaining wall, foot-steps, bridges,

(2) Cemetery approach road,

(3) Creation of village park/recreation centre.

4. ***Capacity Building and administration cost and updating of village data.***
5. ***Strengthening of District Offices and V/C offices:***

(1) Engagement of Technical Staff and Account Assistant on MR basis,

(2) Provision of office furniture for village councils,

(3) Administrative Cost/Office expenses.

In spite of community water storage and rain water harvesting included in the core priority service list, the work activity remain largely centering around priority list No. 3 – construction of foot-path, approach road, foot-steps, and retaining wall. In few cases construction of village council house is undertaken, while in most cases, old and small council house continued to be used. But then the priority list is informative and can be a guide for future endeavor.

There was a Seminar on "Strengthening Panchayati Raj Institutions in Gujarat: Issues Before the 3rd State Finance Commission" on 21 July, 2012 at the Institute of Rural Management Anand (IRMA), particularly focusing on 'Status of Financial Devolution to Panchayat Raj Institutions in Gujarat, and the observations on Budget outlay (Table 6.7-6.11) may be of some help:

Table 6.7: Sources of Revenue for PRI (Figures in Crore)

	2004-05	*2005-06*	*2006-07*	*2007-08*
State Govern-ment Grant	2978.2	3306.38	3564.88	4574.
Govt.of India's Grant	471.36	472.77	740.1	735.9
Own Revenue	108.43	82.23	182.11	713.9
Loans and advances	35.34	47.02	59.91	19.14
EFT/TFC	113.5	136.34	199.66	186.2
	3706.83	**4044.74**	**4746.66**	**6228.**

Source: CAG Report for Local Body audits, 2009-10.

Table 6.8: Source of Revenue for PRI (Figures in per cent)

	2004-05	*2005-06*	*2006-07*	*2007 08*
State Government Grant	80.34	81.75	75.10	73.44
Govt. of India Grant	12.72	11.69	15.59	11.81
Own Revenue	2.93	2.03	3.84	11.45
Loans and Advances	o.95	1.16	1.26	0.31
EFC/TFC	3.06	3.37	4.21	2.99
	100.00	**100.00**	**100.00**	**100.0**

(EFC = Eleventh Finance Commission).

TFC = Twelfth Finance Commission).

Percentage of devolution of PRI finances out of State's Total Budget may be learned from the State of Gujarat which may be seen as follow:

Table 6.9: Percentage Devolution out of State's Total Budget

	Rs in Crore	*Rs in Crore*	*Rs*
State's Total Revenue	*2009-10*	*2010-11*	*2*
	AE	*AE*	*BE*
Tax, NTR & GIA to State	41672.36	52363.64	62
Capital Receipt	14531.65	17055.61	18
Total receipt of State	**56204.01**	**69419.25**	**81**
Total Devolution to PRIs	6524.5	15817.6	95
Percentage of total devolution	**11.61**	**22.79**	**11**

Source: Budget in Brief, 2012-13 and Budget Estimates (Gujarat).

Table 6.10: **Percentage of Devolution of State's Total Tax etc. Budget**

State's Total Revenue	*Rs in crore* 2009-10 AE	*Rs in crore* 2010-11 AE
Tax, NTR, and GIA To State	41672.36	52363.64
Total devolution to PRIs (Functional/Department wise)	6524.50	15817.60
Percentage of Devolution	**15.66**	**30.21**

Source: Budget in Brief, 2012-13 and Budget Estimates (Gujarat).

Below in Table 6.6 can be seen the functional devolution of Budget Estimate to different major departments where Sports, Youth and Cultural activities, and Industries have no allocation.

Table 6.11: Department-wise / functional BE (devolution) / Grant-in-aid to Panchayats (Figures in crore)

Department	*2009-10 ME*	*2009-10 BE %*	*2010-11 BE*	*2010-11 BE %*	*2011-12 BE*
Agriculture & Cooperation Deptt.	107.10	1.64	905.03	5.72	182.54
Education Deptt.	4128.30	63.27	7607.15	48.09	6303.31
General Admn. Deptt.	3.18	0.05	3.47	0.02	5.88
Sprots, Youth & Cultural Activities	0.88	0.01	23.39	0.15	0.00
Health & Family Welfare	405.34	6.21	916.18	5.79	577.61
Women & Child Development	10.00	0.15	285.67	1.81	358.30
Industries & Mining	0.87	0.01	276.29	1.75	18.00
Social Welfare	2.15	0.03	0.00	0.00	0.00
Rural Housing &Rural Dev.	369.36	5.66	1495.95	9.46	921.45
Revenue Department	17.14	0.26	46.09	0.29	12.73
Roads & Buildings	881.50	13.51	762.37	4.82	427.36
Water Supply etc.	0.00	0.00	1319.85	8.34	64.71
Social Justice & Empowerment	111.98	1.72	1339.83	8.47	215.79
Tribal Development	486.70	7.46	836.35	5.29	490.80
Grand Total	**6524.50**	**100.00**	**15817.60**	**100.00**	**9578.49**

Source: *Seminar on "Strengthening of Panchayati Raj Institutions in Gujarat: Issues before the 3rd State Finance Commission" on 2 July, 2012.*

It can be seen that devolution in the case of Education Department is very high, reasonable on Rural Housing, Women and Child Development, Tribal Development and Health and Family Welfare, but very meager in basic items like Water Supply, Roads and Building.

7

Expenditure Analysis

7.1. Administration

The administrative expenditure at the local level cannot be established simply because they do not keep any record of expenditure concerning work items performed by the VC or VEC. But works allotted to them have been carried out by the members of the VC or VEC as the case may be on the basis of honorarium given to those on duty. This is within the sanctioned amount and normally did not create problem. Apart from this, there do not seem to be any administrative expenditure at the local level. At the Directorate level, as far as thirteenth Finance Commission Grant is concerned, during 2010-2011, the Directorate reserved a sum of Rs 24,96,000 for capacity building, Maintenance of Accounts and updating of village data, and in the current budget of 2012-2013 an amount of Rs 1,27,40,400 has been earmarked for capacity building, the break-up of which is as Table 7.1.

As for the MGNREGA, since the State matching share is a problem for Mizoram with no resources of its own, the state government has decided to formulate the Labour Budget under MGNREGA for the year 2012-2013 in the ratio of 80:20 between wages and material including wages for skilled and semi-skilled workers at the wage rate of Rs 136 per person-day as fixed by the state government with effect from 1 April, 2012. Accordingly,

Table 7.1. Proposed Expenditure for Capacity Building/Strengthening of Village Councils: 2012-13

Sl.No.	*Item*
1	Engagement of M/R 9 Nos. Account Assistant 300/ per day
2	Engagement of M/R 2 Nos. of Village Data Operator For Directorate @ Rs 240/ per day
3	Administrative Expenses like T.E
4	Administrative Expenses and Capacity Build Village Councils and other charges: (1)Plastic chairs 3 Nos. each for 756 Village Cc (2)Stationery for Village Councils (3)TFC Cash Book
5	**Grand Total**

Source: Local Administration Department, Mizoram.

the Labour Budget for the year 2012-2013 as per the approved figures of the Labour Budget worked out–Wage and Material in the ratio of 80:20 at the wage rate of Rs 136 per person-day may be seen from Table 7.2.

Table 7.2: Approved Labour Demand in 2012-2013 (in lakhs)

District	*Approved Labour Budget*		
	Employment Demand	*Persondays Generated*	*Exp*
Aizawl	26022	2602200	4689
Champhai	28084	2808400	5060
Kolasib	20556	2055600	3704
Lawngtlai	26809	2680900	4830
Lunglei	34801	3480100	6271
Mamit	18217	1821700	3282
Saiha	13519	1351900	2436
Serchhip	13727	1372700	2473
Total	**181735**	**18173500**	**3274**

Source: *Rural Development Department, Mizoram.*

The methodology for the calculation of item-wise break-up of per centage out of the fund released by the Ministry of Rural Development under MGREGA can be worked out as per the guidelines. The permissible percentage of six per cent out of

Central release fund is now 5.94 per cent only for administration. Since the Labour Budget has been formulated in the ratio of 80:20 between wages and material, the amount of the state matching share to be contributed by the state government has also been reduced, and it is now 4.95 per cent only. Thus, out of any amount of central fund releases, the state government will release 4.95 per cent as matching share. In this way, deduction of funds for administration will now be 5.94 per cent of central release. The expected central release can be seen from Approved Labour Budget.

The method for calculating permissible percentage for administration under MGNREGA, as per the guidelines for MGNREGA at Paragraph 8.1 and the Act at Paragraph 22(1) for the pattern of sharing between the Centre Government and state government will be as follow:

(1) The Centre Government will bear the following costs:

(a) The entire cost of wages for unskilled manual workers;

(b) 75 per cent of the cost of material and wages for skilled and semi-skilled workers;

(c) Administrative expenses as may be determined by the Centre Government. These will include, the salary and allowances of Programme Officers and their supporting staff and work site facilities.(The permissible per centage is six per cent out of the total cost for wages and material etc., now become of course, 5.94 per centin the case of Mizoram);

(d) Administrative expenses of the Centre Employment Guarantee Council.

(2) The state government will bear the following costs:

(a) 25 per centof the cost for material and wages for skilled and semi-skilled workers.

(b) Unemployment allowances payable in case the state government cannot provide wage employment within 15 days of application;

(c) Administrative expenses of the State Employment Guarantee Council.

Since the projected expenditure to be released by the Centre Government is 327,48,65,220, the permissible percentage of

5.94 per cent will work out to be Rs 19,45,26,994 which will go to the Administrative expenditure.

7.2. Civic Functions

MGNREGS is becoming the major scheme for provision of rural employment and developmental works in Mizoram. Mizoram Rural Employment Guarantee Scheme, 2009 has listed types of work in order of priority as follow:

(1) Water conservation and water harvesting,

(2) Drought proofing (including afforestation and tree planting),

(3) Irrigation canals, including micro and minor irrigation works,

(4) Provision of irrigation facility to land owned by household belonging to the Schedule Castes and Schedule Tribes or to land of beneficiaries of land reforms or that of the beneficiaries of Indira Awas Yojana Programme,

(5) Renovation of traditional water bodies including desilting of tanks,

(6) Land Development,

(7) Flood control and protection of works, including drainage in water logged areas,

(8) Rural connectivity to provide all-weather access,

(9) Any other works, which may be notified by the Centre Government in consultation with the state government.

This is in consonant with the all-Indian pattern developed by the National Rural Employment Guarantee Act, 2005 in which the implementing agencies are of two kinds: (a) 50 per cent by Gram Panchayat/VC, and the Programme Oficer or District Programme Co-ordinator may sanction beyond the permissible 50 per cent. (b) Other Implementing agencies are Intermediate and District Panchayats, Line Department, Public Sector undertakings, Cooperative Society and NGO, and Self Help Group.

However, in Mizoram implementing agencies remain to be Village Level implementing agency (VEC now) and Line department and party workers. Empirical field data indicates that less than 50 per cent (VC members state 40 per cent is usual) of the total cost of work items in material component is allotted to the village councils against provision of the Act, and the rest implemented under the control of Line Department. As such selection of possible work items is rather limited to civic amenities like construction of foot-path, retaining wall, public drainage, foot-step, bridges, approach roads to cemetery, and other important places. In this way, items in the high priority list such as water conservation and water harvesting have received scant attention. Thus, the largest part of expenditure under MGNREGS scheme, both wage labour component and material component, had gone to performance of civic functions. Of late, improvement of operational infrastructure particularly construction of village council house and community auditorium has also been taking primacy in few smaller villages such as Lallen and Chamring. As encouragement by the officials, new trend that is observable is that work items for wage labour component have now been extended to private job and vocation within the village. This can be performed only in few villages while others cannot hitherto comprehend the real implication of this.

As for the thirteenth Finance Commission grant, which is also another basic source of fund in rural Mizoram, the priority list already pointed out include Core Services, Improvement of Operational Infrastructure, Civic amenities, capacity building, and strengthening of District offices and *VC offices* in order of priority. But the work items remain to be concentrated on works under Civic Amenities- construction of foot-path, retaining wall, foot-path and approach roads to important places in the village. Overall, civic functions have been given a major share in both the TFC and MGNREGS funded employment and venture.

The following Table 38 indicates utilisation of Grants-in-aid by the village council for the development works against funds released by the Government of India on the basis of Twelfth and Thirteenth Finance Commission's recommendation and achievements during 2007-12. The Government of India released Grants-in-aid of Rs 42.43 crore during the period for rural local bodies. Utilisation of the funds for different items of works is as follow:

Table 7.3: Utilisation of Funds and Achievements during 2007-2012

Year	*Funds released by GOI (in crore)*	*Name of Works*	*Year-Wise Achievement*
2007-2008 to 2009-2010	12.00	Sanitation & drainage	2007-08
			2008-09
			2009-10
		Water supply scheme	2007-08
			2008-09
			2009-10
		Capacity Building	2007-08
			2008-09
			2009-10
	12.00		
2010-2011 to 2011-2012	30.43	Const. of foot path, Retaining wall, Steps, Approach road.	2010-11
			2011-12
		Const. of VC House	2010-11
			2011-12

Source: *Department of LAD, Mizoram, Records.*

According to Finance Commission's guidelines, there should not be any delay beyond 15 days in the release of grants to the local self-governments by the state government from the date of release of the grants by the Centre. The date of release of grants-in-aid to the state government as per recommendations of the Twelfth Finance Commission and thirteenth Finance Commission and transfer o funds by the state department to the implementing agencies is shown below:

Table 7.4: Delay in Release of Funds by LAD Department, Mizoram (in crore)

Release of Grants in Aid by GOI			*Release to tl agencies*	
Recomme-ndations	*Date of release*	*Amount released*	*Due date of release*	*Da rele*
12th FC	Not available	6.00	-	28.
			-	13.
	27.1.2009	6.00	10.2.09	13.
			10.2.09	26.
Sub-Total		**12.00**		
13th FC	15.7.2010	9.39	29.7.10	13.
	16.3.2011	9.16	30.3.11	30.
	01.3.2012	11.88	15.3.12	9.4
Sub-Total		**30.43**		

Source: Department of LAD, Mizoram, Records.

8

General Observation

8.1. Implementation Strategy

The implementation approach and strategy of different development schemes remain largely to be based on centralisation. The state government, while framing the Mizoram Rural Employment Guarantee Scheme, 2009 according to the provision of sub-section(1) of section 4 of National Rural Employment Guarantee Act, 2005 and incorporating the Guidelines clause, "where Part Nine of the Constitution does not apply, local councils/Authorities as mandated by the state concerned will be invested with corresponding responsibilities", there simply is no mention of village council as local body or local authority. On the other hand, it ordered for the creation of Village Employment Council(VEC) where VCP will be the Chairman, Block Employment Council(BEC) and District Employment Council(DEC). It also said, 'all references to the Gram Panchayat and Gram Sabha in the guidelines shall imply VEC'. Therefore, the implementation of MGNREGS, the largest rural developmental scheme in operation, is left at the discretion of VEC guided, of course, by the Block officials. This is one prevaricate to elude empirical reality, and should be corrected. Under the circumstances, democratically elected rural leaders are sidelined, and ignores the basic emphasis on decentralisation and devolution.

Second the implementation process is controlled by the DRDA and BDO officials and as such, the village authority are never in a position to ascertain how much funds will be transferred to them. This remain to be at the discretion of the government officials, and sometimes politicians are very much involved. This is amply demonstrated by empirical case situations. Therefore, the BDO in the name of Technical Staff may undertake the larger portion of development work items, and thus not devolved to village level authorities. Generally, compared to works undertaken by village councils, works performed by technical staff are very much inferior and substandard both in quality and finish. This is definitely in contrast to encouraging participatory decision-making at the micro social level by involving people relating to activities affecting them.

Monitoring is carried out in a confusing and hazy way. In fact, there is nobody to monitor and supervise when the work is undertaken by Technical Staff as the VC has no power and authority. But when the work is done by VC (in earlier occasions) or by VEC, technical officials will have to satisfied himself and certified completion of work. Because of the technical vagueness and imprecision in the process of implementation, the work suffers and remain to be shoddy and poor quality. I have personally seen works performed by the village councils and works performed otherwise involving same amount of fund. The quality of work and finish in the later cases are largely in a pitiable and unfortunate conditions. Some of the Technical Assistants/Contractors may even be from the same village.

8.2. Capacity Building and Training

Efforts for Building capacities of elected representatives or official functionaries of local government institutions began as soon as these institutions had attained institutional status as a result of 73rd constitutional amendment. As the PRIs are assigned increasing responsibilities in both developmental and regulatory functions in other States, there is a growing concern about their capacity. In this way, around 30 lakhs elected representatives and 10 lakhs official functionaries have to be trained every year. National Capacity Building Framework describes the preparatory activities, building up the training infrastructure, developing a pool of resource persons, and other requirements as to sustain a capacity development effort, planning the logistics of implementation and monitoring and evaluation of capacity building efforts. It suggests training in vast areas including

Centrally Sponsored Schemes indicating duration, sequencing and target category with timelines for completion of training programmes.

The overall objectives of National Capacity Building Training (NCBT) include:

- Enabling elected representatives to upgrade their knowledge and skills to better perform their responsibilities.
- Orienting the officials to become more effective technical advisors and implementers of the ideas emerging from the elected representatives.
- Improving the functioning of the Gram Sabha as an important institution of local decision making.
- Sensitising media, political parties, legislatures, civil society institutions and citizen to accept and promote the Panchayati Raj as an essential level of local government and for inclusive and participatory development.

In Mizoram, capacity building and training have been imparted to the elected village council members occasionally but actual modality is yet to be worked out. The training imparted to the elected representatives of local governments so far did not yield expected results as it did not have realistic application.

But the Government of India conducted numerous workshops during 2007-2010 to assist the states in working out the modalities of their capacity building plans primarily for sourcing funds and implementing the Capacity Building Component under BRGF programme. But Capacity Building and Training efforts continue to be intermittent and sporadic consisting of routine lectures by inadequately equipped resource persons. However, as a consequence of continuous efforts of the Centre Government, training coverage has improved from about 33 per cent in 2008-2009 to 36 per cent in 2009-2010, to more than 66 per cent in 2010-2011. Thus, the need for intense capacity building is gaining increasing recognition with the scanty devolution of core functions like Education, Health, Sanitation, etc. Capacity Building is a bedrock on which local governments can stand firmly and deliver basic minimum services. The state will have to prepare itself for genuine capacity building by strengthening SIRD and establishing at least two Extension Training Centres (ETC).

8.3. Computerisation and E-governance

Computer has not been used in the functioning of village councils in Mizoram, although it has been used in both the three Autonomous District Councils and Aizawl Municipal Council and DRDA and BDO offices. E-panchayat is a software product conceptualised, designed and developed by National Informatics Centre, Hyderabad, Andhra Pradesh as a part of its E-governance initiatives. E-panchayat has been designed taking into consideration all the information and knowledge management requirements in a Gram Panchayat. The 1992 Panchayati Raj Act of the Government of India and the success stories of the Gram Panchayats in various states in the country have been taken into consideration while developing e-panchayat. The software is supposed to be citizen-centric. Therefore, the village level functionaries and the citizens are envisaged to benefit by e-panchayat.

It comprises nearly 30 main modules, and nearly 150 sub-modules, in line with 30 sectoral functions of the Gram Panchayat. Applied in the case of village councils in Mizoram, intense training of the functionaries including elected representatives will definitely be required.

The modules facilitate provision of the following information services and should be useful:

- Minutes of meetings,
- Scheduled of Gram Sabha,
- Agenda update,
- Certificates, Licenses,
- Bill payments,
- Attendance monitoring of the Panchayat functionaries,
- Gram Panchayat Meetings Management,
- Gram Panchayat Cleanliness Monitoring,
- Registration Births/Deaths/Marriages, etc.,
- SGSY works monitoring, issue of trade licenses,
- Pension schemes management system,
- Self Help Groups and other villagers welfare schemes management system,

- Assets management, property tax assessment and management,
- Property lost/found reporting system,
- Law and Order management system,
- Encroachments checking and monitoring module,
- Government Orders searching and retrieval system,
- 'Village statistics maintenance and reporting system,
- Intensive sanitation management information system.

8.4. Municipalities

Mizoram is in a very unusual situation. The legal frame of Local Government Institutions in North-east comprise three typologies such as: (1) Sixth Schedule Frame (Meghalaya, parts of Assam, Mizoram and Tripura), (2) State Legislation Frame (Nagaland and Non-council Areas in Mizoram), and (3) National Frame (Arunachal Pradesh, Sikkim, Manipur excluding Hill Areas and Non-council Areas in Assam and Tripura). Accordingly, different constitutional measures will be necessary for any reform in the context of each state. Mizoram falls under both Sixth Schedule Frame and State Legislature Frame. As per the provisional Census, 2011, the population figure of Mizoram district-wise is as follows:

Table 8.1. District-wise Population of Mizoram

Sl.No	District	Population		
		Persons	Males	Females
1	Mamit	85,757	44,567	41,190
2	Kolasib	83,054	42,456	40,598
3	Aizawl	404,054	201,072	202,982
4	Champhai	125,370	63,299	62,071
5	Serchhip	64,875	32,824	32,051
6	Lawngtlai	154,094	79,252	74,842
7	Lawngtlai	117,444	60,379	57,065
8	Saiha	56,366	28,490	27,876
	Total	**1,091,014**	**552,339**	**538,675**

Source: Statistical Handbook, Mizoram, 2012.

The above table designates that Lawngtlai and Saiha districts, where the three Autonomous District Councils locate, encompass a total population of 1,73,810 or 15.93 per cent of the total state population, and the remaining 917, 204 or 84.07 per cent of the population dwell in the non-council area or state Legislation Areas.

Under the Sixth Scheduled provisions, Mizo District Council and Pawi-Lakher Regional Council for the Pawi, Lakher and Chakma tribes were set up in 1952 and 1953 respectively. Both the councils democratised the village administration be enacting the Lushai Hills District (Village Councils) Act, 1953 and the Pawi-Lakher Autonomous Region(Village Councils) Act, 1954 under sub-clause (e) of Clause (3) of the Sixth Scheduled to the Constitution of India. Accordingly, village administration was vested in the democratically elected village councils (VCs) which started functioning from August, 1954. The village councils have very limited functions and powers mostly administrative and judicial of petty nature under the village council Act, 1953 and 1954. The impact of North East Areas (Reorganisation)Act, 1971, Mizo District Council was abolished in 1972 and the Pawi-Lakher Regional Council was trifurcated into three Autonomous District Councils-Lai Autonomous District Council, Mara Autonomous District Council and Chakma Autonomous District Council.

The Lushai Hills District (Village Councils) Act, 1953 and the Pawi-Lakher Regional Council (Village Councils) Act, 1954 have been adapted by the Government of Mizoram, and the three Autonomous District Councils in 1972 for the administration of the rural areas. The administration of the village councils has been put under Local Administration Department and Town Planning and Housing by the Government of Mizoram. At present, village council is operating in both rural areas and the notified/declared urban areas over which the Government of Mizoram and the Autonomous District Councils exercise their jurisdiction independently.

The Mizo Hills District Council enacted the Mizo District (Administration of Town Committee) Act, 1955, but it has neither been introduced by the Mizo District Council nor adapted by the Government of Mizoram in order to get it notified/declared city and towns. Subsequent after attaining statehood of Mizoram in 1987, the Government of Mizoram, however, has formulated and notified 23 towns such as Aizawl, Champhai, Serchhip, Kolasib, Saitual, Khawzawl, Vairengte, Bairabi, N. Kawnpui, Thenzawl, Darlawn, Mamit, Sairang, Zawlnuam, N. Vanlaiphai, Biate, Khawhai, Lengpui, Lunglei, Hnahthial, Tlabung, Lawngtlai, and Saiha, but has not so far endowed with the structure of urban governance administration except in the case of Aizawl (Aizawl Municipal Council). The village councils meant for rural governance have been permitted to continue functioning in the notified towns. Therefore, incorporation of constitutional provisions relating to setting up of municipalities by the Government of Mizoram is very fundamental. However, given the fact that the financial resources of Mizoram Government is frail and fragile, the state government may not be able to fulfill its initial obligation. The centre government may have to come forward to ameliorate the situation and facilitate support for at least five years. There is an urgent need for effective, viable and workable urban decentralised administrative structure in the notified urban areas. Government of Mizoram may, therefore, extend the provisions of Mizoram Municipalities Act, 2007 (as amended in 2009) to the other 20 declared urban areas by suitable amendment/order/notification, excluding Lawngtlai and Saiha which fall on the Sixth Schedule Areas.

Article 243ZC of the Constitution(Seventy-Fourth Amendment) Act, 1992 relating to municipalities is not applicable to Scheduled Areas referred to in clause (1) (Sixth Schedule) and the tribal areas referred to in clause (2) of Article 244 (Fifth Schedule). Mizoram has only two Sixth Scheduled Districts- Saiha and Lawngtlai- where the Autonomous District Councils have been functioning since 1971. To these Sixth Scheduled Areas, the Constitutional provisions of Seventy-Fourth Amendment Act, 1992 concerning municipalities cannot be applicable. The rest of Mizoram comprising six districts such as Aizawl, Lunglei, Champhai, Serchhip, Mamit and Kolasib, does not come under the provision of the Fifth Schedule of the Constitution of India meant for the administration of tribal areas of the country.

Table 8.2: DeclaredTown-Wise Population of Mizoram

Sl.No.	Towns	Persons	Males
1	Zawlnuam	3,730	1,947
2.	Mamit	7,876	4,049
3.	Lengpui	3,203	1,626
4	Vairengte	10,534	5,663
5	Kolasib	24,094	12,002
6	North Kawnpui	7,732	3,896
7	Bairabi	4,336	2,160
8	Darlawn	3,775	1,862
9	Saitual	11,315	5,593
10	Sairang	5,925	2,986
11	Aizawl	291,822	143,803
12	Khawzawl	10,808	5,503
13	Champhai	32,630	16,205
14	Khawhai	2,502	1,264
15	Biate	2,277	1,137
16	Serchhip	21,157	10,770
17	Thenzawl	7,219	3,623
18	North Vanlaphai	3,605	1,806
19	Tlabung	4,414	2,216

Source: Statistical Handbook, Mizoram, 2012.

Extension of PESA

The village councils are designed by the enactments of Government of Mizoram and their provisions are amended by executive and administrative orders. The village council lacks statutory support in its present status. It is a single tier rural administrative institutions having no status of rural self governing entities. The village councils have been denied to the devolution of financial resources, administrative responsibilities, political power, developmentroles, planning and decision-making power. The system lacks devolution of the three Fs-functional devolution, financial devolution and devolution of functionaries. The present village council system, therefore fails to encourage local initiative and democratic participation of the people to bring about the needed changes. The local people respected the persons occupying the office of village councils, but simply do not pay high regard for the office they occupy. Therefore, a revamp and total smarten up is of immediate necessity. Government of Mizoram may go for 73rd constitutional amendment, or else evolve an archetype of the 73rd amendment, appropriately extension of PESA so that we may have village council entity in which provisions for devolution of functions, funds and functionaries as streamlined in (Chapter 2.1) may be evoked. State Legislature may, by law, make such provisions. The hitch here is again the financial predicament of the state government. *The Centre Government may help out by liberal grant to Capacity Building and Training and special Finance Commission grant to overcome initial hurdles. Centre Government may think of extending PESA to Mizoram and other relevant North-eastern States.*

8.4. CSS

Centrally Sponsored Scheme of Mahatma Gandhi National Rural Employment Generation Act (MGNREGA) is operated through the DRDA. However, the District Water and Sanitation Committee (DWSC) and the District Health Society(DHS) have not been effectively functioning at the grassroots level in Mizoram. In view of the immense deficiency in the supply of drinking water and sanitation in almost all the villages, and village councils are responsible for these functions, the DWSC and DHS may be integrated with the activities of the village councils. Central Guidance to this inkling shall be necessary.

8.5. Monitoring and Evaluation System

Monitoring and evaluation system need overhauling and a totally new system required to be evolved. In the existing system, the village council is not given responsibilities and functional role as far as monitoring and evaluation are concerned. The line department/Technical Assistants seem to have taken control of the whole situation. As such the local community is not aware of what transpired in the locality and simply not seriously involved in it.

9

Recommendations and Conclusion

9.1. Principle of Subsidiarity

The principle of subsidiarity proposed by the Second ARC must be incorporated in dealing with the affairs of village councils as promulgated to amend Article 243G: "*Subject to the provision of this Constitution, the Legislatyre of a State shall, be law, vest a Panchayat at the appropriate level with such powers and authority as are necessary to enable them to function as institutions of self government in respect of all functions which can be performed at the local level including the functions in respect of the matters listed in the Eleventh Schedule*". This must be taken into consideration wherever possible.

9.2. Structure of Local Governments

The State Legislature may provide, by law, appropriate structure of Local Bodies as follow:

- There shall be village councils covering a sing village or clusters of village to make it viable. Smaller villages will constitute village council Wards (Gram Sabha constituencies). The existing categorisation of village councils in terms of number of households is as follows:

Table 9.1: Village Councils: Category-wise Number of Household in Each District

Sl.No.	*District*	*I (401 &Above)*	*II (301-400)*	*III (201-300)*
1	Aizawl	17	6	16
2	Lunglei	20	13	21
3	Champhai	21	11	19
4	Serchhip	13	3	5
5	Kolasib	15	4	9
6	Mamit	10	10	15
Total	**6**	**96**	**47**	**85**
7	MADC	2	5	9
8	LADC	6	4	17
9	CADC	3	1	8
Total	**3**	**11**	**10**	**34**
Grand Total		**107**	**57**	**119**

Source: LAD office record, 2012-13.

The present village composition and structure of village councils shows that there are 280 village councils having households of 200 or less, and 85 village councils with households between 201-300 in non-council Areas. The creation of village council in Mizoram probably followed a notion that there should be one village council in each village. Many of them are vastly too small to function as autonomous institutions of local government. It is necessary to restructure them to be economically viable administrative unit, capable of executing manifold and diverse responsibilities. Therefore, a village council has to have a minimum workable size. The principle which may be followed as far as practicable in constituting village council may follow the following pattern. There shall be one village council each in villages under category I and Category II totaling 143 village councils in non-council areas and 164 village councils in Mizoram. Two villages in Category III can be combined to form one Village council which will produce 42 village councils in non-council Areas and a total of 59 village councils in Mizoram. In category IV, three villages can be brought together to create one village council which will generate 51 village councils in non-council Areas and a total of 84 village councils in Mizoram.

Villages in category V are very small ones and four of such villages may combined to make one village council totaling 31 village councils in non-council Areas and a total of 55 village councils. In this way, we shall have 267 (instead of 508) village councils in non-council Areas and 95 (instead of 249)village councils in Council areas, totaling 362 village councils in Mizoram. Each village in Category III, IV and V function as Gram Sabha and will have their own representative(s) in the village council. This may enhance certain factors desired by the Second ARC on the size of rural local bodies such as: (a) Potentiality of resource generation, (b) sustainability of the staff structure, (c) suitability as a unit of planning for core functions, (d) geographical cohesiveness, and (e) communication facility within the village council area. This principles should guide the process of integration of existing categories III, IV and V. As far as practicable, geographical cohesiveness and ease of communication facilicty must be ensured in selecting villages for clustered village councils.

Article 243B of the Constitution defined Gram Sabha as "a body consisting of persons registered in the electoral rolls relating to a village comprised within the area of the Panchayat at the village level". It occupies important place in the entire scheme of locval governance. It is through this body that individual villager participate in the local decision making process. Proper functioning of Gram Sabha is a key to empowerment of village council at the village level. Due to the distance involved in the clustered village councils, each small village may form a Gram Sabha/Ward Sabha of its own with representative(s) at the village council. Big village council can also be divided into such Ward Sabha wherever needed.The Ward Sabha/Gram Sabha shall be assigned the function of identification and prioritisation of beneficiaries under various anti-poverty, social support and wage employment programmes.

- There shall be Block Decvelopment Council with elected members at the Block level to coordinate activities concerning development matters. It may be called 'Block Development Council'. It shall help in Block Level Planning initiated at the village level and other activities.
- There shall be District Planning Committee (non-elected members) to coordinate grass roots planning within the District.

9.3. Electoral Process

Delimitation and conduct of elections and the whole electoral process shall continue to be entrusted to the state election commission.. Terms of office of Local Self-governments (both rural and urban) may be extended to five years.

9.4. Functional Devolution

It is a dictum that state government are reluctant in the past to transfer the 3'F's to elected local bodies. The key issue (as provided in Article 243G of the Constitution for PRIs) here is that at all levels local bodies must function as institutions of self-government rather than as implementing agencies. The suggestion here is that instead of three tier system as operated in other parts of India, there may be two-tier system in Mizoram comprising of village councils and Block Development Councils. However District Planning Committee (DPC) may also be created as a planning coordinating entity. Devolution may be done in relation to functions, funds and functionaries in relation to Block Development Councils and village councils. Devolution is to avoid overlapping jurisdiction of different tiers of government. Accountability must be maintained. It is to be noted that the village council is the local government closest to the people, enjoying financial and functional autonomy, and the devolution should take note of the following principles:

- There should be functional jurisdiction and an independent sphere of action for Block Development Council and village councils. The state government through line departments should not interfere over this sphere except providing guidance. If any activity within this sphere is currently performed by any line department of the state government, that department should cease to perform the activity after devolution.
- Certain spheres should be worked out where the state government and village councils/Block Development Councils should work as equal partners.
- There may be sphere where village councils/Block Development Councils would act as agencies for implementing Union or state government schemes (The difference between partnership mode and agency mode is that the scope of independence in discharging responsibilities is more in partnership mode).

Table 9.2: Status of Devolution of Functions in different States as of November, 2006

State	*Transfer of Subjects through Legislation*	*Subjects covered under Activity Mapping*	*Latest P*
Andhra Pradesh	17 subjects	9 subjects	A Task Special Mapping formulati incorpora accordar of the consider for finali: these di been Governn
Assam	29 subjects	29 subjects	Assam (mapping But, indi operatio executiv functiona recent Panchay has ren mapping map for the curr fiscal de

contd...

contd...

State	*Transfer of Subjects through Legislation*	*Subjects covered under Activity Mapping*	*Latest P*
Bihar	25 subjects	25 subjects	Bihar ha mapping orders Therefor undertak Activity M an NG Committ Commiss Rural D Raj is ur Activity also incl functiona separate Finance constitut on crea Window
Chhatisgarh	29 subjects	27 subjects, except forests and drinking water supply	Althougl complete executiv
Goa	6 subjects	18 subjects	18 funct village P needs

contd...

contd...

State	*Transfer of Subjects through Legislation*	*Subjects covered under Activity Mapping*	*Latest P*
Karnataka	29 subjects	29 subjects	Activity I in respe 2003 fol through 2004.
Kerala	26 subjects	26 subjects	Activity I form of the State mapping mapping Municipa being de devolved
Madhya Pradesh	23 subjects	23 subjects	Activity two stag covered, NGO, S complete remainin been d discussi concern
Maharashtra	18 subjects		There ha activity n has rec

contd...

contd...

State	*Transfer of Subjects through Legislation*	*Subjects covered under Activity Mapping*	*Latest P*
Punjab	7 subjects		Draft a prepared detailed being u such as matrix h Ministry ready fo
Rajasthan	29 subjects	12 subjects	The act started now bee sub-Com August 2 to stren recomme when the
Sikkiim	28 functions		Activity expected 2006.
Tamil Nadu	29 subjects		Tamil N instructic Panchay paper; S water s housing

contd...

contd...

State	*Transfer of Subjects through Legislation*	*Subjects covered under Activity Mapping*	*Latest P*
West Bengal	29 subjects	15 subjects	Activity I and ord subjects
Dadra and Nagar Haveli	29 subjects	29 subjects	Activity I in respe Eleventh amendm Haveli V Regulati
Daman and Diu	18 subjects	18 subjects	The Mini Finance recomm and fun approval Affairs, been tra respect
Andaman and Nicobar Islands	8 subjects	8 subjects	Acitity N for eight marine program and rura
Lakshadweep Islands	25 subjects	25 subjects	Followin Panchay January

Source: Based on Mid-term Appraisal–State of the Panchayats 2006-07(Vol. I) (appeared in the Report of the Second ARC, Rural Governance).

Table 9.2 portraits the picture of actual devolution of functions in different Statesd and Union Territories. Activity Mapping has been tried in almost all the States and Union Territories and completed in a number subjects and departments. We can observe variation in the achivement of functional devolution in different states. In the formulation of activity mapping, agency functions should never be permitted to overshadow the other spheres of action, and local government autonomy must be ensured. Hierarchical relationship between village councils and higher level government must be minimised. Article 243G of the Constitution is intended to ensure that local bodies at all levels function as institutions of self-government rather than as implementing agencies. This exercise has to cover entire range of all the 29 subjects mentioned in the Eleventh Schedule and may be even more. Some states have already devolved all the 29 subjects through State Legislation.

In case of urban local bodies, in addition to the functions enumerated in Twelfth Schedule, the following may be contemplated to be devolved to urban local bodies:

- School Education,
- Traffic management and civic policing activities,
- Urban environmental management,
- Land management including registration.

9.5. Framework Law

Mizoram Government should draft Framework Law for Local Bodies (both rural and urban) and lay down the broad principles of devolution of powers, responsibilities, and functions to local governments bearing in mind the following:

- Principle of Subsidiarity,
- Democratic Decentralisation,
- Delineation of Functions and activities,
- Devolution in Real Terms,
- Convergence,
- Citizen Centricity.

9.6. Activity Mapping

There must be clear and workable Activity Mapping for role clarity and efficient performance. Unbundled activities are to be assigned to village councils and Block Development Councils. In this, economy of scale, externality, equity and heterogeneity will have to play major role in the process. Economies of scale tend to push the service towards higher levels of government. Some activities may be scaled neutral in implementation, and may be pushed down to the lowest level for implementation.

Economies of scope may mean that some services may be linked in ways that make it more efficient for one tier of government to provide all of them more efficiently when bundled together. If an activity impacts an area larger than the jurisdiction of a local body, then such activities ought to be undertaken at a higher level.

Sometimes a particular activity can be undertaken efficiently at the local level, and has no externalities, but in the interests of equity, a uniform growth pattern across jurisdiction may be desirable.

Public accountability is also another crucial factor which guides where an activity ought to be placed.

- *Is the activity discretional*? If so, it will be best performed lower down to enable transparency.
- *Is it transaction intensive*? If so, it is best performed lower down.
- *Who can best judge performance?* If implementation appraisal involves technical skills it could be pushed higher up. The World bank document "India-Inclusive Growth and Service delivery" suggests three important items on service delivery:

(a) The same tier of government should not be responsible for operation and for monitoring and evaluation,

(b) The capability and commitment of higher tiers of government to set standards for outputs and goals for outcomes and to monitor performance and evaluate the impact of alternatives should be strengthened by decentralisation,

(c) There is enormous scope for increasing local control of asset creation and operation.

The Centre Government has been undertaking large fiscal transfers to states in the functional domain of local governments mainly through Centrally Sponsored Schemes and Additional Central Assistance (ACAs). The Ministry of Panchayati Raj has been continually examining the Centrally Sponsored Schemes suggesting changes to make them compatible with the functional assignment to local governments. Activity Mapping is a clear factor in ensuring that local governments are on a sound footing.

When the tasks assigned are clear regarding devolved funds and accountable for their performance of these new responsibilities, they may have a big incentive to demand the capacity required for effective performance. Role clarity catalyses capacity building. But as the Central Finance Commission observes, "the progress made so far in this area is far from satisfactory". The state government, therefore, should constitute a *special task force* to complete this work.

9.7. Extension of PESA

Decentralised governance in North-east states where PRIs do not exist is always problematic. Arunachal is covered by Part IX with no reservation for Scheduled Castes. Six districts of Assam, whole of Meghalaya, part of Tripura and two districts of Mizoram are covered under the Sixth Schedule. The Hill areas of Manipur, whole of Nagaland and six districts of Mizoram are covered by state laws governing village councils, and of these only the Hill areas of Manipur have District Councils. village councils do not exist in the Sixth Schedule areas of Assam and Meghalaya whereas village councils exist in both the District Council areas and non-council areas in Mizoram. The different arrangements of local governments have been allowed to continue during the framing of the constitution, amendments of Sixth Schedule during North-east Re-organisation, and during 73rd constitutional amendment. In Meghalaya and Assam, the District Councils have not legislated for constitution of village councils, and in Tripura there are Village Committees legislated by the District Council. In Mizoram, in the six districts outside the Sixth Schedule areas, village council exist under state law. Inter-Ministerial Team (IMT) of the Government of India and Ministry of Panchayati Raj proposed deepening of decentralised governance through:

- Make village council answerable to Gram Sabha. Recognise Gram Sabha under the law and specify their powers and functions;
- Rationalise the powers of state government and the District Councils in matters of extension and supercession of Councils, make the process transparent and hold elections within six months;
- Reservation for women;

- Mandatory and regular election for the village council through the state election commission;
- Make women members' participation part of the quorum in Gram Sabha and Council meetings;
- Constitution of State Finance Commission;
- Vesting of both developmental and some judicial powers on the village councils, and more powers to village councils and Gram Sabha.

In Mizoram, Gram Sabha is already working successfully in matters concerning MGNREGS. It is, thus, very vital to incorporate the principles of Decentralised Governance within the legal framework set up for each state. The second ARC and the Expert Committee believe PESA to be able to provide guidance in dealing with the problem of governance in North-east Region. Therefore, Panchayat (Extension to Scheduled Areas) Act (PESA) may be extended to non-council Areas of Mizoram. It may thus be suggested that the state government may take steps for adoption of PESA rules with appropriate modifications by legislation, or else go for 73rd amendment as per Constitutional provision. Centre Government may extend PESA to Mizoram and North-east states wherever applicable.

9.8. Urban Local Governments

Suggestion for the creation of urban local bodies in the 22 notified urban centers has already been m Se. state government may extend the provisions of the existing Mizoram Municipalities Act, 2007 (as amended in 2009) as the Act states, *"it shall extend to the whole of the state of Mizoram except the area which has been or may hereafter be declared as, or included in, a panchayat or a village council under provisions of any law in force in Mizoram, but shall not extend to the Mizoram Tribal Areas, as referred to in Part III of paragraph 20 of the Sixth Schedule of the Constitution"* by appropriate notification as per the provision of the Act.

The world today witnesses urban growth. This is mainly because towns and cities are the main beneficiaries of the benefits of globalisation. Millions of people are looking for jobs and migrating to urban areas. For the first time in human history, it is said that more than half of the world's population, i.e., 3.3 billion, is now living in urban complexes. It is estimated that within the next two decades, five billion people of the world's population (about 80 per cent) will be living in cities. The question is, 'just how sustainable our urban conglomerates are? Are our policy makers and civil society with their ill-equipped managerial capacities able to deal with this? For one, preventing environmental degradation and reducing vulnerability of the poor to be key intervention that will determine the quality of life in our towns and cities.

Census of India, 2001 classified two types of towns : (1) Statutory towns: all places with a municipality, corporation, cantonment board or notified town area committee, etc so declared by a state law; (2) Census towns: places which satisfied the following criteria: (a) a minimum population of 5,000; (b) at least 75 per cent of male working population engaged in non-agriculture pursuits; and (c) a density of population of at least 400 persons per sq. km. The constitution allows each state to decide what should be the criteria for classifying an urban centres as town municipal council, city municipal council. This prevents a uniform pattern of categorisation. In spite of this, the category-wise number of urban centres in India as recognised by Census of India, 2001 is as follows:

Table 9.3: Urban Agglomeration / Towns by Class / Category: Census of India, 2001

Class	*Population Size*	*No. of UAs/T*
Class I	1,00,000 and above	393
Class II	50,000-99,999	401
Class III	20,000-49,999	1,151
Class IV	10,000-19,999	1,344
Class V	5,000-9,999	888
Class VI	Less than 5,000	191
Unclassified		10
All Classes		4378

Source: *Census of India, 2001.*

Uniform categorisation is desirable. It is recommended that uniform categorisation would help in adoption of a structured approach leading to a more systematic national planning process and in the devolution of funds through National and State Finance Commissions. Although the 74th amendment lays down three types of Municipal bodies such as: (1) Nagar Panchayat (in transitional area), (2) Municipal Council (small urban area), and (3) Municipal Corporation (large urban area), the census categorisation in Table 9.3 may be adopted.

It is also observed that the present system has two important shortcomings:

- There is little role that average citizen play in his/her own governance,
- Elected representatives as well as officials are not sufficiently accountable and this undermines both efficiency and transparency.

Therefore, keeping in view the 74th amendment towards citizens' participation in urban affairs, the following structure containing the three tiers of urban local bodies, as suggested by Second ARC, may be proposed:

- Municipal Council/city municipal council (by whatever name it is called),
- Ward Committee; and
- Area Committee or Sabha.

However, in Town Panchayats (with a population below 20,000), there would be no need to have three tiers, given the small size in terms of population.

Table 9.4: Recommended Categorisation of Urban Local Governments in India

Size	*Nomencl*
ULGs with a population of up to 20,000	Town Pa
ULGs with a population between 20,000 and 1,00,000	Municipa
ULGs with a population between 1,00,000 and 10,00,000	City Mun
ULGs with a population between 10,00,000 and 50,00,000	Municipa
ULGs with a population above 50,00,000	Metropoli

Thus, in Mizoram, we shall have three categories of Urban Local Governments, namely,

- **One City Municipal Council** (Aizawl Municipal Council),

- **Four Municipal Councils** (Lunglei, Champhai, Kolasib, Serchhip) barring Saiha and Lawngtlai which fall on Sixth Schedule Areas, and
- **Sixteen Town Panchayats** (Saitual, Khawzawl, Vairengte, Mamit, North Kawnpui, Thenzawl, Hnahthial, Sairang, Tlabung, Bairabi, Zawlnuam, Darlawn, North Vanlalphai, Lengpui, Khawhai, Biate).

Area Sabha: An Area Sabha would cover people who are voters in two or more polling stations. In Aizawl Urban areas, they are called Urban local councils replacing village councils. The maximum population of local council may be as decided by the state government.Although Mizoram Municipalities Act, 2007 does not include local councils in its framework, Aizawl Municipal Council makes provisions for the continuation of local councils and elections conducted in 2012. Central Finance Commission also recommended its introduction because it would be the starting point for the other upper echelon(s) of urban governance.

The Second ARC recommended that 'there should be three tiers of administration in urban local governments except in the case of Town Panchayats, where the middle level would not be required. The three tiers should be: (i) Municipal Council/ Corporation, (ii) Ward Committees, (iii) Area Committees of Sabhas(local councils in th case of Mizoram). Ward Committee should be given legitimate functions that could be handled at that level. These may include street lingting, sanitation, water supply, drainage, road maintenance, maintenance of school buildings, maintenance of local dispensaries, local markets, parks, playgrounds, etc. The budget proposed by the Ward Committee in respect to the functions allotted to it should be taken into consideration in formulating the overall municipal budget. Ward Committee should be given a share of the property taxes collected from the ward, and the meetings of Ward Committee should be widely publicised for maximum people's participation. Each Area Sabha or local council should elect its representatives every five years. The Chairman of Area Sabha/local council would represent such specific area in the Ward Committee. The allocation of functional responsibilities between the tiers must be clearly splet out. Broadly, Area Sabha/local council should perform functions similar to the Gram Sabha such as prioritising development activities and identifying beneficiaries under various schemes.

An Area Sabha or local council should be the functional equivalence of Gram Sabha or village council in a village. It should not merely be a political space for opinion formation, but must be endowed with responsibilities formally attached to them. It should be a legitimate, formal space, which would need to be unequivocally defined in terms of constitution, composition, functions, duties and responsibilities.

The term of office of local council may be stretched to five years in consonant with the term of the already existing Aizawl Municipal Council. The allocation of functional responsibilities between the tiers must be clearly spelt out. Activity Mapping similar to the one taken up for village councils must be work out.

9.9. Autonomous District Council

Mizoram Government have already transferred through executive orders and official notifications almost all the relevant subjects. Under paragraph 6(1) of the Sixth Schedule, District Councils have powers to establish, construct and manage primary schools, dispensaries, markets, cattle ponds, ferries, fisheries, roads, road transport and water ways. The councils also have powers to assess, levy and collect revenue in respect of land and buildings, taxes on professions, trades callings and employments, animals, vehicles and boats, toll on passengers and goods carried in ferries, and taxes on maintenance of schools, dispensaries or roads as listed in paragraph 8 of the Sixth Schedule.

The executive functions clarified and elaborated through notifications dated 22nd September, 1993, as also noted by the Report of Expert Committee for Planning for the Sixth Schedule Areas, 2006, have entrusted the following items to the Autonomous District Councils:

(1) Agriculture and horticulture, (5 functional activities)

(2) Fisheries, (grant-in-aid to individual farmers for fish pond development)

(3) Public Health Engineering (2 functional activities)

(4) Industry (3 functional activities)

(5) Sericulture (2 functional activities)

(6) Animal Husbandry and Veterinary (3 functional activities)
(7) Arts and Culture (4 functional activities)
(8) Social Welfare (5 functional activities)
(9) Soil Conservation (3 functional activities)
(10) Local Administration (2 functional activities)
(11) Forest (ongoing projects of forest department)
(12) Transport (separate Transport department)
(13) Sport and Youth Services (separate department)
(14) Cooperation Department (separate department)
(15) Public Works Department (3 functional activities)
(16) Education (3 functional activities)
(17) Rural development (3 functional activities)
(18) DRDA and ICDS (to be clarified)
(19) Relief and Rehabilitation (3 functional activities)
(20) Water ways and inland water transport.

Though the District Councils have been vested with wide powers, the state government continues to undertake works in respect of the same devolved function, without consulting the Councils. In this way, parallel administrative hierarchies are functioning within the Council areas—one headed by the Council which has potentially wide executive and development functions and the other headed and coordinated by the Deputy Commissioner who operate through separate agencies such as the DRDA and state level department officers posted in the district. The observation of the Expert Committee must be noted, *"In Mizoram, these councils, at first glance are over-structured, over-staffed and with patchy empowerment-while they have unbridled unaccountable freedom in one area, they have none in others. The problems of the Councils are also compounded by the fact that they covered very small population of ethnic groups, thereby reducing the scope and scale of their operations"*.

Government departments have pushed out the District Councils from performing most of their mandated functions except in education. The duplication of functions is carried on in an atmosphere of tensions and led to inefficient implementation, detrimental to the state. This has also led to stagnation of decentralisation. Rearrangement of working method must be evolved. state government Notification dated 29 August, 2011 and the instruction (already quoted in page 64) contained therein which reads, '*Administrative departments shall oversee and ensure that these entrusted functions are not again undertaken by their offices in the Autonomous District Council areas and only some skeleton staff are retained there*' must be strictly adhered to operationalisation of transfer of subjects and activities by backing them up with devolution of funds and dismantling of parallel structures that exist is very crucial. In matter of release of allocations to be made to village councils without delay or diversion, a system of less intermediaries be adopted. In order to actualise this, following suggestions of Expert Committee may be considered:

- A database of bank accounts of all village councils may be compiled;
- The state government indicates the overall allocations concerning the scheme that is to be implemented by the village councils, to the District Council. Intimation of this bulk allocation is also made to each village council;
- The District Council lays down the criteria on the basis of which funds can be transferred to each village council and communicates this to the state government in respect of the Scheme concerned;
- The state government transfers the funds directly to the village councils through band transfers, with intimation to the District Councils.

Wide publicity must be given to the release of funds to the village councils.

9.10. Capacity Building

That there is a capacity deficit is a common knowledge particularly in regard to the implementation of flagship schemes such as National Rural Employment Guarantee Act which has become the backbone of rural development in Mizoram. Capacity building in both rural and urban local self governing institutions must attend to both organisation building requirements as well as professional and skills upgradation of individual associated with these bodies, both elected or appointed. State government may encourage local bodies to outsource specific functions to public or private agencies, as may be appropriate, through enabling guidelines and support. This should be backed by development of in-house capacity for monitoring and oversight of outsource activities. Good training requires expertise and resources from different subject matter specific training institutes. Networking of institutions concerned with various subjects such as financial management, rural development, disaster management, and general management. This should be ensure by nodal department in state government.

9.11. Decentralised Planning

Planning starts at the grassroots level. As mandated, District Planning Committee must be constituted within three months of elections to local governments and should become the sole planning body for the district. The DPC should be assisted by planning office with a full time District Planning Officer. State Planning Boards may ensure that the district plans are integrated with the state plans that are prepared by them. In Mizortam, as pointed out earlier, DPC could be a non-elected planning body for the district.

9.12. Transfer of Funds

The main emphasis of the Part IX of the Constitution is structural empowerment of local bodies but the actual strength in autonomy and efficiency is dependent upon their financial position. Panchayats in India are generally receiving funds in the following manner:

- Grants from the Union Government based on recommendations of Central Finance Commission as per Article 280 of the Constitution.
- Devolution from state government based on the recommendations of the State Finance Commission as per Article 243(I).
- Loans/grants from the state government.
- Programme specific allocation under Centrally Sponsored Schemes and Additional Central Assistance.
- Internal Resource Generation (tax and non-tax).

The following figures indicate that Panchayats' own resources are feeble.

Table 9.5: All-India Revenue Structure during 1998-99 and 2002-03

Revenue Source	1998-1999		
	Amount (in crores)	Percentage	A (in
Grants-in-Aid	9744.19	56.34	141
Assignment and Devolution	5222.71	30.20	664
Own Revenue	1167.81	6.75	156
Other sources	1160.97	6.71	164
Total	17295.68	100.00	240

It can be seen that progress in local taxation and non-tax income is very minimal. Most of the revenue buildup comes from taxation of property and profession with minor increment coming from non-tax receipts like rent from property and fees for services. Exercise in this direction will have to be taken seriously taking into account the following:

- Potential for taxation,
- Fixation of realistic tax rates,
- Widening of tax base,
- Improved collection system.

Devolution of funds from the state government and Centre Government forms a major component of the resources. Due to poor resource base and economic activity in rural areas, village council in Mizoram will have to depend on State/Central transfers/grants. As such the role of CFC, SFC, and Central/ State Schemes would continue to be very vital in ensuring that finances available with village councils to harmonise the assigned/ transferred functions.

State Finance Commission may consider initially allotment of fix income for devolution, but may consider devolving share of tax income in later years as Kerala allots three eight of the amount of the basic tax collected by the Government. Thus, income of the village councils increases with the increased tax revenue of the state government. A key step in providing clarity to fund devolution to village councils concerns the creation of village council/Urban Local Bodies/ Sector window in the State budgets. Each department may create separate line items in their budgets for the local bodies earmarking allocations pertaining to responsibilities devolved and schemes entrusted to local bodies (rural and urban). Departments can thus directly send their funds to the local bodies according to ear-marked budget line items. Alternatively, all such earmarked funds could be consolidated by the State Finance Department and send to local bodies in regular installments. Seven States—Chhatisgarh, Gujarat, Karnataka, Kerala, Madhya Pradesh, Maharashtra and Rajasthan—have provided for a separate local body Sector component in their State budgets. The main idea is to prevent mismatch between functional assignments and fiscal transfer.

Own resource generation has a dual purposes of being a source of financial standing and at the same time ensure people's involvement in the affairs of the village councils and also makes the institution accountable to its citizens. Mizoram Government can endorse, by law, the provision of Article 243H which reads, " the Legislature of a State mat, by law—

- Authorise a Panchayat to levy, collect and appropriate such taxes, duties, tolls and fees in accordance with such procedure and subject to such limits;
- Assign to a Panchayat such taxes, duties, tolls and fees levied and collected by the state government for such purposes and subject to such conditions and limits;
- Provide for making such grants-in-aid to the Panchayats from the Consolidated Fund of the State; and
- Provide for constitution of such funds for crediting all moneys received, respectively by or on behalf of the Panchayats and also for the withdrawal of such moneys therefrom as may be specified in the law.

Overall, except for specifically tied major centrally sponsored Schemes and special purpose programmes of the state, all other allocations must be in the form of untied funds. There should contain only brief description of broad objectives and expected outcomes.

9.13. Accountability and Transparency

State government may create Audit Committee and a separate Standing Committee of the State Legislature for the Local Bodies may also be constituted. A local body Ombudsman may also be constituted. It would look into complaints of corruption, maladministration against functionaries, both elected and appointed officials. Local Ombudsman may be a single member body or otherwise two or three members body appointed by a committee consisting of Chief Minister, Speaker of Legislative Assembly, and Leader of opposition in the Assembly from among eminent persons of integrity and should not be serving government officials. Ombudsman shall have authority to investigate cases and submit reports to competent authorities for taking action. This is in addition to social audit and normal audit process.

9.14. Transfer of Functionaries

Staff is an important resource that an organisation must possess to perform its activities. Control over human resource is an important element of autonomy. But local governments in India present a foreboding picture. States are not uniform in this respect. In some states, Local Governments do not have the power to recruit and determine their salaries and other conditions of service. But in some states, they do have such powers, but due to lack of financial resources, such powers are not operated, and have to depend on the officials of the state government. The Central Finance Commission is of the view that as the government at the local level they should have their own staff. They should have full powers with regard to recruitment and service conditions of their own employees within a broad framework of State laws and certain standards. As a transitional measure, it is also suggested that, till such time as the personnel structure of the local governments takes a definite shape, the employees of the state government may be taken on deputation. In Mizoram, village councils cannot be expected to have their own resources to recruit and pay salaries of employees at their own disposal. There are 757 village councils in Mizoram including Council Areas as follows:

Table 9.6: Category-Wise Number of Village Councils, 2012-2013

Name of District	*I (401 and above house-holds)*	*II (301 to 400 house-holds)*	*III (201 to 300 house-holds)*	*IV (101 to 2 househol*
Aizawl	17	6	16	32
Lunglei	20	13	21	39
Champhai	21	11	19	31
Serchhip	13	3	5	12
Kolasib	15	4	9	11
Mamit	10	10	15	29
MADC	2	5	9	39
LADC	6	4	17	33
CADC	3	1	8	26
Total	**107**	**57**	**119**	**252**

Source: Local Administration Department, Mizoram.

These may be compared with the average population of Village Panchayats in other parts of India:

Table 9.7: Demographic Details of Panchayats in States and Union Territories

Sl.No.	*State*	*Rural Population (2001)*	*Nc Vil. Par y*
1	Andhra Pradesh	55401067	21
2	Arunachal Pradesh	870087	1(
3	Assam	23216288	2:
4	Bihar	74316709	8
5	Chhatisgarh	16648056	9
6	Goa	677091	1
7	Gujarat	31740767	13
8	Haryana	15029260	6
9	Himanchal Pradesh	5482319	3
10	Jharkhand	20952088	3
11	Karnataka	34889033	5(
12	Kerala	23574449	9
13	Madhya Pradesh	44380878	23
14	Maharashtra	55777647	27
15	Orissa	31287422	6
16	Punjab	16096488	6
17	Rajasthan	43292813	9
18	Sikkim	480981	1
19	Tamil Nadu	34921681	12
20	Tripura	2653453	5
21	Uttar Pradesh	131658339	52
22	Uttarakhand	6310275	7
23	West Bengal	57748946	3

Source: Based on Mid-term Appraisal-State of the Panchaysts 2006-07 (Vol. I): Planning Commission and Ministry of Panchayati Raj).

Gram Panchayats are further categorised into:

- Tiny Gram Panchayats: Below 2,000: (Arunachal Pradesh 531 to Madhya Pradesh 23,789).
- Small Gram Panchayats: 2,000-5,000: (Madhya Pradesh 2,015 to Rajasthan 4,712).
- Medium Gram Panchayats: 5,000-10,000: (Orissa 5,019 to Bihar 8,773).
- Large Gram Panchayats: Above 10,000: (Assam 10,783 to Kerala 23,789).

In Mizoram, Categories IV and V encompass village councils with a population strength of 200 to 800, and 460 village councils fall into these categories which is 63.36 per cent. In the Autonomous District Council areas, out 249 village councils, 187 village councils fall into these categories accounting for 75.10 per cent, and in non-council areas of Mizoram, out of a total 485 village councils, 273 village councils or 56.28 per cent fall into these categories. It is, therefore, obvious that it may not be realistic for these smaller village councils to keep independent staff of their own. But as suggested in the Structure of Local Governments, a combination of two/three/four smaller villages into one village council to form a custer of such villages for purposes of transferringfunctionaries/staff and planning may be recommended. In this way, we hsall have 267 village councils instead of 508 in non-council areas and 95 village councils instead of 249 in Council areas. Even then clusters of village councils will still be small, and will not be able to raise enough fund to recruit and maintain its own staff, at least initially. Therefore, transfer of officials on deputation or otherwise from state government departments may be contemplated.

9.15. Personal Management

Detailed review of the staffing pattern and systems, with a zero-based approach to local body staffing, may be carefully undertaken. The local bodies may draw staff from the departments/agencies of the state government according to the pattern to be formulated by state government. In future the local bodies must be prepared to have power to recruit personnel and regulate their service conditions subject to such laws and standards as laid down by the state government. The staff posted under their jurisdiction must be placed under their power and must be answerable to them

9.16. Village Councils and State Government

In both Council Areas and Non-council areas, the state government/District Councils command considerable power with regard to review and revision of actions taken by the village councils including power to inquire into the affairs of the village councils and also power to . dissolve the village councils. The village council enactments of state government broadly place state government in a position of command *vis-à-vis* the village councils. There seems to be instances of arbitrary use of this power to dissolve village councils. In this way, local bodies can be victimised on narrow political considerations. However, there could be maladministration, violation of fiscal responsibility norms, misuse of authority, corruption and nepotism which may warrant action against village council or elected representatives. In this respect, state government is to ensure that village councils are carrying out their activities in accordance with law within their domain. The issue is to what extent such controlling powers of the state government should exist in the law. The essence of the matter is to install village councils with autonomous space, and the provision should not anticipate a relationship of subordinate and superior between the two. The state government should not have the power to suspend or annul official resolution passed by the village council or Block Development Council or take action against the elected representatives on any ground, or to supersede/dissolve the village councils. In all such cases, the powers to investigate and recommend action should lie with the local ombudsman who will send his report to the Governor.

9.17. Position of Parastatals

Parastatals may be formed either under specific State enactments or under the Societies Registration Act. These bodies are formed for delivery of specific services, implementation of specific schemes or programmes sponsored by state/Central/ International donor agencies. Some of the important parastatals are District Rural Development Agency (DRDA), District Health Society (DHS), District Water and Sanitation Committee (DWSC). Their functions directly encroach on local institutions. The most important parastatal at the District level in Mizoram and elsewhere is the DRDA. Formed under the Societies Registration Acts, it was created essentially as a semi-autonomous organisation to implement various programmes of livelihood development, wage and employment generation and social support activities of the Centre and state governments. Currently, the funds for most of the Centrally Sponsored Schemes—SGRY, SGSY, IAY are allotted to the DRDA from where it is distributed among implementing agencies at the Block level. In Mizoram, MGNREGA is also included. It has been argued that since the process of democratic decentralisation being in place at all three levels of PRIs, there is no justification for having a separate agency as the DRDA in the district. States like West Bengal, Kerala, and Karnataka, have already merged DRDA with the District Panchayats. In Mizoram, because of lack of democratic decentralisation in the present scenario, DRDA may continue for some more time.

District Water and Sanitation Committee (DWSC) deals with the rural water supply and sanitation schemes. The Union Government has been extending policy, technological and financial support through a Centrally Sponsored Scheme- the Accelerated Rural Water Supply Programme (ARWSP) under which funds are provided to the state governments for implementing rural water supply schemes. Since drinking water and sanitation are included among subjects to be devolved to village councils, DWSC may be introduced as a committee of the District Planning Committee (DPC). Block level committee may also be created. The rural water supply system can be handled, barring few larger investment requiring higher technical and professional support, by the village councils. In Mizoram, Village Water and Sanitation Committee have already been established in most villages. The only drawback is that they have not received any support from ARWSP.

Another area of Parastatal involvement could be Health Care, and the District Health Society (DHS) to look after the programmes of the National Rural Health Mission (NRHM). A major part of the programmes concerns rural sector(running hospital, dispensaries and primary health centres). Rural healthcare is primary concern of village councils, DHS should have true relationship with the District Planning Committee.

But Parastatals should not be allowed, at any level, to undermine the authority of the local bodies.

Democratic governance and citizen sovereignty means that most decisions are taken closest to the people. Such people-oriented governance process enhance participation and legitimacy of our democratic political system. It also ensures greater effectiveness in delivery of services and accountable governance. Three basic issues are important here:

- Democratic institutions need careful nurturing, patience and institutional designs that maximise the benefits and ensure constant self-correction;
- Transfer of power in any form is painful and difficult. Local governments are only now taking roots after 60 years of independence. There is a natural tendency on the part of the state government to hold on to their turf, and resist empowerment of local governments, giving up power is not easy, and is usually resisted, The state should, therefore, be enabled to discover a new and vital role, even of local government become stronger and more vibrant. Political, economic and legal changes completely transformed the Centre's role *vis-à-vis* states, and yet while Union control has declined, its leadership and coordination role are more important than ever. Such a transformation in the role of state *vis-à-vis* local governments is decisive.
- Local government empowerment must ensure continuity and accountability. There cannot be abrupt change and wholesale extinction of existing of current practices overnight. A careful transition and utilisation of the strengths of the arrangements are important. Also, decentralised power should lead to greater efficacy and accountability, and not decentralised corruption and frustration.

9.18. Honorarium to Elected Representatives

The present system of honorarium given to members of village councils can be compared to honorarium given to elected representatives of Kerala state as follows:

Table 9.8: Honorarium of Elected Representatives in Kerala

Local Bodies	*Elected Representatives*
Gram (Village) Panchayat	President
	Vice President
	Standing Committee Chairman
	Members
Block Panchayat	President
	Vice President
	Standing Committee Chairman
	Members
District Panchayat	President
	Vice President
	Standing Committee Chairman
	Members
Municipality	Chairman
	Vice Chairman
	Standing Committee Chairman
	Members
Corporation	Mayor
	Deputy Mayor
	Standing Committee Chairman
	Members

Source: An introduction to Local Self Government in Kerala by Mariamma Sanu George, 2007.

The Kerala example is only an illustration. The questionnaire conducted to the VC members and others associated with village councils reveal the expected remunerations of village council members as follows.

Table 9.9: Expected Honorarium of Village Council Members

Local Bodies	*Elected Representatives*	*Perc respc*
Village Council & Local Council	VC President/ LC Chairman	30.60
		23.46
		20.40
	VC/LC Secretary	20.40
		20.40
		15.30
	VC/LC Members	18.36
		14.28
		14.28

Source: Fieldwork Questionnaire.

Other suggestions for VCP include—2,000 (10 per cent), 3,500 (six per cent), 6,000 (five per cent) and so on. Suggestions for VC Secretary include—2,500 (8.16 per cent), 3,000 (6.20 per cent), 2,400 (six per cent), 1,500 (seven per cent) and so on; and for VC members, suggestions were—3,000 (8.80 per cent), 3,500 (five per cent), 2,500 (five per cent) 1,500 (eight per cent), 4,500 (four per cent) and so on.

The present honorarium expended to members of village councils needs to be re-examined and appraised, and a practicable solution reach.

With local government being a State subject as per Schedule 7 of the Constitution, any legislation reforming the structure of local government has to be enacted at the state level. The task of the state is, therefore, to pass conformity Acts, which either introduce new legislation or amended existing Act to bring the State law into line with the rising aspiration of the people. Such legislation may follow the pattern of the discretionary provisions of 73rd and 74th constitutional amendments which are:

(1) Endow the Gram Sabha with powers and functions at the village level,

(2) Devolve powers and authority to local governments to enable them to function as institutions of self-government. In particular, it calls for the devolution of powers and responsibilities for the preparation of plans and implementation of schemes for development and social justice dealing with wide range of items,

(3) To pass legislation aimed at increasing the financial resources available to rural local bodies by increasing the latter's statutory taxation powers and providing for grants-in-aid from the state government.

Over the years, rural development in India including Mizoram came to be characterised by a proliferation of government schemes and programmes staffed by civil servants who were accountable only to their superiors in the administrative hierarchy, and at upper levels were motivated largely by career concerns. Under this, the increasing flow of funds through local bodies led to the emergence of collusive networks connecting bureaucrats, local and higher level elected representatives, and other members of dominant local elites.

The result was inefficiencies, leakages, and corruption associated with many government schemes undermining the legitimacy of the elected local bodies and wrecked disaster on the performance of various schemes. State legislation may try to remedy these malicious incursion into the administrative affairs of rural local bodies.

Tis report suggests that in spite of constitutional mandate for devolution, transfer of power, responsibilities, functional activities, finance and functionaries has not been achieved in real terms in many States. The overall reasons for the weaknesses of the process of devolution are now identified in Mizoram and elsewhere as follows:

- Lack of Political will of political parties for decentralisation,
- Lack of Public Awareness and vigilance,
- Lack of Orientation of Officials for working with Local Governments,
- Bureaucracies have not learnt to work with the elected Local Governments,
- Decision-making not yet broad-based,
- Rules and procedures not adequately framed.

These are empirically evidenced reality in Mizoram- Lack of Acts, Rules and Procedures; Lack of Political Will of politicians and bureaucrats; Lack of Public awareness—are all very real. It is also a truism in the case of Mizoram (as illustrated by the functioning of Gram Sabha) that we shall be able to overcome the above hurdles once political will is established among the leaders and proper awareness divulged in the public. Wide publicity for awareness people.

APPENDICES

APPENDIX I
THE CONSTITUTION (SEVENTY-THIRD AMENDMENT) ACT, 1992

Statement of the Objects abd Reasons appended to the Constitution (Seventy-Second Amendment) Bill, 1991 which was enacted as the Constitution (73rd Amendment) Act, 1992.

STATEMENT OF OBJECTS AND REASONS

1. Though the Panchayati Raj institutions have been in existence for a long time, it has been observed that these institutions have not been able to acquire the status and dignity of viable and responsive people's bodies due to a number of reasons including absence of regular elections, prolonged suppressions, insufficient representations of weaker section like Scheduled Castes, Scheduled Tribes and Women, inadequate devolution of powers and lack of financial resources.
2. Article 40 of the Constitution which enshrines one of the Directive Principles of State Policy lays down that the State shall take steps to organise village panchayats and endow them with such powers and authority as may be necessary to enable them to function as units of self-government. In the light of the experience in the last forty years and in view of the short-comings which have been observed, it is considered that there is an imperative need to enshrine in the Constitution certain basic and essential features of Panchayati Raj Institutions to impart certainty, continuity and strength to them.

3. Accordingly, it is proposed to add a new Part relating to Panchayats in the Constitution to provide for among other things, Gram Sabha in a village or group of villages; constitution of Panchayats at village and other level or levels; direct elections to all seats in Panchayats at the village and intermediate level, if any, and to the offices of Chairpersons of Panchayats at such levels; reservation of seats for the Scheduled Castes and Scheduled tribes in proportion to their population for membership of Panchayats and office of Chairpersons in Panchayats at each level; reservation of not less than one-third of the seats for women; fixing tenure of five years for Panchayats and holding elections within a period of six months in the event of supersession of any Panchayat; disqualifications for membership of Panchayats; devolution by the State Legislature of powers and responsibilities upon the Panchayats with respect to the preparation of plans for economic developments and social justice and for the implementation of development schemes; sound finance of the Panchayats by securing authorisation from State Legislature for grants-in-aid to the Panchayats from the Consolidated Fund of the State, as also assignment to, or appropriation by, the Panchayats of the revenue of designated taxes, duties, tolls and fees; setting up of a Finance Commission within one year of the proposed amendment and thereafter every five years to review the financial position of Panchayats; auditing of accounts of the Panchayats' powers of State Legislatures to make provisions with respect to elections to Panchayats under the superintendendce, direction and control of the chief Electoral officer of the State; application of the provisions of the said Part to Union Territories; excluding certain States and areas from the application of the provisions of the said Part; continuance of the existing laws and Panchayats until one year from the commencement of the proposed amendment and barring interference by courts in electoral matters relating to Panchayats.

4. The Bill seeks to achieve the aforesaid objectives.

New Delhi. G. Venkat Swamy

The 10th September, 1991

THE CONSTITUTION (SEVEMTY-THIRD AMENDMENT0 ACT, 1992 (20th April, 1993).

An Act further to amend the Constitution of India.

Be it enacted by Parliament in the Forty-third Year of the Republic of India as follows:

1. Short title and commencement: (1) This Act may be called the Constitution (Seventy-third Amendment) Act, 1992. (2) It shall come into force on such date as the Centre Government may, by notification in the Official Gazeete, appoint.
2. Insertion of new Part IX: After Part VIII of the Constitution, the following Part shall be inserted, namely:

PART IX
THE PANCHAYATS

243. Definition: In this Part, unless the context otherwise requires:

(a) "district" means a district in a State;

(b) "Gram Sabha" means a body consisting of persons registered in the electoral rolls relating to a village comprised within the area of Panchayat at the village level;

(c) "Intermediate level" means a level between the village and district levels specified by the Governor of a State by public notification to be the intermediate level for the purposes of this Part;

(d) "Panchayat" means an institution (by whatsoever name called) of self-government constituted under article 243B, for the rural areas;

(e) "Panchayat area" means the territorial area of a Panchayat;

(f) "population" means the population as ascertained at the last preceding census of which the relevant figures have been published;

(g) "village" means a village specified by the Governor by public notification to be a village for the purposes of this Part and includes a group of villages so specified.

243A. Gram Sabha: A Gram Sabha may exercise such powers and perform such functions at the villagelevel as the legislature of a State may, by law, provide.

243B. Constitution of panchayats:

(1) There shall be constituted in every State, Panchayats at the village, intermediate and district levels in accordance with the provisions of the Part

(2) Notwithstanding anything in this clause(1), Panchayats at the intermediate level may not be constituted in a State having a population not exceeding twenty lakhs.

243C. Composition of Panchayats:

(1) Subject to the provisions of this Part, the Legislature of a State may, by law, make provisions with respect to the composition of Panchayats:

Provided that tha ratio between the population of the territorial area of a Panchayat to be filled by election shall, so far as practicable, be the same throughout the State.

(2) All the seats in a panchayat shall be filled by persons chosen by direct election from territorial constituencies in the Panchayat area and; for this purpose, each panchayat area shall be divided into territorial constituencies in such manner that the ratio between the population of each constituency and the number of seats allotted to it shall, so far as practicable, be the same throughout the Panchayat area.

(3) The Legislature of a State may, by law, provide for the representation—

(a) of the Chairpersons of the Panchayats at the village level, in the panchayats at the intermediate level or in the case of a State not having Panchayats at the intermediate level, in the Panchayats at the district level;

(b) of the Chairpersons of the panchayats at the intermediate level, in the Panchayats at the district level;

(c) of the members of the House of the People and the members of the Legislatiuve Assembly of the State representing constituencies which comprise wholly or partly a Panchayat area at a level other than the village level, in such Panchayat;

(d) of the members of the Council of States and the members

of the Legislative Council of the State, where they are registered as electors within—

(i) a Panchayat area at the intermediate level, in Panchayat at the intermediate level;

(ii) a Panchayat area at the district level, in Panchayat at the district level.

(4) The Chairperson of a panchayat and other members of a Panchayat whether or not chosen by direct election from territorial constituencies in the Panchayat area shall have the right to vote in the meetings of the Panchayats.

(5) The Chairperson of—

(a) a Panchayat at the village level shall be elected in such manner as the Legislature of a State may, by law, provide; and

(b) a Panchayat at the intermediate level or district level shall be elected by, and from amongst, the elected members thereof.

243D. Reservation of Seats:

(1) Seats shall be reserved for:

(a) The Scheduled Castes; and

(b) The Scheduled tribes,

In every Panchayat and the number of seats of reserved shall bear, as nearly as may be, the same proportion to the total number of seats to be filled by direct election in that Panchayat as the population of the Scheduled Castes in that Panchayat area or of the Scheduled tribes in that Panchayat area bears to the total population of that area and such seats may be allotted by rotation to different constituencies in a Panchayat.

(2) Not less than one-third of the total number of seats reserved under clause (1) shall be reserved for women belonging to the Scheduled Castes or, as the case may be, the Scheduled Tribes.

(3) Not less than one-third (including the number of seats reserved for women belonging to the Scheduled Castes and the Scheduled tribes) of the total number of seats to be filled by direct election in every Panchayat shall be reserved for women and such seats may be allotted by rotation to different constituencies in a panchayat.

(4) The offices of the Chairpersons in the Panchayats at the village or any other level shall be reserved for the Scheduled Castes, the Scheduled tribes and women in such manner as the Legislature of a State may, by law, provide:

Provided that the number of offices of Chairpersons reserved for the Scheduled Castes and the Scheduled Tribes in the Panchayats at each level in any State shall bear, as nearly as may be, the same proportion to the total number of such offices in the Panchayats at each level as the population of the Scheduled Castes in the State or of the Scheduled Tribes in the State bears to the total population of the State:

Provided further that not less than one-third of the total number of offices of Chairpersons in the Panchayats at each level shall be reserved for women:

Provided also that the number of offices reserved under this clause shall be allotted by rotation to different Panchayats at each level.

(5) The reservation of seats under clause (1) and (2) and the reservation of offices of Chairpersons (other than the reservation for women) under clause(4) shall cease to have effect on the expiration of the period specified in article 334.

(6) Nothing in this Partshall prevent the Legislature of a State from making any provision for reservation of seats in any Panchayat or offices of Chairpersons in the Panchayats at any level in favour of Backward class of citizens.

243E. Duration of Panchayats, etc.

(1) Every Panchayat, unless sooner dissolved under any law for the time being in force, shall continue for five years from the date appointed for its first meeting andf no longer.

(2) No amendment of any law for the time being in force shall have the effect of causing dissolution of a Panchayat at any level, which is functioning immediately before such amendment, till the expiration of its duration specified in clause (1).

(3) An election to constitute a Panchayat shall be completed,

(a) before the expiry of its duration specified in clause (1);

(b) before the expiration of a period of six months from the date of its dissolution;

Provided that where the rermainder of the period for which the dissolved Panchayat would have continued is less than six months, it shall not be necessary to hold any election under this clause for constituting the Panchayat for such period.

(4) A Panchayat constituted upon the dissolution of a Panchayat before the expiration of its duration shall continue only for the remainder of the period for which the dissolved Panchayat would have continued under clause (1) had it not been so dissolved.

243F. Disqualifications for Membership:

(1) A person shall be disqualified for being chosen as, and for being, a member of a Panchayat:

(a) If he is so disqualified by or under any law for the time being in force for the purposes of elections to the Legislature of the State concerned;

Provided that no person shall be disqualified on the ground that he is less than twemty-five years of age, if he has attained the age of twenty-one years;

(b) If he is so disqualified by or under any law made by the Legislature of the State.

(2) If any question arises as to whether a member of a Panchayat has become subject to any of the disqualifications mentioned in clause (1), the question shall be referred for the decision such authority and in such manner as the Legislature of a State may, by law, provide.

243G. Powers, Authority and Responsibilities of Panchayats:

Subject to the provisions of this constitution, the legislature of a State may, by law, endow the panchayats with such powers and authority as may be necessary to enable them to function as institutions of self-government and such law may contain provisions for the devolution of powers and responsibilities upon Panchayats at the appropriate level, subject to such conditions as may be specified therein, with respect to—

(a) the preparation of plans for economic development and social justice;

(b) the implementation of schemes for economic development and social justice as may be entrusted tothem including those in relation to the matters listed in the Eleventh Schedules.

243H. Powers to Improve Taxes by, and Funds of, the Panchayats:

The Legislature of a State may, by law—

(a) authorise a Panchayat to levy, collect and appropriate such taxes, duties, tolls and fees in accordance with such procedure and subject to such limits;

(b) assign to a Panchayat such taxes, duties, tolls and fees levied and collected by the state government for such purposes and subject to such conditions and limits;

(c) provide for making such grants-in-aid to the Panchayats from the Consolidated Fund of the State; and

(d) provide for constitution of such Funds for crediting all moneys received, respectively, by or on behalf of the Panchayats and also for the withdrawal of such moneys therefrom, as may be specified in the law.

243-I. Constitution of Finance Commission to Review Financial Position:

(1) The Governor of a State shall, as soon as may be within one year from the commencement of the Constitution (Seventy-third Amendment) Act, 1992, and thereafter at the expiration of every fifth year, constitute a Finance Commission to review the financial position of the Panchayats and to make recommendations to the Governor as to—

(a) the principles which should govern—

(i) the distribution between the State and the Panchayats of the net proceeds of the taxes, duties, tolls and fees levliable by the State, which may be divided between them under this Part and the allocation between the Panchayats at all levels of their respective shares of such proceeds;

(ii) the determination of the taxes, duties, tolls and fees which may be assigned to, or appropriated by, the Panchayat;

(iii) the grants-in-aid to the Panchayats from the Consolidated Fund of the State;

(b) the measures needed to improve the financial position of the panchayats;

(c) any other matter referred to the Finance Commission by the Governor in the interests of sound finance of the Panchayats.

(2) The Legislature of a State may, by law, provide for the composition of the commission, the qualifications which shall be requisite for appointment as members thereof and the manners in which they shall be selected.

(3) The Commission shall determine their procedure and shall have such powers in the performance of their functions as the Legislature of the State may, by law, confer on them.

(4) The Governor shall cause every recommendation made by the commission under this article together with an explanatory memorandum as to the action taken thereon to be laid before the Legislature of the State.

243J. Audit of Accounts of Panchayats:

The Legislature of a State may, by law, make provisions with respect to the maintenance of accounts by the Panchayats and the auditing of such accounts.

243K. Elections to the Panchayats:

(1) The superintendence, direction and control of the preparation of electoral rolls for, and the conduct of, all elections to the Panchayats shall be vested in a state election commission consisting of a state election commissioner to be appointed by the Governor.

(2) Subject to the provisions of any law made by the Legislature of a State, the conditions of service and tenure of office of the state election commissioner shall be such as the Governor may by rule determine:

Provided that the state election commissioner shall not be removed from his office except in like manner and on the like grounds as a Judge of a High Court and the conditions of service of the state election commissioner shall not be varied to his disadvantage after his appointment.

(3) The Governor of a State shall, when so requested by the Statre Election Commission, make available to the state election commission such staff as may be necessary for the discharge of

the functions conferred on the state election commission by clause(1).

(4) Subject to the provisions of this Constitution, the Legislature of a State may, by law, make provision with respect to all maters relating to, or in connection with, elections to the Panchayats.

243L. Application to Union Territories:

The provisions of this Part shall apply to the Union territories and shall, in their application to a Union territory, have effect as if the references to the Governor of a State were references to the Adminstrator of the Union territory appointed under article 239 and references to the Legislature or the Legislative Assembly of a State were references, in relation to a Union territory having a Legislative Assembly, to that Legislative Assembly:

Provided that the President may, by public notification, direct that the provisions of this Part shall apply to any Union territory or part thereof subject to such exceptions and modifications as he may specify in the notification.

243M. Part not to Apply to Certain Areas:

(1) Nothing in this Part shall apply to the Scheduled Areas referred to in clause (1), and the tribal areas referred to in clause (2), of article 244.

(2) Nothing in this part shall apply to—

(a) the State of Nagaland, Meghalaya and Mizoram;

(b) the Hill Areas in the State of Manipur for which District Councils exist under any law for the time being in force.

(3) Nothing in this part—

(a) relating to Panchayats at the district level shall apply to the hill areas of the District of Darjeeling in the State of West Bengal for which Darjeeling Gorkha Gill Council exists under any law for the time being in force;

(b) shall be construed to affect the functions and powers of the Darjeeling Gorkha Hill Council constituted under such law.

(4) Notwithstanding anything in this Constitution—

(a) the Legislature of a State referred to in sub-clause (a) of clause (2) may, by law, extend this Part to that State, except the areas, if any, referred to in clause (1), if the Legislative Assembly of that State passes a resolution to that effect by a majority of the total membership of that House and by a majority of not less than two-thirds of the members of that House present and voting;

(b) Parliament may, by law, extend the provisions of this part to the Scheduleed Areas and the tribal areas referred to in clause (1) subject to such exceptions and modifications as may be specified in such law, and no such law shall be deemed to be an amendment of this Constitution for the purposes of article 368.

243N. Continuattion of Existing Laws and Panchayats:

Notwithstanding anything in this part, any provision of any law relating to Panchayats in force in a State immediately before the commencement of the Constitution (Seventy-third Amendment) Act, 1992, which is inconsistent with the provision of this Part, shall continue to be in force until amended or repealed by a competent Legislature or other competent authority or until the expiration of one year from such commencement, whichever is earlier:

Provided that all the Panchayats existing immediately before such commencement shall continue till the expiration of their duration, unless sooner dissolved by a resolution passed to that effect by the Legislative Assembly of that State or, in the case of a State having a Legislative Council, by each House of the Legislature of that State.

243-O. Bar to Interference by Courts in Electoral Matters:

Nothwithstanding anything in this Constitution—

(a) the validity of any law relating to the delimitation of constituencies or the allotment of seats to such constituencies, made or purporting to be made under article 243K, shall not be called in question in any court;

(b) no election to any Panchayat shall be called in question except by an election petition presented to such authority and in such manner as is provided for by or under any law made by the Legislature of a State:

Constitution, after sub-clause (b), the following sub-clause shall be inserted, namely:—

"(bb) the measures needed to augment the Consolidated Fund of a State to supplement the resources of the panchayats in the State on the basis of the recommendations made by the Finance Commission of the State".

Constitution, the following Schedule shall be added, namely:—

"ELEVENTH SCHEDULE (Article 243G).

1. Agriculture, including agricultural extension.
2. Land improvement,implementation of land reforms, land consolidation and soil conservation.
3. Minor irrigation, water management and waterswhed development.
4. Animal husbandry, dairying and poultry.
5. Fisheries.
6. Social Forestry and farm forestry.
7. Minor forest produce.
8. Small scale industries, including food processing industries.
9. Khadi, village and cottage industries.
10. Rural Housing.
11. Drinking water.
12. Fuel and Fodder.
13. Roads, culverts, bridges, ferries, waterways and other means of communication.
14. Rural electrification, including distribution of electricity.
15. Non-conventional energy sources.
16. Poverty alleviation Programme.
17. Education, including primary and secondary schools.
18. Technical training and vocational education.
19. Adult and non-formal education.
20. Libraries.
21. Cultural activities.
22. Markets and fairs.
23. Health and sanitation, including hospitals, primary health centres and dispensaries.
24. Family Welfare.
25. Women and child welfare.
26. Social Welfare, including welfare of the handicapped and mentally retarded.

27. Welfare of the weaker sections, and in particular, of the Scheduled castes and the Scheduled Tribes.
28. Public Distribution System.
29. Maintenance of Community Assets.

APPENDIX II
THE CONSTITUTION (SEVENTY-FOURTH AMENDMENT) ACT, 1992

Statement of Objects and Reasons appended to the Constitution (73rd Amendment) Bill, 1991 which was enacted as the Constitution (74th Amendment) Act, 1992.

STATEMENT OF OBJECTS AND REASONS

In many States local bodies have become weak and ineffective on account of a variety of reasons, including the failure to hold regular elections, prolonged supersessions and inadequate devolutiuon of powers and functions. As a result, Urban Local Bodies are not able to perform effectively as vibrant democratic units of self-government.

2. Having regard to these inadequacies, it is considered necessary that provisions relating to Urban Local Bodies are incorporated in the Constitution particularly for—

(i) putting on a firmer footing the relationship between the state government and the urban Local Bodies with respect to—

  (a) the functions and taxation powers; and

  (b) arrangements for revenue sharing;

(ii) Ensuring regular conduct of elections;

(iii) ensuring timely elections in the case of supersessions; and

(iv) providing adequate representation for the weaker sections like Scheduled Castes, Scheduled Tribes and women.

3. Accordingly, it is proposed to add a new Part rerlating to the Urban Local Bodies in the Constitution to provide for—

  (a) constitution of three types of Municipalities:

(i) Nagar panchayats for areas in transition from rural area to urban area;

(ii) Municipal Councils for small urban areas;

(iii) Muncipal Corporation for larger urban areas.

The broad criteria for specifying the said areas is being provided in the proposed article 243-O;

(b) Composition of Municipalities, which will be decided by the Legislature of a State, having the following features:

(i) persons to be chosen by direct elections;

(ii) representation of Chairpersons of Committees, if any, at ward or other levels in the Municipalities;

(iii) representation of persons having special knowledge or experience of Municipal Administration in Municipalities (without voting rights);

(c) election of chairpersons of a Municipality in the manner specified in the State law;

(d) constitution of Committees at ward level or other level or levels within the territorial area of a Municipality as may be provided in the Statre law;

(e) reservation of seats in every Municipality—

(i) for Scheduled Castes and Scheduled tribes in proportion to their population of which not less than one-third shall be for women;

(ii) for women which shall not be less than one-third of the total number of seats;

(iii) in favour of backward class of citizens if so provided by the Legislature of the State;

(iv) for Scheduled Castes, Scheduled Tribes and women in the office of Chairpersons as may be specified in the State law;

(f) fixed tenure of five years for the Municiplity and re-election within six months of end of tenure. If a Municipality is dissolved before expiration of its duration, elections to be held within a period of six months of its dissolution;

(g) devolution by the State Legislature of powers and responsibilities upon the Municipalities with respect to preparation of plans for economic development and social justice, and for the implementation of development schemes as may be required to enable them to function as institution of self-govertnment;

(h) levy of taxes and duties by Municipalities, assigning of such taxes and duties to Municipalites by state governments and for making grants-in-aid by the State to the Municipalities as may be provided in the State law;

(i) a Finance Commission to review the financés of the Municipalities and to recommend principles for—

(1) determining the taxes which may be assigned to the Municipalities;

(2) Sharing of taxes between the State and Municipalities;

(3) grants-in-aid to the Municipalities from the Consolidated Fund of the State;

(j) audit of accounts of the Municipal Corporations by the Comptroller and Auditor-General of India and laying of reports before the Leghislature of the State and the Municipal Corporation concerned;

(k) making of law by a State Legislature with respect to elections to the Municipalities to be conducted under the superintendence, direction and control of the chief electoral officer of the State;

(l) application of the provisions of the Bill to any Union territory or part thereof with such modifications as may be specified by the President;

(m) exempting Scheduled areas referred to in clause (1), and tribal areas referred to in clause (2), of article 244, from the application of the provisions of the Bill. Extension of provisions of the Bill to such areas may be done by Parliament by law;

(n) disqualifications for membership of a Municiplaities;

(o) bar of juriusdiction of Courts in matters relating to elections to the Municipalities.

4. The Bill seeks to achieve the aforesaid objectives.

New Delhi Sheila Kaul

The 11th September, 1991.

THE CONSTITUTION (SEVENTY-FOURTH AMENDMENT) ACT, 1992 (20th April, 1993)

An Act further to amend the Consitution of India

Be it enacted by Parliament in the Forty-third Year of the Republic of India as follows:

1. Short Title and Commencement:

(1) This Act may be called the Constitution (Seventy-fourth Amendment) Act, 1992.

(2) It shall come into force on such date as the Centre Government may, by notification in the Official Gazette, appoint

2. Insertion of New Part IXA: After Part IX of the Constitution, the following Part shall be inserted, namely:—

PART IXA

THE MUNICIPALITIES

243P. Definition:

In this Part, unless the contex otherwise requires:

(a) "Committee" means a Committee constituted under article 243S'

(b) "district" means a district in a State;

(c) "Metropolitan area" means an area having a population of ten lakhs or more, comprised in one or more districts and consisting of two or more Municipalities or Panchayats or other contiguous areas, specified by the Governor by public notification to be a Metropolitan area for the purposes of this Part;

(d) "Municipal area" means the territorial area of a Municipality as is notified by the Governor;

(e) "Municipality" means an institution of self-government constituted under article 243G;

(f) "Panchayat" means a Panchayat constituted under article 243B;

(g) "Population" means the population as ascertained at the last preceding census of which the relevant figures have been published.

243G. Constitution of Municipalities:

(1) There shall be constituted in every State,

(a) a Nagar Panchayat (by whatever name called) for a transitional area, that is to say, an area in transition from a rural area to an urban area;

(b) a Municipal Council for a smaller urban area; and

(c) a Municipal Corporation for a larger urban area,

In accordance with the provisions of this Part:

Provided that a Municipality under this clause may not be constituted in such urban area or part thereof as the Governor may, having regard to the size of the area and the municipal services being provided or proposed to be provided by an industrial establishment in that area and such other factors as he may deem fit, by public notification, specify to be an industrial township

(2) In this article, "a transitional area", " a smaller urban area" or "a larger urban area" means such area as the Governor may, having regard to the population of the area, the density of the population therein, the revenue generated for local administration, the per centage of employemt in non-agricultural activities, the economic importance or such other factors as he may dim fit, specify by public notification for the purposes of this Part.

243R. Composition of Municipalities:

(1) Save as provided in clause (2), all the seats in a Municipality shallbe filled by persons chosen by direct election from the territorial constituencies in the Municipal area and for this purpose each Municipal shall be divided into territorial constituencies to be known as wards.

(2) The Legislature of a State may, by law, provide—

(a) for the representation in a Municipality of—

(i) persons having special knowledge or experience in Municipal administration;

(ii) the members of the House of the People and the members of the Legislative Assembly of the State representing constituencies which comprise wholly or partl;y the Municipal area;

(iii) the members of the Council of States and the members of the Legislative Council of the State registered as electors within the Municipal area;

(iv) the Chairpersons of the Committee consatituted under clause (5) of article 243S;

Provided that the persons referred to in paragraph (i) shall not have the right to vote in the meetings of the Municipality;

(b) the manner of election of the Chairperson of a Municipality.

243S. Constitution and Composition of Wards Committees, etc.

(1) There shall be constituted Wards Committees, consisting of one or more wards, within the territorial area of a Municipality having a population of three lakhs or more.

(2) The Legislature of a State may, by law, make provision with respect to—

(a) the composition and the territorial area of a Wards Committee;

(b) the manner in which the seats in a Wards Committee shall be filled.

(3) A member of a Municipality representing a ward within the territorial area of the Wards Committee shall be a member of that Committee.

(4) Where a Wards Committee consists of—

(a) one ward, the member representing that ward in the Municipality; or

(b) two or more wards, one of the members representing such wards in the Municipality elected by the members of the Wards Committee, shall be the Chairperson of that Committee.

(5) Nothing in this article shall be deemed to prevent the Legislature of a State from making any provision for the constitution of Committees in addition to the Wards Committee.

243T. Reservation of Seats:

(1) Seats shall be reserved for the Scheduled Castes and the Scheduled Tribes in every Municipality and the number of seats so reserved shall bear, as nearly as may be, the same proportion to the total number of seats to be filled by direct election in that Municipality as the population of the Scheduled Castes in the Municipality area or of the Scheduled Tribes in the Municipal area bears to the total population of that area and such seats may be allotted by rotation to different constituencies in a Municipality.

(2) Not less than one-third of the total number of seats reserved under clause (1) shall be reserved for women belonging to the Scheduled Castes or, as the case may be, the Scheduled tribes.

(3) Not less than one-third (including the number of seats reserved for women belonging to the Scheduled Castes and the Scheduled Tribes) of the total number of seats to be filled by direct election in every Municipality shall be reserved for women and such seats may be allotted by rotation to different constituencies in a Municipality.

(4) The offices of Chairpersons in the Municipality shall be reserved for the Scheduled Castes, the Scheduled Tribes and women in such manner as the Legislature of a State may, by law, provide.

(5) The reservation of seats under clauses (1) and (2) and the reservation of offices of Chairpersons (other than the reservation for women) under clause (4) shall cease to have effect on the expiration of the period specified in article 334.

(6) Nothing in this Part shall prevent the Legislature of a State from making any provision for reservation of seats in any Municipality or offices of Chairpersons in the Municipalities in favour of backward class of citizens.

243U. Duration of Municipalities, etc.

(1) Every Municipality, unless sooner dissolved under any law for the time being in force, shall continue for five years from the date appointed for its first meeting and no longer:

Provided that a Municipality shall be given a reasonable opportunity of being heard before its dissolution.

(2) No amendment of any law for the time being in force shall have the effect of causing dissolution of a Municipality at any level, which is functioning immediately before such amendment, till the expiration of its duration specified in clause (1).

(3) An election to constitute a Municipality shall be completed,

(a) before the expiry of its duration specified in clause (1(;

(b) before the expiration of a period of six months from the date of dissolution:

Provided that where the remainder of the period for which the dissolved Municipality would have continued is less than six months, it shall not be necessary to hold any election under this clause for constituting the Municipality for such period.

(4) A Muncipality constituted upon the dissolution of a Municipality before the expiration of its duration shall continue only for the remainder of the period for which the dissolved Municipality would have continued under clause (1) had it not been so dissolved.

243V. Disqualifications for Membership:

(1) A person shall be disqualified for being chosen as, and for being, a member of a Municipality—

(a) if he is so disqualified by or under any law for the time being in force for the purposes of elections to the Legislature of the State concerned:

Provided that no person shall be disqualified on the ground that he is less than twenty-five years of age, if he has attained the age of twenty-one years;

(b) if he is so disqualified by or any law made by the Legislature of the State.

(2) If any question arises as to whether a member of a Municipality has become subject to any of the disqualifications mentioned in clause (1), the question shall be referred for the decision of such authority and in such manner as the Legislature of a State may,by law, provide.

243W. Powers, Authority and Responsibilities of Municipalities, etc.

Subjec to the provisions of this Constitution, the Legislature of a State may, by law, endow—

(a) the Municipalities with such powers and authority as may be necessary to enable them to function as institutions of self-government and such law may contain provisions for the devolution of powers and responsibilities upon Municipalities, subject to such conditions as may be specified therein, with respect to—

(i) the preparation of plans for economic development and social justice;

(ii) the performance of functions and the implementation of schemes as may be entrusted to them including those in relation to the matters listed in the Twelfth Schedule;

(b) the Committee with such powers and authority as may be necessary to enable them to carry out the responsibiolities conferred upon them including those in relation to the matters listed in the Twelfth Schedule.

243X. Power to Impose Taxes by, and Funds of, the Municipalities:

The Legislature of a State may, by law:—

(a) authorise a Municipality to levy, collect and approipriate such taxes, duties, tolls and fees in accordance with such procedure and subject to such limits;

(b) assign to a Municipality such taxes, duties, tolls and fees levied and collected by the state government for such purposes and subject to such conditions and limits;

(c) provide for making such grants-in-aid to the Municiplaities from the Consolidated Fund of rhe State; and

(d) provide for constitution of such Funds for crediting all moneys received, respectively, by or on behalf of the Municipalities and also for the withdrawal of such moneys therefrom, as may be specified in the law.

243Y. Finance Commission:

(1) The Finance Commission constituted under article 243-I shall also review the financial position of the Municipalities and make recommendations to the Governor as to—

(a) the principles which should govern—

(i) the distribution between the State and the Municipalities of the net proceeds of the taxes, duties, tolls and fees leviable by the State, which may be divided between them under this Part and the allocation between the Municipalities at all levels of their respective shares of such proceeds;

(ii) the determination of the taxes, duties,tolls and fees which may be assigned to, or appropriated by, the Municipalities;

(iii) the grants-in-aid to the Municipalities from the Consolidated Fund of the State;

(b) the measures needed to improve the financial position of the Municipalities;

(c) any other matter referred to the Finance Commission by the Governor in the interests of sound finance of the Municipalities.

(2) The Governor shall cause every recommendation made by the Commission under this article together with an explanatory memorandum as to the action taken thereon to be laid before the Legislature of the State.

243. Z. Audit of Accounts of Municipalities:

The Legislature of a State may, by law, make preovisions with respect to the maintenance of accounts by the Municipalities and the auditing of such accounts.

243A. Eledction to the Municipalities:

(1) The superintendence, direction and control of the preparation of electoral rolls for, and the conduct of, all elections to the Municipalities shall be vested in the state election commission referred to in article 243K.

(2) Subject to the provisions of this Constitution, the Legisdlature of a State may, by law, make provision with resopect to all matters relating to, or in connection with, elections to the Municipalities..

243ZB. Application to Union Territories:

The provisions of this Part shall apply to the Union territories and shall, in their application to a Union territory, have effect as if the references to the Governor of a State were references to the Administrator of the Union territory appointed under article 239 and references to the Legislature of the Legislative Assembly of a State were references in relation to a Union territory having a Legislative Assembly, to that Legislative Assembly.

Provided that the President may, by public notification, direct that the provisions of this Part shall apply to any Union territory or part thereof subject to such exceptions and modifications as he may specify in the notification.

243ZC. Part not to Apply to certain Areas:

(1) Nothing in this Part shall apply to the Scheduled Areas

referred to in clause (1), and the tribal areas referred to in clause(2), of article 244.

(2) Nothing in this part shall be construed to affect the functions and powers of the Darjeeling Gorkha Hill Council constituted under any law for the time being in force for the hill areas of the Darjeeling in the State of West Bengal.

(3) Notwithstanding anything in this Constitution, Parliament may, by law, extend the provisions of this part to the Scheduled Areas and the tribal areas referred to in clause (1) subject to such exceptions and modifications as may be specified in such law, and no such law shall be deemed to be an amendment of this Constitution for the purposes of article 368.

243ZD. Committee for District Planning:

(1) There shall be constituted in every State at the district level a District Planning Committee to consodidate the plans prepared by the Panchayats and the Municipalities in the district and to prepare a draft development plan for the district as a whole.

(2) The Legislature of a State may, by law, make provision with respect to—

(a) the composition of the District Planning Commission;

(b) the manner in which the seats in such Committee shall be filled;

Provided that not less than four-fifths of the total number of members of such Committee shall be elected by, and from amongst, the elected members of the Panchayat at the district level and of the Municipalities in the district in proportion to the ratio between the population of the rural areas and of the urban areas in the district;

(c) the functions relating to district planning which may be assigned to such Committees;

(d) the manner in which the Chairpersons of such committees shall be chosen.

(3) Every District Planning Committee shall, in preparing the draft development plan:—

(a) have regard to—

(i) matters of common interest between the Panchayats and

the Municipalities including spatial planning, sharing of water and other physical and natural resources, the integrated development of infrastructure and environmental conservation;

(ii) the extent and type of available resources whether financial or otherwise;

(b) consult such institutions and organisations as the Governor may, by order, specify.

(4) The Chairperson of every District Planning Committee shall forward the development plan, as recommended by such Committee, to the Government of the State.

243ZE. Committee for Metropolitan Planning:

(1) There shall be constituted in every Metropolitan area a Metropolitan Planning Committee to prepare a draft development plan for the Metropolitan area as a whole.

(2) The Legislature of a State may, by law, make provision with respect to—

(a) the composition of the Metropolitan Planning Committee;

(b) the manner in which the seats in such Committee shall be filled:

Provided that not less than two-thirds of the members of such Committee shall be elected by, and from amongts, the elected members of the Municipalities and Chairpersons of the Panchayats in the Metropolitan area in proportion to the ratio between the population of the Municipalities and of the Panchayats in that area;

(c) the representation in such committees of the Government of India and the Government of the State and of such organisations and institutions as may be deemed necessary for carrying out the functions assigned to such Committees;

(d) the functions relating to planning and coordination for the Metropolitan area which may be assigned to such Committees;

(e) the manner in which the Chairpersons of such Committees shall be chosen.

(3) Every Metropolitan Planning Committee shall, in preparing the draft development plan—

(a) have regard to—

(i) the plans prepared by the Municipalities and the Panchayats in the Metropolitan area;

(ii) matters of common interest between the Municipalities and the Panchayats, including co-ordiated spatial planning of the area; sharing of water and other physical and natural resources, the integrated development of infrastructure and environmental conservation;

(iii) the overall objectives and priorities set by the Government of India and the Government of the State;

(iv) the extent and nature of investments likely to be made in the Metropolitan area by agencies of the Government of India and of the State and other available resources whether financial or otherwise;

(b) consult such institutions and organisations as the Governor may, by order, specify.

(4) The chairperson of every Metropolitan Planning Committee shal forward the development plan, as recommended by such committee, to the Government of the State.

243ZF. Consinuance of Existing Laws and Muncipalities:

Notwithstanding anything in this Part, any provision of any law relating to Municipalities in force in a State immediately before the commencement of the Constitution (Seventy-fourth Amendment) Act, 1992, which is inconsistent with the provisions of this Part, shall continue to be in force until amended or repealed by a competent Legislature or other competent authority or until the expiration of one year from such commencement, whichever is earlier;

Provided that all the Municipalities existing immediately before such commencement shall continue till the expiration of their duration, unless sooner dissolved by a resolution passed to that effect by the Legislative Assembly of that State or, in the case of a State having a Legislative Council, by each House of the Legislature of that State.

243ZG. Bar to Interference by Courts in Electoral Matters:

Notwithstanding anything in this Constitution—

(a) the validity of any law relating to the delimitation of constituencies or the allotment of seats to such constituencies, made or purporting to be made under article 243ZA shall not be called in question in any court;

(b) no election to any Municipality shall be called in question except by an election petition presented to such authority and in such manner as is provided for by or under any law made by the Legislature of a State.

3. Amendment of article 280:

In clause (3) of article 280 of the Constitution, sub-clause (c) shall be relettered as sub-clause (d) as so relettered, the following sub-clause shall be inserted, namely—

"(c) the measures needed to augment the Consolidated Fund of a State to supplement the resources of the Municipalities in the State on the basis of recommendations made by the Finance Commission of the State,".

4. Addition of Twelfth Schedule:

After the eleventh Schedule to the Constitution, the following Schedule shall be added, namely—

"TWELFTH SCHEDULE

(Article 243W)

1. Urban planning including town planning.
2. Regulation of land-use and construction of buildings.
3. Planning fo economic and sical development.
4. Roads and bridges.
5. Water supply for domestic,industrial and commercial purposes.
6. Public health, sanitation conservancy and solid waste management.
7. Fire Services.
8. Urban forestry, protection of the environment and promotion of ecological aspects.
9. Safeguarding the interests of weaker sections of society including the handicapped and mentally retarded.
10. Slum improvement and upgradation.
11. Urban poverty alleviation.

12. Provision of urban amenities and facilities such as parks, gardens, playgrounds.
13. Promotion of cultural, educational and aesthetic aspects.
14. Burial and burial grounds; cremations, cremation grounds and electric crematoriums.
15. Cattle ponds; prevention of cruelty to animals.
16. Vital statistics including registration of births and deaths.
17. Public amenities including street lighting, parking lots, bus stops and public conveniences.
18. Regulation of slaughter houses and tanneries.

APPENDIX III
THE PROVISIONS OF THE PANCHAYATS (EXTENSION TO THE SCHEDULED AREAS) ACT, 1996

(Came into force on the 24th December, 1996)

(An Act to provide for the extension of the provisions of Part IX of the Constitution relating to the Panchayats to the Scheduled Areas).

Be it enacted by Parliament in the Forty-seventh Year of the Republic of India as follows:

Short title

1. This Act may be called the Provisions of the Panchayats (Extension to the Scheduled Areas) Act, 1996.

Definition

2. In this Act, unless the context otherwise required,- "Scheduled Areas" means the Scheduled Areas as referred to in clause(1) of Article 244 of the Constitution.

Extension of Part IX of the Constitution

3. The provisions of Part IX of the Constitution relating to Panchayats are hereby extended to the Scheduled Areas subject to such exceptions and modifications as are provided in Section 4.

Exceptions and Modifications to Part IX of the Constitution

4. Notwithsatnding anything contained under Part IX of the Constitution, the Legislature of a State shall not make any law under that Part which is inconsistent with any of the following features, namely:—

(a) a State legislation on the Panchayats that may be made shall be in consonance with the customary law, social and religious practices and traditional management practices of community resources;

(b) a village shall ordinarily consist of a habitation or a groupo of habitations or a hamlet or a group of hamlets comprising a community and managing its affairs in accordance with traditions and customs;

(c) every village shall have a Gram Sabha consisting of persons whose names are included in the electoral rolls for the Panchayat at the village level;

(d) every Gram Sabha shall be competent to safeguard and preserve the traditions and customs of the people, their cultural identity, community resources and the customary mode of dispute resolution;

(e) every Gram Sabha shall—

(i) approve of the plans, programmes and projects for social and economic development before such plans, Programmes and projects are taken up for implementation by the Panchayat at the village level;

(ii) be responsible for the identification or selection of persons as beneficiaries under the poverty alleviation and other programmes;

(f) every Panchayat at the village level shall be required to obtain from Gram Sabha a certification of utilisation of funds by that Panchayat for the plans, programmes and projects referred to in clause(e);

(g) the reservation of seats in the Scheduled Areas at every Panchayat shall be in proportion to the population of the communities in that Panchayat for whom reservation is sought to be given under Part IX of the Constitution:

Provided that the reservation for that Scheduled Tribes shall not be less than one-half of the total number of seats;

Provided further that all seats of Chairpersons of Panchayats at all levels shall be reserved for the Scheduled Tribes;

(h) the state government may nominate persons belonging to such Scheduled Tribes as have no representation in the Panchayat at the immediate level or the Panchayat at the district level:

Provided that such nomination shall not exceed one-tenth of the total members to be elected in that Panchayat;

(i) the Gram Sabha or the Panchayats at the appropriate level shall be consulted before making the acquisition of land in the Scheduled Areas for development projects and before re-setling or rehabilitating persons effected by such projects in the Scheduled Areas; the actual planning and implementation of the projects in the Scheduled Areas shall be coordinated at the State level;

(j) planning and management of minor water bodies in the Scheduled Areas shall be entrusted to Panchayats at the appropriate level;

(k) the recommendations of the Gram Sabha or the Panchayats at the appropriate level shall be made mandatory prior to grant of prospecting licence or mining lease for minor minerals in the Scheduled Areas;

(l) the prior recommendation of the Gram Sabha or the Panchayats at the appropriate level shall be made mandatory for grant of concession for the exploitation of minor minerals by auction;

(m) while endowing Panchayats in the Scheduled Areas with such powers and authority as may be necessary to enable them to function as institutions of self-government, a State Legislature shall ensure that the Panchayats at the appropriate level and the Gram Sabha are endowed specifically with—

(i) the power to enforce prohibition or to regulate or restrict the sale and consumption of any intoxication;

(ii) the ownership of minor forest produce;

(iii) the power to prevent alienation of land in the Scheduled Areas and to take appropriate action to restore any unlawfully alienated land of a Scheduled Tribes;

(iv) the power to manage village markets by whatever name called;

(v) the power to exercise control pver money lending to the Scheduled Tribes;

(vi) the power to exercise control over institutions and functionaries in all social sectors;

(vii) the power to control over local plans and resources for such plans including tribal sub-plans;

(n) the State Legislations that may endow Panchayats with powers and authority as may be necessary to enable them to function as institutions of self-government shall contain safeguards to ensure that Panchayats at the higher level do not assume the powers and authority of any Panchayat at the lower level or of the Gram Sabha;

(o) the State Legislature shall endeavour to follow pattern of the Sixth Schedule to the Constitution while designing the administrative arrangements in the Panchayats at the district levels in the Scheduled Areas.

Continuance of existing laws on Panchayats:

5.Notwithstanding anything in Part IX of the Constitution with exceptions and modifications made by this Act, any provision of any law relating to Panchayats in force in the Scheduled Areas, immediately before the date on which this Act receives the assent of the President, which is inconsistent with the provisions of Part IX with such exceptions and modifications shall continue to be in force until amended or repealed by a competent Legislature or other competent authority or until the expiration of one year from the date on which this Act receives the assent of the President;

Provided that all the Panchayats existing immediately before such date shall continue till the expiration of their duration unless sooner dissolved by a resolution passed to that effect by the Legislative Assembly of that State or, in the case of a State having Legislative Council, by each House of the Legislature of that State.

K.L. Mohanpuria

Secy. to The Government of India

APPENDIX IV

Amendments Proposed in the PESA Act

Sl.No.	*Reason for Amendment*	*Proposed Amendme*
1.	Some terms used in the Act have not been defined in Section 2, which has resulted in lack of implementation in keeping with the spirit of the Act	The following defini **Section 2** of the Act **(ii) Community** resources include la and other resources domain of the comm **(iii) Consultation**: mandatory consulta requisite informatior shall be binding on t unless modified or r recorded in writing. **(iv) Panchayat** Panchayat at appr lowest tier of Panch particular function particular rescource
2.	Section 4 stipulates that the Legislature of a State shall not make any law which is inconsistent with the features of PESA. This formulation does not clearly state the rights of the Gram Sabha and panchayats. It needs to be made	It is proposed that r under PESA may b The wording in Sec changed to: 'Notwithsatding any or any other law in fc (i)the following shall powers entrusted tc Panchayat at the ap (ii)the Legislature of

Sl.No.	*Reason for Amendment*	*Proposed Amendme*
5.		(ii)the Gram Sabha may, if so supporte majority of each constitute a Pargan existing, inform th writing about its e Parishad shall cor representatives of e Gram Sabha.
6.	There is need to explicitly state that the Gram Panchayat or any other village level committee will function under the overall superiuntendence and control of the Gram Sabha	The following may b (i) The Gram S Standing/ad hoc Cc their respective resp the members. (ii) The members of Gram Sabha shall meeting of the Gr members of the Grai (iii) The Gram Pancl committee constitut executive instructio department or any purpose, shall superintendence, co Gram Sabha
7.	Section 4(d) deems the Gram Sabha to be	The following may b Provided that any r

Sl.No.	*Reason for Amendment*	*Proposed Amendme*
8.	The role of the Gram Sabha in scrutiny of activities of various agencies including Panchayats, government departments and corporate bodies through social audit needs to be defined explicitly.	The following may b iii. conduct regular programmes taken Panchayat, State, agency whatsoever;
9.	The words 'be required to' in Section 4(f) are unnecessary	Words 'required to' i • be deleted.
10.	Section 4(i) does not articulate clearly that the Gram Sabha as well as Panchayats at the appropriate level have to be consulted before land acquisition and the consent of the Gram Sabha is mandatory. Further, it also needs to be clarified that all Gram Sabhas affected by land acquisition	Section 4(i) needs tc (i)the Gram Sabhas Panchayats at t depending on the g proposed activity,in t land acquisition pe before taking a d notification for the a Scheduled Areas regarding the rehab livelihood plan. Full f zone of influence, i rehabilitation and su shall be placed befo

Sl.No.	Reason for Amendment	Proposed Amendme
11.	Section 4(j) provides that the planning and management of minor water bodies in the Scheduled Areas shall be entrusted to Panchayats at the appropriuate level. It needs to be clarified that these shall vest with the Gram Sabha, and if necessary, with the Panchayats at the appropriate level.	Section 4(j) be repla Planning and mana bodies in the Schec Gram Sabha an panchayats at t depending on the sp
12	In Section 4(K) and 4(l) provide that the recommendations of the Gram Sabha or the Panchayats at the appropriate level shall be made mandatory prior to grant of prospecting license or mining lease for minor mineral, and concession for exploitation of minor minerals respectively.	Section 4(k) may am The recommendatio necessary, the Panc level depending c proposed project sh grant of prospecting for minerals in the S Provided that the re Sabha shall be b reversed by a c reasons to be re approved by the Sta Section 4(l) may be

Sl.No.	*Reason for Amendment*	*Proposed Amendme*
15.	Section 5 needs to indicate a time line whereby all Acts inconsistent with its amendment Act shall cease to be valid.	In Section 5, the f inserted after the pro • Provided furthe any law relatin in the Schedu before the amendment Ac the President, this amendme be in force until a competent competent a expiration of o which this Ame assent of the F
16.	PESA does not confer rule making powers to the State Government. Since a major problem in implementation of the Act has been that such rules have not been framed, and subject laws have not been amended, this needs to be made mandatory.	Section 6 may be follows: • It shall be Governments t Act and for t Governments t per the provisi months of this not framed by within six mont Act, the mod PESA by the C apply(Appendix

APPENDIX V
MODEL RULES FOR THE PANCHAYATS(EXTENSION TO THE SCHEDULED AREAS) ACT, 1996

Provision of PESA Act	*Topic*
01	Short title and scope of rules
02	Definition
II COMPOSITION AND FUNCTIONING OF GRAM SAB	
03	Composition of the Gram Sabha
04	Declaration of Village
05	Gram Panchayat to the Executive Comn
06	Secretary, office, etc. of Gram Sabha
07	Gram Sabha meetings to be in public
08	Method of taking decision
09	Date and time of meetings of Gram Sabl
10	Proceeding of the meetings of Gram Sal
11	Presence in Gram Sabha
12	Special meetings of Gram Sabha
13	Standing Committee of Gram Sabha
14	Parallel Bodies
15	Procedure of the Standing Committees (
16	Complaint against Gram Sabha
17	Joint Meetings of Gram Sabhas
18	Committee of Gram Panchayat to execu
III GRAM SABHA ACCOUNTS	

30	Punishment by Gram Sabha
31	Role of Police
32	Arrest and bail
33	Action by a person or persons not sat the Gram Sabha regarding dispute resolution
V MANAGEMENT OF NATURAL RESOURCES, AGF	
34	Gram Sabha to safeguard Natural res(
35	Resource Planning and Management '
36	Gram Sabha to plan for farming
37	Land Management
38	Prevention of Land alienation
39	Restoration of alienated land
40	Consultation before land acquisition
41	Planning and management of water re
42	Management of irrigation
43	Management of land of ponds
44	Fishing etc.
VI MINES AND MINERALS	
45	Gram Sabha to plan for minor mineral:
46	Used by individual vilaegrs
47	Mining lease for minor minerals

IX MINOR FOREST PRODUCE	
61	Consultation with Gram Sabha for depa Forests
62	Management of minor forest produce
63	Gram Sabha to decide purchase of m royalty
64	Official Management of minor forest proc
65	Scheme for minor forests
X MANAGEMENT OF MARKETS	
66	Control over markets
67	Market Committee
XI MONEY LENDING	
68	Control over money lending transaction:
69	Review of agreements
70	Rescheduling of loan repayment
71	No attachement or auctioning of land wit Sabha
72	Seeds and granary
XII POWERS OF IDENTIFICATION OF BENEFICIAR OF PLANS SUPERVISION etc.	
73	Gram Sabha to identify beneficiaries
74	Approval of programmes by Gram Sabha

MODEL RULES FOR THE PANCHAYATS (EXTENSION TO TRHE SCHEDULED AREAS) ACT, 1996

I. INTRODUCTION

1. Short title and scope of rules

(1) These rules may be called the Model Rules for the Panchayat (Extension to Scheduled Areas) Act, 1996

(2) These rules are formulated under the Panchayats (Extension to Scheduled Areas) Act, 1996

(3) These rules shall apply to all the areas covered under the panchayat(Extension to the Scheduled Areas) Act, 1996

2. Definitions

(1) Gram Sabha:- Gram Sabha means a village assembly, comprising all adult members of a village.

(2) Minor water body:- Minor water body means water body used for fetching drinking water, construction of check dams of any and irrigating land up to 40 hectares.

(3) Scheduled Areas:- Scheduled areas means the Scheduled Areas referred to in clause (1) of article 244 of the Constitution.

(4) Village:- Village means a habitation or group of habitations or a hamlet or a group of hamlets comprising a community and managing its affairs in accordance with tradition and customs.

(5) Minor forest produce:- Minor forest produce includes all non-timber forest produce of plant origin including bamboo, brush wood, stumps, cane, tussar, cocoons, noney, wax, lac, tendu, or kendu leaves, medicinal plants and herbs, roots, tubers and the like.

II. COMPOSITION AND FUNCTIONING OF GRAM SABHA

3. Compositiomn of the Gram Sabha

All the people included in the electoral rolls of a village shall be the members of the Gram Sabha of that village.

4. Declaration of Village

(1) In conformity with the provision of Section 4(b) of PESA Act, a village shall consist of a habitation or a group of habitations, or a hamlet or a group of hamlets, comprising a

community and managing its affairs in accordance with its traditions and customs.

(2) If the people of any habitation are of the opinion that their habitation should be recorded as a village, and is not so recorded, they may pass a resolution to this effect and forward it to the Sub-Divisional Magistrate (SDM).

(3) The SDM will enquire into the merits of the resolution. In the case of favourable outcome of the inquiry, the habitation shall be notified as a village.

5. Gram Panchayat to be the Executive Committee of Gram Sabha

(1) The Gram Panchayat shall be deemed to be the Executive Committee of the Gram Sabha

(2) The Gram Panchayat shall function under the general superintendence, control and direction of the Gram Sabha.

6. Secretary, Office, etc. of Gram Sabha

(1) The Secretary of the Gram Panchayat will be deemed to be the Secretary of the Gram Sabha. In a situation where there are more than one Gram Sabhas in a Gram Panchayat, the Secretary of the Gram Panchayat will be the Secretary of all the Gram Sabhas.

(2) The Gram Sabha may appoint an Assistant Secretary from its members apart from the Secretary. But the Assistant Secretary will not be entitled to any pay, honorarium etc. He or she will execute his duties honorarily.

(3) The duties of the Assistant Secretary will be to help the Secretary and work in collaboration with him. In the absence of the Secretary, the Assistant Secretaryt will discharge the duties on his behalf.

(4) The office of the Gram Panchayat will be the office of the Gram Sabha.If there is more than one Gram Sabha in a Gram Panchayat, apart from the headquarter of the Gram Panchayat, each Gram Sabha will have its own office in its village, such as the house of an ordinary person. Rent will not be paid in any form for this office.

7. Gram Sabha Meetings to be in Public

(1) Every meeting or proceeding of the Gram Sabha will be conducted in public.

(2) Even if a meeting of the Gram Sabha is to be held in a closed building, there will not be any provision of closing the doors or prohibiting entry.

8. Method of Taking Decision

(1) As far as possible, the working of the Gram Sabha will be done with consensus.

Note:'Consensus' means the people present either agree with the proposal or are neutral, and none of them is an opponent.There is a compulsion of the quorum for a consensus.

(2) In the condition of non-consensus on any issue in a meeting, that matter will be discussed in the meeting to be held after one week or later, as decided by the Gram Sabha.

(3) If there is no consensus in the second meeting also, a decision will be taken on the basis of a majority. But there is a compulsion of quorum in such meetings. In the absence of quorum the matter will be considered void. The issue may subsequently be decided by a majority whenever the quorum is completed.

9. Date and Time of Meetings of Gram Sabha

(1) Gram Sabha will hold a meeting at least once in two months. The Gram Sabha may decide a fixed date (means English date, Indian date or the day of the week), time and place of the meeting permanently. In such a case there would be no need to provide any type of information for specific meetings.

(2) However, if the Gram Sabha decides to fix each meeting separately, or decides to hold a meeting on a particular day, within three days of the decision, an announcement will be made in the whole village.

10. Proceedings of the Meeting of Gram Sabha

(1) A Chairperson will be selected for the meeting of the Gram Sabha for one year. From the members present, only a member of Scheduled Tribe will be so selected.

Provided that in villages where the population of the Scheduled Trtibes is less than 10 per cent, a chairperson may be selected from among persons, who do not belong to the Scheduled tribes.

Provided further that no Sarpanch or Panch of the Panchayat shall be eligible to act as the chairperson of the Gram Sabha.

(2) Selection of chairperson will be done with consensus to the extent possible. In the case of non-consensus, amongst the members present, the oldest lady from the Scheduled Tribes would be the chairperson.

(3) In case the Gram Sabha is not satisfied with the performance of the chairperson, it will have the right to recall him/her by a simple majority and select a new chairperson.

(4) The quorum of the meeting of the Gram Sabha will be one fifth of the total members. There shall b e a separate quorum for women, which will be one third of the general quorum.

(5) In the absence of the quorum, the meeting would be considered postponed. But from amongst the present members may decided to hold a meeting within a week.The quorum will be necessary even in the postponed meeting.

(6) A detailed statement of the complete record of income, expenditure of the last month, muster roll of wortkers, sale and purchase will be produced in the meeting of the Gram Sabha. The quality of the works undertaken may be discussed and necessary action taken as per the decisions of the Gram Sabha to improve the situation.

(7) While concluding the meeting, a brief statement of the decisions taken in the Gram Sabha will be prepared by the Secretary/Additional Secretary and in their absence, a person nominated by the Gram Sabha. After a consensus about th correctness of the statement, the Chairperson, Secretary or the writer will sign or put a mark. In the case of disposal of disputes, the members of the judicial committee will sign or stamp that statement.

11. Presence in Gram Sabha

The Gram Sabha can ensure the mandatory presence of at least one member from every family of the village for the executrion of its works. The concerned family may be penalised if the member is absent without proper reason.

12. Special Meeting of Gram Sabha

(1) Apart from its regular meetings, in the following circumstances special meetings of the Gram Sabha may be held:

(i) If it is so decided in the general meeting of the Gram Sabha

(ii) If there is a proposal in the Panchayat which needs to be considered by the Gram Sabha

(iii) If an Officer requests the Sarpanch.

(iv) On the basis of the written information given to the Secretary by at least five per cent of total members of Gram Sabha or 25 members, whichever is more.

(2) Except in situation (1), the Secretary will call for a meeting within seven days after consulting the Sarpanch, and public information thereof will be given in the village 3 days prior to the fixed date through announcement and other methods.

Provided that if the Secretary is of the opinion that the Sarpanch is hindering holding a meeting, he will hold a meeting despite the negative advice of the Sarpanch.

Provided that, in the absence of Secretary/Assistant Secretary or lack of action to hold a meeting within a week, three members from among the people who request in writing to organise a meeting may inform the Sarpanch and organise the meeting by giving notice of at least three days.

(3) The decisions taken in a particular meeting shall not be challenged anywhere else except in the next meeting. The decisions of the Gram Sabha will be final.

13. Standing Committee of Gram Sabha

(1) The Gram Sabha may constitute Standing Committee viz. Peace Committee,Justice Committee, Resource Planning and Management Committee, Intoxication Control Committee, Debt Control Committee, Market Committee, Sabha Kosh Committee and others as deemed appropriate by the Gram Sabha in order to fulfill its responsibilities regarding various aspects of the working of the village. Besides, temporary and ad-hoc committees may be constituted as per requirement.

(2) The members of the Standing Committees of the Gram Sabha shall be elected in an open meeting of the Gram Sabha among members of the Gram Sabha. As per the spirit of the participatory democracy, that to the extent possible, every member of the Gram Sabha will be included in some Committee and discharge some responsibility.

(3) The tenure of all the Standing Committees will be of one or two years as decided by the Gram Sabha. For this purpose

on the decided date all the members of the Committees will be relieved of their duties. Gram Sabha will then take a decision to assign them responsibility in the same or some other Standing Committee.The Gram Sabha is competent to reconstitute the Committees.

(4) There will be a President and Secretary in each Standing Committee. The Committee concerned will appoint them from among the members with consensus.

Provided that if the Standing Committee is not able to form a consensus, a decision will be taken through simple majority.

(5) The responsibility to implement the decisions taken by the Gram Sabha on various subjects will be of the concerned Standing Committee. But the responsibility of the works to be carried out from the amount received from the Government in any form will be of the Gram Panchayat and its concerned committees.

14. Parallel Bodies

(1) If under any Act on any subject such as forest, irrigation management etc., a body or committee is constituted by any government department, the same will be treated as a Standing Committee of Gram Sabha on that subject. Notwithstanding the provisions in the concerned Act, the body or committee will be accountable to Gram Sabha.

(2) Any instructiuons issued by any agency other than the Gram Sabha will not be treated as legal instructions to the Gram Sabha or Gram Panchayat. Such instructions will be treated merely as "advisory".

(3) The concerned committee will put up such "instructions: before Gram Sabha and the final decision to implement them in the same or revised form or not to implement them will be of the Gram Sabha.

15. Procedure of the Standing Committee of Gram Sabha

The procedure of the Standing Committees of Gram Sabha will be the same as of Gram Sabha as follow:

(1) Meetings of all Committees including Gram Panchayat will be in open.

(2) Notice of every meeting of the Standing Committee, specifying the date, time and place thereof and business to be transacted thereat shall be given by the Secretary of the Standing Committee at least three days in advance.

(3) The quorum necessary for the meeting of the Standing Committee shall be one-half, including the President.

(4) A member of Gram Sabha may attend any meeting of Standing Committee. He may ask any question on the topic of the dfiscussion with the permission of the chair. But he or she will not have the right to vote at the time of final decision.

(5) All the decisions of the Standing Committees will be taken as per the procedure for the Gram Sabha.

(6) The gist of the important decisions taken in the meetings of the Standing Committees will be recorded.

16. Complaint against Gram Sabha

(1) Any complaint, allegation or objection made about any action taken by the Gram Sabha may be put up in the general meeting of the Gram Sabha for reconsideration.

(2) If the complainant or any other person is of the opinion that an observer is necessary to assist the Gram Sabha in resolving the complaint, he may make a request to the District Collector to direct an observer to attend the Gram Sabha meeting.

(3) If the District Collector is satisfied about the need for an observer, he may depute an observer for the meeting of the Gram Sabha under intimation to the complainants.

(4) The observer as appointed shall felicitate the redressal of the grievance of the complainant.

(5) If the issue is not addressed, the complainant or the the observer may refer the issue to the Ombudsman whose decision shall be final.

17. Jount Meetings of Gram Sabhas

(1) Every Gram Sabha is competent to execute its functions in its jurisdiction. But in matters like management of resources, construction of roads etc. in which working with other Gram Sabhas is required, a joint meeting of all Gram Sabhas falling under the jurisdiction of the Gram panchayat can be conducted.

(2) The Joint meeting of Gram Sabhas would be conducted as per the rules of Gram Sabha as if all the Gram Sabhas were a single entity.

(3) The Joint meeting would be chaired by the Sarpanch of the Village Panchayat.

(4) In the Joint meeting, attendance of a minimum of 5 per centmembers or 10 members from each Gram Sabha, whichever is less, would be mandatory. In case there is no quorum, the date of next meeting would be finalised on the same day and the same would be sent to all Gram Sabhas.

(5) The decision making process would be the same as in the case of a single Gram Sabha.

(6) The area wise allocation for Government programmes in the Gram Panchayat will be made in the joint meetings for which the proposal will be made by the Gram Panchayat. The decision of the Joint Gram Sabha would be final.

18. Committee of Gram Panchayat to Execute Works in Gram Sabha

The Gram Panchayat may constitute a Standing Committee to execute the works of a Gram Sabha after obtaining agreement from the concerned Gram Sbha. All the 'Panch' or members elected from the Gram Sabha will be the members of this Committee and one of them will act as coordinator. This Standing Committee will be competent to execute all the works of that Gram Sabha on behalf of the Panchayat.

III. GRAM SABHA CCOUNTS

19. Gram Sabha Kosh

(1) The Gram Sabha will maintain a Gram Sabha Kosh.

(2) This Kosh will consist of the contribution received in any form including voluntary contributions of cash and goods and labour of villagers; amount received through the government from minor forest produce, minor minerals etc; and surcharges imposed on the consumption of the resources or fines levied by the Gram Sabha.

(3) The Kosh will be under the control of Gram Sabha. The Gram Sabha will have the complete right of its usage as per its own decisions.

(4) The Kosh will be operated by a Gram Sabha Kosh Committee comprising of at least three members nominated with consensus or elected by the Gram Sabha. At least one member out of the three members would be a woman. One member will be incharge of the deposited amount of kosh. Another member will take care of the accounts. The third member will take care of the transaction of money or expenditure.

20. Cask Box

(1) The cash available with the Gram Sabha may be kept in a box under lock and key upto Rs 3,000 and in a bank for higher amount.

(2) In case of the cash kept in a box, and the key to the lock of the box will be kept with different persons.

21. Accounts to be Maintained

(1) The accounts of the Gram Sabha kosh shall be maintained in a register by a member of the Gram Sabha Kosh Committee.

(2) The accounts of the Kosh will be produced in the monthly meeting of the Gram Sabha every month.

22. Gram Sabha-wise Accounts

For every Gram Sabha, the Gram Panchayat will keep a separate account of the expenditures incurred from the funds of the Panchayat, which would be certified only by the concerned Gram Sabha.

IV. PEACE AND SECURITY AND DISPUTE RESOLUTION

23. Role of Gram Sabha in Maintaining Peace and Dispute Resolution

(1) In keeping with community traditions and the spirit of the Constitution, law and relevant rules, it will be the fundamental duty of the Gram Sabha to maintain peace and order in its area.

(2) Gram Sabha is competent for the following action/works in its region:

(i) To maintain a peaceful atmosphere where there is no fear,

(ii) To safeguard self respect and maintain the freedom of expression of every citizen, and

(iii) To counter the vices of antisocial elements including indecent behavior with women, fighting/quarrelling in public place etc.

(iv) Resolve disputes.

24. Peace Committee

(1) The Gram Sabha may constitute a Peace Committee. The Peace Committee shall have at least 33 per cent women, and a minimum of 50 per cent STs.

(2) The Peace Committee shall maintain a healthy relationship with the neighbouring villages, and ensure that in matters of common interest and interdependence of neighbouring villages, any action taken will be based on consultation with the neighbouring villages.

(3) The Gram Sabha may empower the Peace Committee to:

(i) Inquire into incidents that vitiate peace of the village and report to Gram Sabha for a decision.

(ii) Counsel those breaking peace and arbitrate.

(iii) Take immediate action where necessary, and subsequently report to Gram Sabha.

(iv) With the approval of the Gram Sabha make a report/ request to the Sub-Divisional Magistrate for suitable action.

25. Peace and Security Corps

(1) Gram Sabha may constitute a Peace and Security Corps in order to protect life and property. This team will function under the guidance of the Peace Committee.

(2) Youth of the village from the age-group 18 years to 30 years may voluntarily join the Peace and Security Corps. But in any extraordinary situation or owing to any special reason, Gram Sabha on its own may induct any youngster in the team.

(3) The leader of the Peace and Security team will be an ex-officio member of the Peace Committee.

(4) The Peace and Security Corps will form small groups to fulfill their responsibilities that may be allotted any work including night patrolling.

(5) If the members of the team come to know about any untoward incident or the possibility of its occurrence, whether

themselves or throug any other medium, then without making any delay they will take the matter to the coordinator of the Peace Committee or any of its members, and act as per his instructions.

(6) The members of the team will not use force in any form except in circumstance where they have to use their right of self-defence and that too only when there is no other way out and they are completely helpless.

26. Matters Relating to Superstition, Sorcery, etc.

(1) matters related to superstition, sorcery or magic will be deliberated upon in open meetings of the Gram Sabha.

(2) The matters of superstition will be discussed in two continuous meetinsg of the Gram Sabha so that everyone gets an opportunity to think over the matter.

(3) When such matters are discussed, any member fo the Gram Sabha may make a request to the District Collector for the presence of an observer. Upon receiving such a request, the District Collector shal depute an observer.

(4) It will be the duty of the observer so deputed to provide factual and scientific information about the matter to the Gram Sabha

27. Disputes to be Heard by Gram Sabha

(1) Whenever any dispute is brought to the Gram Sabha by the Peace Committee or any person or persons, the Gram Sabha will consider it immediately or fix a date for hearing.

(2) The Gram Sabha or a Committee authorised by it will be competent to hear cases and levy punishment as indicated in Annexure–I.

28. Justice Committee

(1) To carry out the proceedings/hearings of the disputes, Gram Sabha may constitute a Justice Committee comprising of three to twelve members.

(2) Judicious senior citizens will be included in the Committee. At least 50 per cent of the members will be from among Scheduled tribes and at least 50 per cent will be women and two persons will be from the Peace Committee who will act as its representatives.

(3) Cases will be heard by a bench of three members as decided among the Justice Committee. There will be at least one woman in each bench.

29. Process of Dispute Resolution

(1) While resolving a dispute, the Gram Sabha, Justice Committee or the Peace Committee will take action as per its tradition, keeping in mind the principles of natural justice.

(2) The hearing of any dispute will take place only in public. Before arriving at the final decision, persons from both the parties and other people actively involved in the proceedings, if any, will be given ample opportunity to express their views.

(3) After listening to the views of all the people, the bench of the Justice Committee, after deliberating on the matter, shall present its conclusion and proposal for further action to the Gram Sabha.

(4) All the members of the Gram Sabha will have an opportunity to give their views on the conclusions and proposals of the Justice Committee.

(5) After getting the reactions of the Gram Sabha, the Justice Committee, after making appropriate amendments, if necessary, will present its conclusion and proposal again to the Gram Sabha again. These will be accepted as the decision of the Gram Sabha on the basis of consensus or a majority vote as the case may be.

(6) If the conclusions or proposals of the Justice Committee do not get a majority vote in the Gram Sabha, the matter shall be sent to the Peace Committee. After having an informal talks with the parties, the Peace Committee shall, again present the matter in the next meeting of Gram Sabha.

(7) In case the proposal of the Peace Committee fails to get a majority, the Justice Committee and Peace Committee will take a decision as per their discreation and their decision will be considered to be the decision of the Gram Sabha and will have to be accepted by both the parties.

(8) The main objective of resolving any dispute will be to eliminate the dispute completely and create an atmosphere of harmony in the village.

30. Punishment by Gram Sabha

(1) The Gram Sabha may provide for punishment as follows:

(i) In cases where there is no intent to cause harm, to accept one's mistake, regretting it in front of the Gram Sabha, apologising for the wrong committed, and promising not to repeat the mistake will be considered a suitable punishment.

(ii) In other cases, penalty may be levied by the Gram Sabha upto the Maximum limit indicated in Annexure-I. The penalty will be in proportion to the economic condition of the person found guilty.

(iii) In case the matter is extremely serious, a complaint may be made to the Competent Authority with the approval of Gram Sabha.

31. Role of Police

(1) If the local police receives information regarding a possibility of disruption of peace in the area of any Gram Sabha, then except in cases in which immediate action by the police is mandatory, the polic officer concerned will present a detailed report of the matter to the Gram Sabha or to the Peace Committee. Arbitration in such matters or preventive measures against any person will be taken only with the concurrence of the Gram Sabha.

(2) If the police receives information regarding any crime, then except in case of serious crime or in an extraordinary situation where immediate action by the police is required, after the report is registered in the police station, a copy of the same will be sent to Gram Sabha or Peace Committee. If necessary, an effort will be made to resolve the matter in Gram Sabha's special meeting or in its forthcoming meeting. In case the matter is not resolved in three months, the Gram Sabha will inform the police for further action.

Note: Those crimes shall be considered to be serious for which there is a provision of punishment of 2 or more years in the Indian Penal Code.

32. Arrest and Bail

(1) Before arresting any person as far as possible, the concerned officer will present the matter in Gram Sabha for its

views on the matter. If the Gram Sabha is not in agreement with the police, the arrest would be made only after stating the reason for it in writing.

(2) In cases where the police has to make arrests without consulting the Gram Sabha or Peace Committee, it will be the responsibility of the prolice to present the matter in detail to the Peace Committee or Gram Sabha at the earliest and in any case in two weeks.

(3) At any time of arrest, the presence of the Coordinator of the Peace Committee or any of its other members will be mandatory.

(4) The police will have to give full information within 48 hours regarding the custody of any person to the Gram Sabha or well wisher of the person concerned nominated by the Gram Sabha.

33. Action by a Person or Persons not Satisfied with the Decision of the Gram Sabha Regarding Dispute Resolution

If a person or group of persons affected by any decision of the Gram Sabha feels that there has been a violation of his human rights and in following the decision a punishable offence and the affected person registers a report in the police station, then in such cases, before initiating action as per normal procedure, the concerned officers shall contact the Gram Sabha or Peace Committee for full information regarding the decision.

34. Gram Sabha to Safeguard Natural Resources

(1) Gram Sabha is competent to safeguard and preserve the natural resources located in its area as well as those over which it enjoys traditional rights including water, forest, land and mineral as per local tradition and the spirit of the laws of the Central and state governments. To fulfill this role, the Gram Sabha may play active role in their management.

(2) The Gram Sabha will ensure that resources are utilised in such a way that:

(i) Livelihood means are sustained.

(ii) Inequality among the people does not increase.

(iii) Resources are not confined to a few people.

(iv) There is full utilisation of local resources, in keeping with sustainability.

(3) Though as per the prevalent rules individual rights over natural and other resources will be suitably honoured, their management will be done keeping in view the inherent spirit of the community legacy.

35. Resource Planning and Management Committee

(1) There will be a Standing Resource Planning and Management Committee (RPMC) of Gram Sabha. Representatives of all departments will function as advisers to the RPMC and attend its meetings.

(2) RPMC will chalk out a plan for the best possible use of all the resources within the territory of the village and those in the surrounding and will advice and cooperate with Gram Sabha members to make use of them accordingly.

(3) The RPMC will consider all the aspects, including difference of opinion or dispute about the management or use of the resources. The Gram Sabha may authorise the RPMC to resolve such disputes. If the RPMC is not able to resolve the same these will be considered in the meetings of Gram Sabha. The decision of Gram Sabha will be final.

(4) The RPMC may constiutute sub-committees on specific issues such as farming, minor minerals, to assist in its functions.

36. Gram Sabha to Plan for Farming

(1) Gram Sabha is competent to plan and take action about the farming of its village in such a way to make farming economically viable for the farmer.

(2) The decisions of Gram Sabha, inter-alia, may include the following major points:

(i) To prevent the soil erosion,

(ii) To regulate grasing in order to protect crops and enhance the capacity of meadows,

(iii) To accumulate rain water, use it for farming and provide for its distribution,

(iv) With mutual cooperation or otherwise, to ensure provision of seeds, manure etc. as well as knowledge sharing,

(v) Promotion of organic manures, fertilisers and insecticides.

37. Land Management

(1) The Gram Sabha may undertake the following activities with respect to the land in the village:

(i) Review of records of the entire land of the village in meetings of Gram Sabha to ensure that the farmer's names are correctly recorded and records are properly maintained.

(ii) Measures to ensure that farming land does not remain fallow due to any reason and to provide for the farming on lands of migrating people, dependents and minors etc. and to determine the conditions for the tillers of such land.

(iii) make arrangements so that the lands of migrating people can be farmed by landless or needy people and decide the conditions for such farming.

(2) It shall be mandatory for village officials to take permission from Gram Sabha prior to any kind of transfer of land.

Note: Any kind of devolution includes sale, mortgage, lease-contract etc. in which the owner or tiller of the land changes.

(3) All matters regarding mortgage of land will be put up before Gram Sabha. Gram Sabha may take action to prevent such mortgage or decide the conditions of such mortgage.

38. Prevention of Land Alienation

(1) The Gram Sabha will ensure that no land belonging to Scheduled Tribes is transferred to non ST persons.

(2) The Gram Sabha shall be competent to enquire into any land transactions, or authorise the Peace Committee to do so, on the basis of complaints or *suomotto*.

(3) The Peace Committee shall place its findings before the Gram Sabha.

(4) If the Gram Sabha is of the opinion that attempts are being made to alienate lands belonging to STs, it may issue instructions to prohibit the transaction.

(5) The decision of the Gram Sabha in such cases shall be final.

39. Restoration of Alienated Land

(1) If Gram Sabha finds that any person other than a member of the aboriginal tribe, is in possession of any land of a Bhmiswami belonging to an aboriginal tribe, without any lawful authority, it shall restore the possession of such land to that person to whom it originally belonged and if that person is dead to his legal heirs.

(2) In case of dispute regarding the land to be restored, the Gram Sabha will follow its process of dispute resolution.

40. Consultation before Land Acquisition

(1) When the government considers land acquisition under any Act, the government or the concerned authority will submit to the Gram Sabha the following written information along with the proposal:—

(i) The complete outline of the proposed project including the possibility impact of the project,

(ii) Proposed land acquisition,

(iii) New people likely to settle in the village and possible impact on the area and society, and

(iv) The proposed participation, amount of compensation, job opportunities, for the people of the village.

(2) After getting complete information the concerned Gram Sabhas will be competent to summon the representatives of the concerned authorities and the government to examine them either individually or collectively. It will be mandatory for all such persons summoned to furnish point-wise clear and correct information.

(3) The Gram Sabha after considering all the facts, shall make a recommendation regarding the proposed land acquisition and rehabilitation plan of persons displaced.

(4) The recommendation of the Gram Sabha shall be considered by the Land Acquisition Officer.

(5) In case the Land Acquitision Officer is not in agreemtn with the recommendations of the Gram Sabha, he will send the case again to the Gram Sabha for reconsideration.

(6) If after a second consultation, the Land Acquisition Officer passes an order against the recommendations of the Gram Sabha, he shall record the reasons for doing so in writing.

(7) In case of industrial projects, all the Gram Sabhas that are influenced by such projects shall be consulted.

41. Planning and Management of Water Resources

(1) The management and use of water resources will be such that these are kept intact for future generations, and all the villagers have equal rights over this resource.

(2) Water bodies within a Gram Panchayat will be managed by the Gram Panchayat, those extending to more than one Gram Panchayat by the'Block Panchayat' and those extending to more than one Block Panchayat by Zilla Panchayat.

(3) The Gram Panchayat or the Block or District Panchayat as the case may be, after consulting the Gram Sabha, keeping in view its traditions and the spirit of prevalent laws, will regulate the use of available water in the village for various purposes and also decide about the priority of use.

(4) It will be mandatory for Panchayats at all levels to consult the RPMC or the Gram Sabha consensus before taking any decision regarding water body.

42. Management of Irrigation

(1) The Gram Panchayat or the Blochk or District Panchayat as the case may be, regulate the use of water for irrigation after taking the advice of the RPMC.

(2) The use of water for irrigation will be such that equal access is allowed to all.

(3) Any dispute will be put up before the RPMC or Gram Sabha. The decision of Gram Sabha will be final and binding for all.

43. Management of Land and Ponds

The Gram Panchayat or Block or District Panchayat as the case may be, will make arrangement for the farming of land available as a consequence of the reduction of water level of ponds meant for the irrigation and other purposes, in consultation with RPMC and concerned departments. It will also decide about the levy rate on that land, keeping in view state government rules.

44. Fishing, etc.

(1) All persons will have equal rights to fishing as per the convention in the water resources located within the territory of the village.

(2) Keeping in view the local traditions the Gram panchayat will impose necessary conditions regarding any aspect of fishing to ensure that one or more persons do not increase their jurisdiction in an unjust manner and also to maintain the availability of the fish.

VI. MINES AND MINERALS

45. Gram Sabha to Plan for Minor Minerals

(1) Gram Sabha is competent to plan and control the excavation and use of all the minor minerals including soil, stones, sands etc t be found in its area.

(2) The RPMC shall discharge this responsibility.

46. Use by Individual Villagers

(1) The villagers may use minor menerals for their individual needs as per the traditional practice. But

(i) the permission of Gram Sabha will be compulsory for use of minerals,

(ii) Gram Sabha may decide the extent of use of the local materisl such as stone, sand, etc. for making pucca houses different from the traditional dwellings and may also impose royalty.

(2) The Gram Sabha may fix the responsibilities such as filling up pits, planting trees, constructing ponds etc. by persons undertaking excavation to compensate for the general or special ill effects of excavation.

47. Mining Lease for Minor Minerals

(1) The Panchayat or the Government department concerned may award mining lease for minor minerals only in consultation with Gram Sabha.

(2) Gram Sabha may impose conditions for protecting the environment, employment, etc. in the lease of minor minerals.

48. Protection of Environment

(1) In villages having commercial feasibility of minor mioneral production, before permitting the minor minerals to be used commercially, it will be the responsibility of the Mineral Department to consult Gram Sabha.

(2) If any condition has been imposed by the Government for the protection of the environment etc, the concerned officer will provide emplete information to the Gram Sabha in this regard.

(3) The condition imposed by Gram Sanbha about the environment can not be relaxed at any level.

(4) The plan for exploitation of minor minerals: This will include arrangements such as excavation area, the type of area, managing of ill effects of excavation such as existence of pits, water shortage, reduction in vegetation, effect of ash or smoke on fields, etc. the nullify all these effects by filling up the pits, planting trees, etc.

49. Grant of Concession for Exploitation of Minor Minerals by Auction

If any concession is given by any Government department for the exploitation of minor minerals, it shall be mandatory of the said department to obtain the permission of the Gram Sabha.

VII. MANPOWER

50 Gram Sabha to Plan for Labour Force

(1) Gram Sabha is competent to undertake activities in order to ensure that there is full utilisation of the village labour force including under the National Rural Employment Guarantee Scheme and forest related works.

(2) The Gram Sabha may take any action which encourages cooperation among the people, sharing each others knowledge, work, etc.

51. Workers taken Outside the Village

(1) It will be mandatory for all persons taking workers outside the village for jobs to provide complete information to Gram Sabha about the written or oral agreement specifying natue and conditions of work, and take its permission before taking any workers outside the village.

(2) Gram Sabha or Peace Committee will ensure that all persons going out for work have complete and correct information about the work and any agreements made if they are to be given an advance sum of money as the condition of going out or otherwise, the amount will be given before Gram Sabha or Peace Committee.

(3) Only after getting the permission of the Gram Sabha as per the procedure mentioned above, will it be possible to take the people out for work.

(4) Gram Sabha will be competent to make such an arrangement as it deems fit to ensure that girls do not get entrapped. Apart from the establishment of the govetnmental and organised sector, it will be mandatory for managers of private or unorganised sector to keep the Gram Sabha concerned informed from time to time about the well being of the girls.

52. Accounting of Birth, Death, etc.

(1) Gram Sabha is competent to maintain separate registers for the details of the (i) births (ii) deaths (iii) marriages (iv) festivals (v) persons going outside the village to make livelihood.

(2) The same will be certified by Chairperson and Secretary in meetings of the Gram Sabha and the details of this cetrtification will be recorded in the proceedings of the meeting.

(3) In case of dispute, the particulars prepared by Gram Sabha will be treated as proofs.

53. Wages for Work

(1) If in a village, the work is to be got done by a Government or non-governmental institution on the basis of measurement of work instead of daily wages, the work rates will have to be submitted in the general meeting of the Gram Sabha.

(2) Gram Sabha, inter-alia, will be informed about the name of the officer deciding the rate, the name of the Act, data and modalities of how it was decided.

(3) Gram Sabha, after taking into account those details, if required, may ask the department to reconsider it citing the reasons for the same.

(4) These wage rates will be displayed on a board at a common place in the village.

54. Muster Roll to be Submitted to Gram Sabha

Muster Roll of the labourers pertaining to all kinds of works to be conducted by Department or institutions will be submitted in the monthly general meeting of the Gram Sabha for its information, review and certification.

VIII INTOXICATION CONTROL

55. Regulation of Intoxication

The Gram Sabha is competent to have full control over all the aspects related to any type of intoxicant within its jurisdiction. It means that the Gram Sabha may:

(i) completely stop the relaxation of allowing tribals to make local liquor for their own use or impose any type of ban on it in the village.

(ii) give instructions to stop the sale of any type of intoxicant from a shop or in any other manner. Provided that these instructions would come into force from the forth coming financial year.

(iii) impose a ban on bringing in any type of intoxicant or taking it outside the village territory.

(iv) prohibit or impose a limit on the storage of intoxicants at any place.

(v) completely stop the use of liquor or other intoxicants in its village territory or impose any restriction.

(vi) prohibit the sale of Mahua, Jaggery, etc., which are used in making liquor in the village or in the market.

(vii) regulate the use of Taadi, Sulphi, etc.

56. Intoxication Control Committee

(1) The Gram Sabha may constitute an Intoxication Control Committee to inquire into complaints related to intoxicants and either on the basis of complaints or suo motto, make suitable suggestions regarding the control of intoxicant for the benefit of the people.

(2) At least half of the members of the Intoxication Control Committee shall be women.

(3) The responsibility of the Intoxciation Control Committee would include:

(i) To ensure that the factories manufacturing any type of intoxicants adhere to all the conditions mentioned in the license and in case of any infringements, report to competent authorities.

(ii) To aske the owner of the concerned factory to present all matters related to the welfare of the people including manufacture of liquor, distriobution system, its environmental impact etc. before the Gram Sabha.

(4) Gram Sabha may take advice and help from the Excise Department for the smooth functioning of the Intoxication Control Committee.

57. Insatructions by Gram Sabha to Manufactures of Intoxicants

(1) The Gram Sabha may give appropriate instructions to the owner of any factory manufacturing intoxicants of any type on matters related to the welfare of people, and also ask the Excise Department to intervene if it considers necessary.

(2) If the problems of the welfare are not solved even after departmental intervention, the matter will be referred to the District Collector.

58. Opening a New Factory or Shop

(1) Without the concurrence of the Gram Sabha, no new factory for manufacturing liquor or other intoxicants may be established.

(2) All proposals to construct a factory to manufacture liquor or other intoxicants or to open a new shop for the sale of liquor in the jurisdiction of a Gram Sabha, by the Government or any other agency, would be required to be presented to the Gram Sabha.

(3) Such proposals will be presented for information in the Gram Sabha meeting, but would be considered in the next meeting or in a special meeting by the Gram Sabha.

(4) The decision of the Gram Sabha will be final.

(5) In case the Gram Sabha remains undecided on the issue or if the proposal is not considered, then the proposal will be deemed to be unacceptable.

(6) In the absence of a complete quorum, the above mentioned proposal cannot be considered in the meeting of the Gram Sabha.

59. Continuance of Liquor shop

(1) In order to continue a liquor shop for any year, a proposal would have to be presented by the Excise Department in the Gram Sabha meeting before the month of December of the previous year.

(2) A liquor shop may continue only if a resolution is passed in the Gram Sabha to allow continuing the sale of liquor.

(3) If such a proposal is not received from the Excise Department till the Gram Sabha meeting of the month of December or a proposal is received but there is no decision in the Gram Sabha regarding allowing the shop to continue, then this will be considered to be an order to close the shop from 1st April. In such a case, it will be mandatory for the shopkeeper to close the shop from 1st April.

(4) If such a shop is not closed by the shopkeeper voluntarily, the Intoxication Control Committee by its own discretion will be competent to take appropriate action to close the shop.

60. Views of Women to be Crucial

(1) On any of the above mentioned topics, the views of the female members present in the Gram Sabha will be considered to be the views of the Gram Sabha and action will be taken in this regard according to those views.

(2) In the Intoxication Control Committee in case of any difference of views the views of the women mebers will be held to be the views of the Committee.

IX MINOR FOREST PRODUCE

61. Consultation with Gram Sabha for Departmental Programmes of Forests

Before chalking out the Departmental Programme for forests and exploitation of forest produce, it will be compulsory for the Forest Department to consult the Gram Sabha.

Notes: In this consultation it will be ensured that the exploitation of the forest is in consonance with the scheme chalked out with people's consent, and no such plants/trees are cut which are useful to the local people and there is no illegal export of the forest yield.

62. Management of Minor Forest Produce

(1) Despite any provision about minor forest produce in any Act, the management of such produce will be done to protect the right of ownership access to collect, use and dispose of minor forest produce which has been traditionally collected within or outside village boundaries of forest dwelling Scheduled Tribes and other forest dwellers in consonance with section 3 of Forest Rights Act, 2006.

(2) The Gram Sabha may chalk out an action plan about the use or exploitation of small forest producer in consultation with the forest officer concerned.

(3) Gram Sabha may, in case of limited quantity of a minor forest produce, make a cyclic arrangement for its collection and use by a few people such as re-sourceless and economically weaker groups.

(4) Gram Sabha is competent to ensure strict compliance of rules in the exploitation of minor forest produce and that collectors of minor forest produce do not commit any act which demages the forest.

63. Gram Sabha to Decide Purchase of Minor Forest Produce and Royalty

(1) One or more Gram Sabhas together, in consultation with the Forest Department, may decide the minimum price for the purchase of minor forest produce or exchange rates for other commodities such as chiraunji and salt.

(2) Gram Sabha may determine the royalty payable by the collector or the trade on minor forest produce. This amount will be deposited in Sabha Kosh.

(3) It will be mandatory to give details to Gram Sabha before taking any minor forest produce outside the area of the Gram Sabha collected by any department or institution on the basis of any Act, rule or administrative instructions, and obtain clearance from it for the same.

64. Official Management of MInor Foreest Produce

(1) If the state government organises the trade of any minor

forest produce in order to protect tribal interests, that trade will be treated as trade carried out on behalf of people.

But prior approval of the Graqm Sabha will be needed for the proposed arrangement. On the basis of suggestions of the Gram Sabha, necessary changes may be carried out.

(2) In the above trade, Gram Sabha and the collectors will have complete right over net profit.

65. Scheme for Minor Forests

(1) For meeting the village requirements such as grasing, fuel wood, making houses and ploughs, Gram Sabha will chalk out a minor forest scheme for the use of forest resources used traditionally by the people in consultation with the concerned Forest Officers. Under this scheme every person will be able to use the resources after getting permission letter from the RPMC.

(2) Gram Sabha may make rules to ensure that the interest of the poor persons for picking up fuel wood and livelihood are protected.

(3) Gram Sabha may chalk out suitable programmes to conserve the forest, improve the environment and enhance employment at local level in their respective areas.

(4) Gram Sabha is competent to make enquiries, despite the departmental permit, about the wood or the forest produce passing through their areas.

(5) If there is a doubt of illegal operations on enquiry, Gram Sabha is competent to stop it on the spot.

X MANAGEMENT OF MARKETS

66. Control Over Markets

Gram Sabha is competent to control and manage the markets within its territory, including the following:

(1) make available water, sheds and other physical facilities to the shop keepers and the consumers in the market.

(ii) prohibit the inflow and sale of harmful objects in the market.

(iii) ensure that the weight, measurement and payment in the transactions are genuine.

(iv) obtain and share information about the prices being charged.

(v) prohibit all unfair practices, including cheating or misinformation regarding prices.

(vi) prohibit gambling, betting,testing luck, cock-fighting etc. in the market or its surrounding area.

(vii) impose tax on the shopkeepers of the market.

Provided that no tax shall be levied on small vendors coming to the market to sell the yield. The Gram Sabha will be competent to decided who qualifies as a small vender.

67. Market Committee

(1) Gram Sabha of villages which share a common market may constitute a Market Committee for the management of the market of the village. Market Committee will be accountable for the arrangement of the market.

(2) Peace Corps of the village in which the market is held at the instructions of Market Committee will be responsible for ensuring smooth functioning of the market without any conflict or quarrel.

(3) In case of any dispute the decision of the Market Committee can be challenged in Gram Sabha. The decision of Gram Sabha will be final.

XI MONEY LENDING

68. Control over Money Lending Transaction: Scope and Process

(1) Despite any provisions in any Act or law, according to the sapirit of section 4 (m) of the Extension Act, Gram Sabha is competent to control money lending transdacrtions of all the villagers. For this, it may institute a Debt Control Committee.

Note: Money lending transactions include loan etc. extended by Government, co-operative money lenders, banks and other institutions under an Act or privately or informally, as per the convention or otherwise.

(2) Gram Sabha is competent to decide the condition of maximum interest and repayment in the matters of private transaction.

(3) Gram Sabha may ask for any information regarding the

loan extended by any person or institution to the villagers, its condition, repayment status etc. In these matters, on being asked for the information, the concerned person or institution will provide complete information to the Gram Sabha within the prescribed time.

(4) A villager may put up his case in writing or orally before the Gram Sabha or Debt Control Committee rtegarding any kind of irregularity, corruption in transaction, the recovery proceeding, inability to repay the loan etc. in respect of the loan extended by any institution or person. If there is an oral complaint, it will be the duty of Secretaryt of Gram Sabha or debt Control Committee to prepare a memo in this regard and to keep the same in records.

(5) After considering the application mentioned above if the Gram Sabha itself or on the basis of the conclusions of the Debt Control Committee finds that there has been injustice with the applicant, it may instruct the concerned institution/person to redress the injustice.

(6) Gram Sabha, especially in the case of the tribals, may instruct a bank, society or any lending that loans be disbursed only in presence of Gram Sabha or its Debt Control Committee.The same instructions may be issued about the repayment of the loan.

(7) Instructions of Gram Sabha will be binding.

(8) If the concerned institution has any doubt about it, it may appeal to the District Collector. The District Collector shall appoint an arbiter, who will resolve the complaint.

69. Review of Agreements

Gram Sabha is competent to review written, oral and informal agreements of all kinds of labourers in the village and ensure that there is no forced labour as repayment of loan.

70. Rescheduling of Loan Repayment

(1) A debtor may apply to the Gram Sabha for the rescheduling of his loan.

(2) While considering any application for waiver or concession regarding a loan on the basis of the information and other facts submitted, Gram Sabha will, iner-alia, consider the following points:—

(i) The amount of loan and the date on which received by the applicant.

(ii) The installments already paid.

(iii) Whether the applicant has received the loan or grant in time and as per his requirement for the programme concerned.

(iv) Whether the applicant has received any aid from the credit institution or the Government department in circumstances beyond his understanding.

(v) Whether the applicant received desired benefit after taking the loan.

(vi) Whether the social and economic condition of the applicant have been considered while deciding the installments for recovey and accordingly making the recovery.

71. No Attachment or Auctioning of Land without Permission of Gram Sabha

No legal action including attachment of property for recovery of any loan may be taken without the permission of the Gram Sabha. If such an action is being taken against any person he may give application to Gram Sabha about it. After considering the application, Gram Sabha may also instruct to stop that action till the decision is taken.

72. Seeds and Granary

(1) Gram Sabha is competent to store seeds granary in the village with mutual cooperation for the following purposes:—

(i) To make available grains and other produce in the required quantity to meet the requirements of the villagers, and

Note: 'The requirements of a village' includes the provision for emergency and seeds etc. in case of crop failure due to any reason

(ii) To provide facility of advance to those persons who have shortage of food.

(iii) To provide relief to the farmers from compulsion of selling at low price.

(2) Gram Sabha may make rules regarding the contribution in the storage by its members and the purchase of the grains from granary.

(3) Gram Sabha is competent to decide conditions for providing grains etc. to its members from the storage in the form of loan, as per conventions and principles of natural justice.

XII. POWERS OF IDENTIFICATION OF BENEFICIARIES, APPROVAL OF PLANS SUPERVISION ETC.

73. Gram Sabha to Identify Beneficiaries

(1) The Gram Sabha is competent to finalise rules and criteria for identification of beneficieries on the basis of the economic condition of the family for development programmes from among the people of the village, in keeping with government rules.

(2) Beneficiaries for all developmental programmes will be selected by the Gram Sabha.

74. Approval of Programmes by Gram Sabha

(1) It will be mandatory for the Gram Panchayat to obtain the approval of all the Gram Sabhas on plans and projects for the village.

(2) Before beginning any programme or project in the village the Gram Panchayat, any government department or any other institution will present it before the Gram Sabha for its approval.

(3) The concerned institution will present complete information related with that programme before the Gram Sabha including the following:

(i) the relevance and importance of the programme with reference to the objectives finalised for the development of the village.

(ii) The full financial details of the programme, such as expenditure by government, loan or aid.

(iii) In matters regarding construction works, their dimension, construction material, use of technology and machines, participation of the local workers, the role of contractors, etc.

(4) It will be the right of the Gram Sabha to:—

(i) Approve the plan, programme or project in the form in which it is presented by the concerned institution or put conditions.

(ii) While giving an approval for programme, making necessary modifications keeping in mind the situation of the village.

(5) The decision of the Gram Sabha will be final.

75. Compliance of Decision of Gram Sabha by Government Departments and Gram Panchayat

(1) The Gram Panchayat and its committees will work under control and direction of Gram Sabha and they will be wholly accountable to Gram Sabha.

(2) The functioning of Gram Panchayat will be carried out as per the general rules if made, by the Government. But in case of conflict between these rules and directives of the Gram Sabha, the latter will have supremacy.

(3) While using its rights, if the Gram Sabha takes a decision which causes hindrance or there is possibility of hindrance in the official work of any department or officer, then action will be taken as follows:—

(i) The representative of the concerned department the officer will postpone the action on the disputed matter and present his point of view to the Gram Sabha and with a request to reconsider its decision.

(ii) If the department is not satisfied with the decision of the Gram Sabha, it will refer the matter to District Collector whose decision will be final.

76. Certification of Expenses

(1) It will be mandatory for th Gram Panchayat to obtain a certification of utilisation of all funds from Gram Sabha for works undertaken in its area.

(2) Gram Sabha is competent to give a certificate that the amount given in any form or the work taken up by any department or institution under any head in the village is spent properly.

(3) The certificate given by the Gram Sabha will be considered valid during the audit process.

77. Details Regarding Works to be given to Gram Sabha

(1) In the meetings of the Gram Sabha the complete details

regarding every work going on in the village will be given by all the agencies working in the area.

(2) Any objection pertaining to the quality of the work, certification of the expenditure etc. may be placed before Gram Sabha. Gram Sabha may examine the issue and give proper instruction for improvement and its decision will be final.

(3) On completion of any programme or the complete details thereof will be produced before the next meeting of Gram Sabha.

78. Enquiries of Panchayat, etc.

(1) Any enquiry into the functioning of Gram Panchayat by any officer under aPanchayat Act or any other Act will not be made without consulting Gram Sabha.

(2) Before finalising the results of the enquiry undertaken after consulting Gram Sabha, the results would be presented before Gram Sabha. Keeping in mind the consultations with Gram Sabha in this regard, if found necessary, suitable amendments would be made in the results and the report would be forwarded for proper action.

(3) During the review of all institutions, the procedure desribed above in (2) would be followed.

79. Review of Social Sector

(1) The Gram Sabha shall be competent to review social sector schemes as well as local institutions such as schools, hospitals etc. from time to time.

(2) The Gram Sabha may constitute special Committees to assist in its review.

(3) The instructions given by the Gram Sabha to improve the implementation of social sector schemes of local institutions will have to be followed by the concerned functionaries.

80. State legislation to be in Keeping with Customary Law, Social, Religious and Traditional Management Practices of Community

(1) If a Gram Sabha is of the opinion that any State Legislation is not in consonance with the customary law, social and religious practices and traditional management practices of the Communitty resources it may pass a resolution to that effect.

(2) The resolution so passed shall be forwarded to the District Collector by the Gram Sabha, who shall forward it to the state government.

(3) All such resolutions of Gram Sabhas shall be considered by the a Committee constituted by the state government chaired by the Minister for tribal affairs, and comprising Scheduled Tribe MLAs, and NGO representatives and activitss working in Scheduled Tribe areas. The Committee will make its recommendations on the resolution of the Gram Sabha after due consideration to the state government.

(4) The state government shall take necessary action on the recommendations made by the above mentioned Committee.

XIII NOMINATION IN BLOCK AND DISTRICT PANCHAYATS

81. State Government to Nominate Scheduled Tribe Representatives in Block and District Panchayats

(1) The state government may nominate members of Scheduled Tribes to a block or district Panchayats, provided that the number of persons so nominated shall not exceed 10 per centof the toal strength of the panchayats.

(2) Provided members from among different tribes shall be nominated by rotation.

Annexure – 1

Offences under IPC triable by Gram Sabha under PESA Rules:

Sl. No.	*Sections Under IPC*	*Offences*	*Max*
1	160	Affray	Fine
2	264	Fraudent use of false instruments for weighing	Fine
3	265	Fraudulent use of false weight or measure	Fine
4	266	Being in possession of false weight or measure	Fine
5	267	Making or selling false weight or measure	Fine
6	269	Negligent act likely to spread infection of disease dangerous to life	Fine
7	277	Fouling water of public spring or reservoir	Fine
8	283	Danger or obstruction in public way or line of navigation	Fine
9	285	Negligent conduct with respect to fire or combustible matter	Fine
10	286	Negligent conduct with respect to explosive substabce	Fine

Sl.No	Sections under IPC	Offences
19	341	Wrongful Restraint
20	352	Assault or criminal force otherwise than on grave provocation
21	374	Unlawful compulsory labour
22	379*	Theft
23	403*	Dishonest misappropriation of property
24	411*	Dishonestly receiving stolen property
25	417*	Cheating
26	426	Mischief
27	427	Mischief causing damage to the amount of fifty rupees
28	428	Mischief by killing or maiming animal of the value of ten rupees

*Provided that the amount of property does not exceed Rs 250.

References and Bibliography

All India Congress Committee (AICC) (1954), *Report of the Congress Village Panchayat Committee,* New Delhi.

Ambasht, N.K. (1997), "Tribal Panchayats: A case for rejuvenation (with special reference to Oraon) in Pfeffer, G., and D.K.Behera (eds) *Contemporary Sociewty: Tribal Studies,* New Delhi: Concept Publishing Company.

Areeparampil, Mathew (1995), *Tribals of Jharkhand: Victims of Development,* New Delhi: Indian Sopcial Institute.

Asoka Mehta Committee (1977), *Report of the Committee on Panchayati Raj Institutions,* New Delhi.

Association of Voluntary Agencies for Rural Development (AVARD) (1962), *Report of a Study Team on Panchayati Raj in Rajasthan,* New Delhi.

Bardhan, Pranab and Dilip Mookherjee (ed) (2006), *Decentralisation and Local Governance in Developing Countries,* Cambridge: Massachusetts Institute of Technology.

Chaube, Shibanikinkar (1973), *Hill Politics of North-east India,*Calcutta, Orient Longman Ltd.

Cheema, G. Shabbir and Dennis A. Rondinelli (ed) (2007), *Decentralising Governance,* Harvard: Ash Institute for Democratic Governance and Innovation.

Committee to Review the Existing Administration Arrangements for Rural Development and Poverty Alleviation Programme (CAARD), (1985) Report, Department of Rural Development Ministry of Agriculture, New Delhi.

Dholakia, Ravindra H. (2000), 'Liberalisation in Gujarat' *Economic and Political Weekly*, 35(35-36) 3121-25, 26 August-2 September (2003) 'The Role of the state government in Promoting Private Sector Growth: The case of Gujarat' in Stephen Howes *et al.* (eds.) *State Level Reforms in India-Towards more Effective Government*, New Delhi: MacMillan India Ltd.

Doornbos, Martin (2001), 'Good Governance- the rise and decline of a Policy Metaphor' *Journal of Development Studies*, 37(6) August.

Dutta, Sujit Kumar and Dilip Kumar Ghosh (2006), *Institutions for Development (The Case of Panchayats)*, New Delhi: Mittal Publications.

Gandhi, M.K. (1942), "My Idea of Village Swaraj" *Harijan*, 26 July, 1942.

Gait, G.A., (1926), *A History of Assam*, Cacutta: Thaker Spink and Co.

Ghosh, Buddhadeb (2000), *Panchayati Raj:Evolution of the Concept* New Delhi: Institute of Social Sciences.

Government of India (GOI) (2002a), *Tenth Five Year Plan, 2003-2007*, Vol. II, New Delhi: Planning Commission.

Haokip, George T. (ed) (2012), *Human Rights and Social Security in North-East India*, New Delhi: Mittal Publications.

Hidayatulleh, M. (1979), *The Fifth and Sixth Schedules to the Constitution of India*, Guwahati: Ashok Publishing House.

Howes, Stephen, A.K. Lahiri and N.Stern (ed) (2003), *State-Level Reforms in India-Towards More Effective Government*, New Delhi: MacMillan India Ltd.

Jagadish, K. Patnaik (ed) (2008), *Mizoram: Dimensions and Perspectives*, New Delhi: Concept Publishing Company.

Jain, L.C. *et al.* (1985), *Grass without Roots*, New Delhi: Sage Publications.

Kothari, Rajni (1988), *State Against Democracy: Humane Governance.* New Delhi: Ajanta Publications.

Lalthangliana, B. (1992), *Hmasang Zonun*, Aizawl: RTM Press.

Lalzawnga, R. (2010), "Panchayati Raj in India" in Laskar, Baharul Isalm (ed.) *Mizoram: The Emerging Issues of Development*, Guwahati: DVS Publishers.

Malaviya, H.D. (1956), *Village Panchayats in India,* Economic and Political Research Department, All India Congress Committee, New Delhi.

Mander, Harsh and Mohammed Asif (2004), *Good Governance-Resource Book,* Bangalore: Books for Change.

Mooij, Jos (2001), 'Economic Reforms and Political Interpretations' Working Paper 41, Hyderabad Centre for Economic and Social Studies.

Mukarji, Nirmal and Datta, Abhijit (1996), *New Perceptions on Local Government.* New Delhi: Institute of Social Sciences

Nachane, D.M. (ed) (2011), *India Development Report,* New Delhi: Oxford University Press.

Narayan, Jayaprkash (1970), *Communitarian Society and Panchayati Raj,* Edited by Brahmanad; Varanasi: Navchetana Prakashan.

Nayar, K.R. (2004), 'Kerala-Confusing New Approach to Public Services' *Economic and Political Weekly,* 39(21) 22 May.

Nunthara, C. (1989), *Impact of the Introduction of Grouping of Villaghes in Mizoram,* New Delhi: Omsons Publication.

Nunthara, C. (1996), *Mizoram: Society and Polity,* New Delhi: Indus Publishing Company.

Nunthara, C. (2013), 'State Formation Processes among the Mizos in the Pre-colonial Times' in Battercherjee, J.B and David R. Syiemlieh (ed.) *Early States in North-east India,* New Delgi: regency Publications.

Oommen, T.K. (2004), *Nation, Civil Society and Social Movements.* New Delhi: Sage Publications.

Parry, N.E. (1931), 'Notes on the Lushais', *Census of India 1931,* Assam, Report Part I, Vol. 3.

Patnaik, Jagadish K. (ed.) (2008), *Mizoram: Dimensions and Perspectives (Society, Economy and Polity)* New Delhi: Concept Publishing Company.

Polaski, S., M. Panda and A Ganesh-Kumar (2008), 'Policy Dilemmas in India: The Impact of Changes in Agricultural Prices on Rural and Urban Poverty' IGIDR Working Paper No. 2008-12.

Rao, Adityendra (1988), *Tribal Social Stratification,* Udaipur: Himansu Publications.

Rao, R.S. (1998), 'World Bank and Economy of Andhra Pradesh' *Economic and Political Weekly*, 30(25): 1499-1502, 20 June.

Roy Burman, B.K. (1995), *Panchayati Raj and Tribals* New Delhi" Institute of Social Sciences.

Sachdeva, Pardeep (2011), *Local Government in India*, Delhi: Pearson

Salamon, Lester M. (ed) (2002), *The Tools of Government-A Guide to the New Governance.* Oxford: Oxford University Press.

Santha, E.K. (1999), *Political Participation of Women in Panchayati Raj.* New Delhi: Institute of Social Sciences.

Sinha, Haredra (2012), *Bureaucracy and Rural Development in Mizoram*, New Delhi: Concept Publishing Company Pvt. Ltd.

Shakespeare, J. (1912), *The Lushai-Kuki Clans*, London: MacMillan and Co.

Shukla, L.P. (1964), *A History of Village Panchayats in India*, Dharwar: Institute of Economic Research.

Songate, Hranglien (1956), *Hmar History*, Imphal: Mao Press.

United Nations Development Programme (2002), *Human Development Report.* New Delhi: Oxford University Press.

Vanlawma, R. (1975), 'Mizo lalte leh an Khua leh tui' Mizo Academy of Letters, *Mizo Ziarang*, Aizawl.

Venkatarangaiya, M. and M.Pattabhiram (eds) (1969), *Local Government in India: Select Readings*, Mumbai: Allied Publishers

Widmalm, Sten (2008), *Decentralisation, Corruption and Social Capital*, New Delhi: Sage Publications.

World Bank (1992), *Governance and Development*, Washington, D.C.

World Bank (1994), *Governance-The World Bank Experience*, Washington D.C.

World Bank (2002), *Globalisation-Growth and Poverty-Building an Incentive World Economy*, A World Bank Policy Research Report: New York: Co-Publication of the World Bank, Washington and Oxford University Press.

World Bank (2004), *Reforming Public Institutions and Strengthening Governance: A World Bank Strategy* (www.worldbank.org/public sector/strategy htm 4 Oct. 2004.

Zatluanga (1968), *Mizo Chanchin* (Mizo History) Aizawl: Khuma Printing Press.

Index